3361

Hail to the Chiefs

Books by RUTH MONTGOMERY

HAIL TO THE CHIEFS

HERE AND HEREAFTER

A SEARCH FOR THE TRUTH

FLOWERS AT THE WHITE HOUSE

A GIFT OF PROPHECY: The Phenomenal Jeane Dixon

MRS. LBJ

ONCE THERE WAS A NUN

Hail to the Chiefs

My Life and Times with Six Presidents

by Ruth Montgomery

COWARD-McCANN, INC.
New York

Library of Congress Catalog Card Number: 77-127951

PRINTED IN THE UNITED STATES OF AMERICA

VAN REES PRESS • NEW YORK

To my brother
Paul J. Shick
who encouraged me to write this book

and with grateful acknowledgment to my husband
Robert H. Montgomery
who helped me live its nostalgic pages

Foreword

WRITING a book about the most meaningful quarter century of one's life must be somewhat akin to relaxing on a psychoanalyst's couch. I have never tried the latter, but the former awakens a flood of half-forgotten memories which prompt tantalizing and conflicting emotions: nostalgia, exhilaration, frustration, pique, laughter, love, happiness. And tumbling questions. Where has the time gone? Was that person really I? Where did I find the bounding energy? Am I truly twenty-six years older than when it all began?

I have loved life, including my own life. I have enjoyed nearly every moment of it, but I would not want to live it over again. I might not be so fortunate the second time around and might not be blessed with such a rich profusion of indulgent editors and delightful friends. Writing again of those marvelous characters who strode vigorously across the world stage from 1944 to 1970, I hold them close to my heart and sorely miss the many who have passed on to still greater adventures in the life beyond.

Perhaps I have recaptured here a little of their wonderful pomposities, sparkling witticisms, whimsical eccentricities, and undying charm—Franklin Delano Roosevelt and his remarkable Eleanor; Harry S. Truman and warm, motherly Bess; Dwight David Eisenhower and bubbling Mamie; John F. Kennedy and beautiful, imperious Jacqueline; Lyndon Baines Johnson and his loyal, long-suffering Lady Bird; Richard M. Nixon and unflappable, capable Pat. Is it possible that I have known them all so well!

This, then, is a personalized account of my life and times during six Presidential administrations. It was fascinating to live it and a rewarding experience to write it. I hope that it will be enjoyable to read as well.

7

Contents

Hail to the Chiefs

CHAPTER I

In the Beginning

I WANTED no part of Washington. The war was on, and my husband had joined the chair-borne brigade at the Navy Department, but I was having a glorious time at the Chicago *Tribune* as a newspaper reporter. Say what you will about Colonel Robert R. McCormick's peculiar penchant for editorialized journalism, no reporter on the city side of the *Tribune* was expected to slant a murder case or sexy court trial. And since crime unfortunately was rampant on the home front, we were often crowding World War II from the banner headline with our by-lined staccatos.

Too, there was a little matter of wounded feminine pride. Bob, my good-looking husband, rather fancied himself as Uncle Sam's newest Navy lieutenant that day in 1943 when he waved good-bye. Like most newly commissioned officers, he had been secretly practicing salutes to the mirror until his uniform arrived, and, as we sallied forth along Michigan Avenue, he alternated between stolen glimpses of himself in store windows and a furtive search of the rush-hour crowds for some scrambled-egg cap to salute.

Suddenly a lady marine saluted him smartly at an intersection, and in his flustered surprise Bob nearly missed the curbing. He had forgotten that mere women wear uniforms. A few minutes later, when we joined newspaper friends in Tom's Bar for a farewell martini, my devoted spouse made a point of commending one of the star reporters whose husband was already fighting the war from Stateside: "Rita, I certainly admire the way you have refused to become a camp follower," he extolled. "I don't want Ruth trying to follow me around."

Famous last words! Within a month he was as tired of the male companionship, the war, and the monotonous garb as the rest of the civilians turned warriors. When I visited him that Christmas in Virginia, where he was suffering the rigors of war at luxurious Williamsburg Inn, which the Navy had requisitioned for officers' quarters, he rather sheepishly urged me to stay. With some asperity I replied that I was no camp follower, and I returned to my pleasant perch at the Chicago *Tribune*.

Shortly afterward Bob was transferred to the Navy Bureau of Ordnance in Washington, and his pleas became more urgent. When was I going to give up my silly career and join him in Washington, where I belonged? He usually had to telephone several times before finding me at home. Our reportorial hours were noon until 9 P.M., and after the excitement of our days a few of us often gravitated to a nearby bar to talk it over with a beer.

The last straw, as far as Bob was concerned, came when he tried all one night to reach me. My telephone still rang unanswered at 7 A.M., and he left for the Navy Department in an anything but contented mood. How was he to know that the *Tribune* had suddenly dispatched me to Grand Rapids, Michigan, to cover the racy trial of a young man accused of burning to death his high school sweetheart in a lonely lovers' tryst? My telegram to that effect reached him too late to restore his lost sleep, but it did arouse the dominant male. Bob ordered me to Washington, and armed with several bylined, eight-column front-page headlines to prove my reportorial experience, I reluctantly went.

How could I then know that during the next quarter century I would hobnob with Presidents who called me by my first name, dine with the world's mighty, interview dozens of heads of state, travel around the world, tour Russia and Siberia with a future President, fly to Europe and the Middle East with the blasé of a regular commuter, cover revolutions, travel on Presidential campaign trains, win journalism awards, and amass two honorary Doctors of Law degrees?

Chicago *Tribune* policy prohibited women in its Washington bureau, a lucky break for me, although I scarcely thought so at the time. Unwilling to let wartime Washington go to press without me, I dashed off a note to Richard W. Clarke, executive editor of the New York *Daily News* (the *Tribune*'s sister paper), and the next day Washington bureau chief John O'Donnell wired me a cryptic "How much?"

Except for my loquaciousness, I would have started work on the *Daily News* immediately. Rita, however, had already joined her desk-soldiering husband in Washington, and when she announced her firm intention of becoming a lady of leisure, I confided that I had contacted the New York *Daily News* bureau about a job. My friend promptly rushed to Mr. O'Donnell with her own application and began pulling wires which I did not have.

A special brand of guardian angel must watch over fools and talkative women, because a week later I, not Rita, became a Washington correspondent for the New York *Daily News*. Rita then accepted a less tantalizing job, which had previously been offered to me, as a local reporter for the Washington *Times-Herald*. Thanks to the war, which had called so many men to active duty, newspaper doors in Washington were grudgingly swinging open to feminine scribes.

CHAPTER II

Wartime Washington

THE morning that Bob met his wife and much-traveled cocker spaniel at Union Station, I gazed across the beautiful plaza, saw the United States Capitol framed by the lacy greenery of early June, and decided that I was there to stay. Bob was later to learn how right I was. After spending six months urging me to come to Washington, he tried for a year after the war to lure me away, before finally conceding defeat and becoming a government official.

During this era Eleanor Roosevelt was holding weekly press conferences at the White House with the giddy informality of an Aunt Nellie. We newspaperwomen, clutching Secret Service identification cards on which our photographs resembled gun molls, assembled each Monday morning in the Green Room of the Executive Mansion. Promptly at 11 A.M. we trooped up the broad staircase to the historic Monroe Treaty Room, and as soon as we were assembled, Mrs. Roosevelt strode into the room, followed by Miss Malvina Thompson, her private secretary, and Mrs. Edith Helm, her social secretary.

Mrs. Roosevelt's high-pitched voice caroled greetings as she fluttered around the room, extending a limp hand to each female scribe. After she had fluted her fantastically crowded schedule for the coming week, the question period began, and although no question disconcerted her, some of her answers which appeared afterward in print evoked squirming discomfort from Steve Early, the President's press secretary.

Did Mrs. Roosevelt think it was right for her to accept an $11,000 mink coat during wartime, a gift from Canadian mink ranchers? Mrs. Roosevelt assured us that she did, since there were no legal restrictions against a President's wife receiving presents. In fact, King Ibn Saud of Saudi Arabia had sent her and daughter Anna some extravagant harem dresses, which they had gleefully modeled for each other the night before. Did she really favor birth control for poor families, in view of the Roman Catholic Church's stern disapproval? The First Lady shrugged that she did and that her own Episcopal Church had issued no ban against it.

Her headlined utterances harassed the male side of the White House, but Eleanor gaily went her chattering way. Once, when FDR blasted newspaper columnists as "excrescences" and a reporter reminded that his wife was writing a "My Day" column, he grinningly retorted that that was different.

Franklin Delano Roosevelt was renominated for a fourth term the week after my arrival in Washington, and I attended my first Presidential press conference. Never before had I so throbbed to history in the making. I could scarcely concentrate on Mr. Roosevelt's words for pinching myself. Was I actually on the scene at such a moment of world history? There we reporters stood, perspiringly squashed together for half an hour, while FDR tauntingly dismissed the more embarrassing questions as "iffy" and emphasized the points that he wished to stress with a jab of his long cigarette holder. He obviously enjoyed these fencing matches with the press and handled them adroitly. We liked them, too, since they were a proven path to a front-page by-line, even though we had to assemble in jumbled lineup outside the President's door for an hour or so beforehand, twice a week, awaiting his summons to the inner sanctum.

Congress was wrangling over black marketeers and the problems of reconversion to be faced when peace came, and I covered those fiery hearings, along with the Truman Committee's probes of war profiteering. The 1944 election campaign began, and with a neat flair for dramatics, FDR made a headlined trip to Hawaii to confer with his Far Eastern commanders. Beauteous Congresswoman Clare Boothe Luce promptly took the House floor to blast the trip as political, and Representative Harold Knutson solemnly announced that a U.S. destroyer had had to swing back in mid-Pacific to pick up the President's dog, allegedly left behind at some Aleutian telephone pole.

There was never a dull moment in Washington in those days. Roosevelt laughingly defended "my little dog Fala" in a political speech before the International Brotherhood of Teamsters at the Statler Hotel, and immediately afterward six labor goons mauled a battle-scarred naval officer who refused to say whether he would vote for his Commander in Chief. What a hero we reporters made of that officer, with our interviews at his bedside!

As expected, Roosevelt won reelection in November and announced that for the first time the Presidential oath of office would be administered at the south portico of the White House, rather than on the Capitol steps. With other shivering members of the press corps, I stood ankle-deep in thawing snow that gray January day while the President, leaning heavily on the supporting arm of his eldest son, James, pledged to work for "a just and durable peace." Senator Harry S. Truman, an inconspicuous little man in metal-rimmed spectacles, succeeded Henry A. Wallace as Vice President in thirty seconds flat. The audience paid little heed to the future President, and one line in my inaugural story took care of his role in the event.

At a Presidential press conference shortly after the inauguration, FDR told us that he was leaving for a Big Three conference at Yalta and was taking his daughter Anna Boettiger, along as secretary. We of the press obeyed orders to suppress the news for security reasons until the historic meeting officially began in the Russian Black Sea resort. On FDR's return, I covered his dramatic personal report to a joint session of Congress, and it was there that the ailing leader finally dispensed with the myth that he was a well man as he entered the House chamber by wheelchair. How wan he looked. The ruddy glow was gone, but the inspiring voice still vibrated from his flabby throat.

Speaking from a cushioned red velvet chair, he confidently extolled the Yalta agreement as "a turning point in American history" which spelled "the end of the system of unilateral action and exclusive alliances and spheres of influence and balances of power, and all the other expedients which have been tried for centuries, and have failed." The dying man could not foresee the fallacy of his cheerful prognostication.

A day or two later FDR held a press conference, and from my tightly wedged standing position beside his gadget-littered desk, it was plain to see that the fire was ebbing rapidly. That evening I wrote Mother and Dad that the President "looks so gray and drawn that he resembles an old, old woman more than a man." His face was like waxed parchment, worn translucent by time. The President went to Warm Springs without Mrs. Roosevelt, and on April 12 she held her last press conference as First Lady, although unknowingly so.

Two months previously I had been elected president of Mrs. Roosevelt's Press Conference Association, an honor which the First Lady would probably have preferred to see bestowed on a correspondent of a more friendly newspaper. My publisher, Joseph Medill Patterson, an enthusiastic backer of FDR during the New Deal days, had broken with him over the issues of lend-lease and a third term and, along with publishers McCormick and William Randolph Hearst, had become his severest critic. But newswomen elected their own officers, and Mrs. Roosevelt politely invited me and the four members of my executive board to tea in the White House family quarters.

The chief topic of conversation over the teacups was her recrimination of my Washington bureau chief, John O'Donnell, whose editorial column reflected our publisher's changed view of the President. Mrs. Roosevelt complained that she could not understand how John could turn against her husband's administration "after all those letters of introduction we gave him for a European trip before the war." What she refused to see was that at the time of John's journey Roosevelt had not declared for a third term and had not yet launched the lend-lease program which many observers believed would lead to our active involvement in the war. My own relations with Mrs. Roosevelt remained pleasant, if distant, and immediately after her press conference in April, 1945, a crisis arose within our press association.

The First Lady had put part of her answer to a question off the record, but one of our members had reported the full text in a

Washington paper. Mrs. Roosevelt's secretary called me to complain about the woman's violation of conference rules, and I promptly scheduled a meeting of our executive board to determine what action should be taken against our colleague. The meeting was never held. Late that afternoon, as I was preparing to leave the office, news tickers throughout the press building clanged a three-bell alert. Dated Warm Springs, where only wire service reporters had been permitted to accompany the President, the bulletin read: "Roosevelt is dead."

Our hearts stood still, but not our feet. News editor Ted Lewis dispatched me on the run to the White House two blocks away, where other shocked reporters were also converging on the west lobby. Soon Steve Early, red-eyed from emotion, beckoned us into his office. There, in choked tones, he recounted the sequence of events leading to the President's fatal stroke and also the steps which had been taken to notify Vice President Truman that he was now President.

Mrs. Roosevelt had been attending a Thrift Club benefit when Steve telephoned her to return to the White House at once. Then Steve and Admiral Ross T. McIntire, the President's personal physician, sadly trudged to her upstairs sitting room to break the news of her widowhood. Magnificent in her grief, she was the calmest of them all. Ten minutes later when the bereaved woman received Truman, who had been located in Speaker Sam Rayburn's office having a bourbon-and-branchwater, her first words to him were: "What can we do to help you, Mr. President?"

The swearing-in of the new Chief Executive was delayed another half hour while his wife and daughter, Margaret, rushed to the White House. Then, with several New Deal officials weeping softly and Mrs. Truman's eyes welling with tears, Harry S. Truman took the time-honored oath in the Presidential office that was now his own.

We worked far into that hectic night, and the next morning's papers duly recorded that the new First Family, alone except for Secret Service guards in their unpretentious five-room apartment on Connecticut Avenue, had found themselves without food for dinner, since all social engagements were automatically canceled. A simple man of the people, the new President solved the dilemma by knocking on an adjoining apartment door and borrowing sandwich ingredients from the neighbor.

Franklin Delano Roosevelt, the only President whom a generation of youngsters had known, was dead. A stunned nation nursed its grief, while Mrs. Roosevelt flew to Warm Springs to board the hastily assembled funeral train for the sad journey back to the capital. Mrs. Elizabeth Shoumatoff, a Russian artist who was painting the President's portrait at the moment of his cerebral hemorrhage, departed abruptly and could not be located for two days. My newspaper, with laudable journalistic enterprise and $10,000 cash, obtained from her the exclusive first publishing rights to her uncompleted canvas, but not until nearly a quarter century later did Jonathan Daniels, in his book *Washington Tapestry,* disclose that Lucy Rutherford, FDR's intimate friend, also had been present at his death and had fled with Mrs. Shoumatoff. It was the best-kept secret of the war years.

The morning after Roosevelt's death, Jonathan Daniels held a press conference to brief us on funeral plans. Daniels, who had been taking over as press secretary from Steve Early, said that since so many dignitaries from here and abroad wanted to attend the funeral and space was limited, press coverage would have to be pooled by ten newsmen, one of whom could be a woman. As president of Mrs. Roosevelt's Press Conference Association, I was chosen to represent distaff reporters, a memorable assignment for a girl who had been covering the Washington political scene for only ten months.

Early that somber morning of April 14, 1945, I slipped through the thousands of massed mourners who were keeping solemn vigil outside the White House gates. As the flag-draped casket was gently carried from the black caisson to its place of honor in the East Room, below the portraits of George and Martha Washington, we pool reporters slipped in quietly to begin our note-taking. The gold walls of the room, which had been the scene of so many gala balls in happier times, were banked high with floral tributes. The venetian blinds were closed, but from three massive crystal chandeliers light played softly on the closed coffin.

The room began to fill with dignitaries: British Foreign Secretary Anthony Eden, who had hastily flown the Atlantic, the Earl of

Athlone and Princess Alice, the sober-visaged diplomatic corps all in black, the Supreme Court Justices whom FDR had appointed one by one to replace the "Nine Old Men" who distrusted his New Deal innovations, and the sad-eyed Presidential Cabinet. A stir swept the quiet room as the dying Harry Hopkins, rushed from his hospital bed at Mayo Clinic, entered with his wife. The former Louise Macy attracted almost as much attention as her red-eyed husband, for in the room of soberly clad mourners, her bare arms in a sleeveless black dress evoked disapproving murmurs. Governor Thomas E. Dewey, FDR's fourth-term rival, slipped into an assigned seat near the rear, and James F. Byrnes and James A. Farley, who had feuded with their chief and departed the Washington scene, were back to pay him final homage.

The new President of the United States, entering with Mrs. Truman and Margaret, solemnly found his seat of honor at the head of the coffin. Then came Mrs. Roosevelt, wearing deep mourning and a widow's veil, followed by daughter Anna, son Elliott, and four daughters-in-law. Dry-eyed, she strode in queenly solitude to the family seats at the foot of the casket, across the aisle from the new First Family.

After the twenty-three-minute service, we pool reporters met our waiting colleagues in the teeming west lobby and gave them a full report on the historic rites. Walter Trohan, Washington correspondent of the Chicago *Tribune,* preferred to skip the fill-in and write his own account of the services. As a consequence, his by-lined story the next day described the "peaceful half-smile" on the lips of the departed leader. The casket lid was never raised, so we could not know how he looked, but perhaps Walter had guessed correctly.

Our next few weeks were supercharged with reportorial excitement. President Truman had visited old friends on Capitol Hill during his first day in office and, spotting a group of us who had covered him in the Senate, said gravely, "I hope you fellows will pray for me. I don't know whether any of you ever had a whole load of hay or a bull fall on you or not, but I felt as though the moon and a couple of planets had fallen on me last night when I received the news of the President's death." The new President also had to stop in at a bank to secure a loan until his first check as Chief Executive came through.

Less than a week after the funeral Mrs. Roosevelt vacated the White House, with thirteen army trucks removing the Roosevelt mementos of more than twelve years to Hyde Park. President Truman went to Capitol Hill to deliver his first address to a joint session of Congress and received thunderous applause. I happened to ride up in a private elevator of the Capitol with Mrs. Truman that day and used the opportunity to express the hope that she would continue the press conferences which Mrs. Roosevelt had inaugurated. She smiled and chatted amiably but did not commit herself.

Mrs. Truman, a virtual unknown to the nation, had become front-page news overnight, and American women hungered to know more about the motherly-looking woman and her blond daughter. I wrote a prophetic article which began: "Shy, diffident Bess Wallace Truman, as First Lady of the land, is destined to contrast sharply with her dynamic, globe-trotting predecessor. Grey-haired, motherly Mrs. Truman is like someone you knew back in Oshkosh. Her tears and choking sobs as she sought to tell Mrs. Roosevelt of her grief at the President's death heightened their essential difference. Mrs. Roosevelt, tall and slim, was the dry-eyed mistress of her emotions."

The new First Family, bowing to worried Secret Service agents, moved from their simple apartment to Blair House, the historic mansion across the street from the White House where Robert E. Lee had refused President Abraham Lincoln's entreaty to command Union troops during the Civil War. Now it was used as the official guest house for foreign VIP's, but it became home to the Trumans until the White House could be redecorated.

President Truman's first press conference, held five days after he assumed the nation's highest office, was as bombastic as any that were to follow. Truman's trigger-quick replies made it difficult for the 348 reporters to keep pace with their pencils. Standing instead of sitting behind a bare desk swept clean of the dozens of model ships and tiny donkeys assembled by his gadget-loving predecessor, Truman in eleven whirlwind minutes said that he wanted to meet with Soviet Premier Joseph Stalin, British Prime Minister Winston

Churchill, Chinese President Chiang Kai-shek, and French leader Charles de Gaulle, but had as yet initiated no arrangements; that he expected Soviet Foreign Minister V. M. Molotov to call on him en route to the Japanese peace conference in San Francisco; and that he had no plans for bringing James F. Byrnes back into government, although he shortly thereafter named him Secretary of State. Truman, who had not even known that an atomic bomb was in the making until he became President, also had numerous other pronouncements on the prosecution of the war and our home front problems.

We had been prepared for the exhausting hour-long wait on our feet outside the Presidential door, but Truman proved to be a punctual man. Promptly at the appointed hour the doors swung open, and we swept one another along in our dash for the coveted front places around his desk. The new President, a nonsmoker, needed no tapering cigarette holder to emphasize his points. Using his two hands like meat choppers, he rattled off his replies almost before our tumbling queries had reached their question marks.

Later, chastened by world-shattering reactions to some of his too-quick replies about atomic bombs and foreign affairs, Truman learned to have briefing sessions with advisers in advance of the news conferences and to temper his abrupt replies, but the spring of 1945 was a field day for White House correspondents. Once, after reporters had tried to outrun one another to the telephones, Truman paused to survey the wreckage. A crippled correspondent lay on the Presidential rug, his crutches yards apart. Another time, United Press correspondent Merriman Smith, dashing ahead of his wire service rivals, turned the well-worn corner of the doorway too sharply and fractured his note-taking hand.

On May 7, 1945, I spent all day at the White House, which was clogged with reporters and photographers awaiting the imminent German collapse. Peace-hungry pedestrians jammed Pennsylvania Avenue outside, and Capitol Hill was in readiness for a V-E Day announcement, with loudspeakers set up in the House to carry the radioed announcement from President Truman. Here was the moment for which the nation had long waited, but it was not until the next day that the announcement finally came.

The war in Europe was over, exactly eleven months after I had become a Washington correspondent, and what a thrill-packed time it had been! More was yet to come. With remarkable rapidity, one Cabinet head after another began to fall. Byrnes replaced Ed Stettinius at State. Fred Vinson took over from Henry Morgenthau at Treasury. Tom Clark replaced Francis Biddle as Attorney General, and Truman's old Missouri friend Robert E. Hannegan became Postmaster General.

Representative Clinton P. Anderson had been holding House hearings critical of our agricultural policies and was told by the President, "All right, if you know so much about running the Department of Agriculture, you're it," and Claude Wicker stepped down. Frances Perkins, the first woman to hold a Cabinet appointment, vanished from the Washington scene and was replaced at Labor by L. B. Schwellenbach. By the end of the year only Henry A. Wallace and James Forrestal remained, as Secretaries of Commerce and the Army, respectively.

In June, 1945, General Dwight D. Eisenhower flew into Washington for the warmest homecoming the capital had paid a war hero since the return of "Black Jack" Pershing twenty-five years before. Outside the Statler Hotel, cheering throngs all but mobbed the popular liberator of Western Europe, and on Capitol Hill where the five-star general addressed a joint session, I wrote that "members of Congress abandoned all pretense at dignity. When General Eisenhower was escorted into the House chamber, the legislators whistled, stomped and cheered."

The most fascinating part of that historic day came later when Ike held a no-holds-barred press conference at the Pentagon. I sat immediately behind Mrs. Eisenhower in the second row, and Mamie, a little flowered hat perched atop her famous bangs, sparkled like a starry-eyed bride. A reporter asked Ike about his immediate plans, and with an affectionate glance toward his wife, he quipped, "I'm going to have a little furlough, or there'll be a rebellion around here." Then someone inquired whether the general planned to take his wife back with him to Germany for the occupation assignment, and Mamie literally caught her breath. No one in that crowded room yearned to know his answer as much as the woman who had had no single moment alone with her hero husband since he flew in from Europe that morning. Ike, this time avoiding her eyes, hesitated only a moment before replying gravely, "That would be out of character, until every GI can have the same advantage."

While the smile vanished from Mamie's piquant face and her shoulders perceptibly sagged, the general added, "Wives cannot go in the immediate future, because Germany is destroyed. It is a hostile nation, and it is short of food." Ike returned shortly to Europe, and the future First Lady resumed her lonely vigil in her Wardman Park apartment.

Historians until the end of time will remember that summer of 1945 as the date when the world's greatest democracy dropped two atomic bombs on its enemy, Japan. The pros and cons of President Truman's fateful decision will be debated for as long, but in August the war was over, and a tenuous peace returned to our weary planet. Three days after V-J Day, a delightful little old lady visited the White House and captured the fancy of the nation with her independent quips. President Truman, bareheaded and proud, skipped up the ramp of the famous *Sacred Cow* plane, which had flown his predecessor to Yalta, and buoyantly greeted his ninety-two-year-old mother, Mrs. Martha Truman. While we reporters watched, they emerged from the plane together, and when the salty old rebel, who had defiantly flown the Confederate flag above her door for years after the Civil War, glimpsed the assembled photographers, she chided, "Fiddlesticks! If I'd known that, I wouldn't have come."

The nation could chuckle again.

It was my obligation, as the last president of Mrs. Roosevelt's Press Conference Association, to try to persuade Mrs. Truman to continue our weekly news sessions, but telegrams, letters, and personal pleas failed to move the adamant new First Lady. Mrs. Truman personally escorted us through the refurbished White House, as Mrs. Roosevelt had once done, but she refused to speak for quotation. The distaff side of the Executive Mansion could be covered only by rumor and backstairs gossip.

Press relations deteriorated to such an extent that when Madame Chiang Kai-shek, paying a farewell call on President Truman, told reporters afterward that Mrs. Truman was in Missouri and could not receive her, feminine scribes nursed their wounds at being scooped by a visiting dignitary. On checking, however, I learned that the First Lady was very much in residence at the White House. Publisher Joseph Medill Patterson had meanwhile selected me to be our syndicated Washington columnist whenever John O'Donnell was vacationing or ill, and the farewell visit of China's dynamic First Lady coincided with one of my columning stints.

Describing the unfortunate mix-up in my column, I wrote: "Most Washingtonians are convinced that Mrs. Truman intended no slight in not receiving Madame Chiang. It is the sort of misunderstanding which could have been cleared up overnight—long before the rumor mills began grinding out their bitter chaff—if the distaff side of the White House maintained any sort of 'diplomatic relations' with the press. Unfortunately, most such news thus far has reached reporters by way of backstairs gossip for lack of any regular channel."

The day that my column appeared in New York and Washington papers, our Women's National Press Club held a tea in honor of Mrs. Truman. While I chatted with her on noncontroversial subjects, a friend rushed over and breathlessly asked the First Lady, "Did you read Ruth's column today?"

"Yes, I did." Mrs. Truman smiled enigmatically.

Time magazine led its press section that week with a feature about my career and quoted from my column on the First Lady. The day that it appeared on the newsstands I flew to Independence, Missouri, on the press plane to cover the First Family's visit to their hometown. As Mrs. Truman deplaned in Kansas City, my heart sank to see her wave a copy of *Time* at me. Was I permanently in the Truman doghouse?

The next evening Judge Henry Bundschu of Independence, a lifelong friend of the Trumans, gave a dinner party in my honor at a local country club. Significantly, the other guests were Mrs. Kitty Accola, a former Missouri friend of the Trumans who had flown out from Washington with them, and Mr. and Mrs. Mize Peters, the Trumans' closest friends from childhood. All of them had read the *Time* article and seemed rather shocked that I should have dared to criticize the First Lady, but they soon began to see my point. By the end of the evening the five of us were warm friends, and they had assigned themselves the task of conveying my logical viewpoint on press conferences to Mrs. Truman.

Early the next morning the Peters slipped into the "Little White House" at Independence and spent an hour with the First Family. Shortly after my return to Washington, the First Lady sent me a charming note concerning a column that I had written about the trip, saying: "I read with much interest the column you wrote about your brief visit to Independence. I am so glad you enjoyed your visit here. You certainly made a hit with our friends."

Mrs. Truman remained briefly in Independence, but on her return to the White House she established regular press conferences, with social secretary Edith Helm and personal secretary Reathel Odum serving as her stand-ins. Once again news flowed through regular channels.

CHAPTER III

Party Time in Wartime

LET no business tycoon contend that during the daylight hours he toils more arduously than our legislators and policy planners. But then comes sundown! Washington is an early-to-bed town without real nightclubs, but as dusk settles softly along the Potomac, the public cocktail lounges bulge with lobbyists, party lights begin to twinkle in Georgetown's eighteenth-century salons, and Embassy Row teacups rattle to the staccato of popping champagne corks. Playtime is at hand!

Even the war, the food shortages, the gas rationing, and the vanishing supply of scotch whisky could not affect the party tempo. Evalyn Walsh McLean, the undisputed queen of the Washington social whirl during the frenetic forties, threw open the hospitable doors of her fabulous estate Friendship once a week for soldiers and their girlfriends, but this generous gesture merely added one more soiree to her already crowded social calendar. As music drifted lazily from the drawn curtains of her Georgetown mansion, Cabinet officers, Senators, local cave dwellers, Supreme Court Justices, and Pentagon high brass jostled one another in bantering camaraderie through her expansive doors.

Evalyn, wearing her incredible Hope diamond and perennial dark glasses, was waiting just inside the private ballroom to receive the political elite of the nation. Party axes, like swords in knighthood days, were checked in the foyer, and for a few fleeting hours a Demo-

29

cratic Senator who had just blasted a Republican colleague could pay gallant court to his bedecked spouse.

My own first evening at Friendship in 1944 had spelled pure enchantment. Fresh from the Middle West, I trod in unbelieving fantasy up the curving canopied steps, through the broad entrance hall with its clublike checkrooms, past the merrymaking in the lavish bar, and along the carpeted sweep to the ballroom. Two concert grand pianos, dwarfed by the magnificent proportions of the columned room, poured forth their muted harmony as Mrs. McLean pressed my hand in welcome. The famous Star of India, one of the world's greatest diamonds, sparkled in her dark tresses like the headlight of an oncoming train in the night. Her arms and tapering fingers were paved with lesser stones which could have financed a battleship, and from a diamond-studded chain around her aging throat hung, in solitary splendor, the forty-five-carat blue Hope diamond which had once graced the crown of Marie Antoinette.

Butlers carrying gleaming trays of champagne and whiskey snaked through the festive throng. When dinner was announced, I continued my Alice in Wonderland journey through a mirror-shelved salon crammed with figurines of cats, past another luxurious drawing room, and into the vast dining salon beyond. A life-sized oil portrait of Warren G. Harding, the ill-starred Chief Executive who used to play golf at the McLean estate, beamed benignly from one wall. Gold and silver services glittered on alternate tables, and strolling musicians filled our fairyland with song. How could I have then dreamed that six short years later Bob and I would buy and remodel one section of that sparkling old mansion into a townhouse, as our own residence!

That first evening I found my place at one of the gold-bedecked tables and peeped through lowered lashes at my fellow dinner partners. There, directly opposite, sat "Princess" Alice Roosevelt Longworth, glamorous daughter of President Theodore Roosevelt and widow of House Speaker Nicholas Longworth. One seat removed from Alice was—could it be possible—her arch social rival from the Hoover administration, Dolly Gann. How well I remembered the details of that much publicized feud, which had occurred long before

I was old enough to vote. Dolly, the official hostess for her unmarried brother, Vice President Charles Curtis, had publicly declared that she should outrank the wife of Speaker Longworth. Alice had just as publicly declared that a wife always outranked a mere sister, and since each had declined to sit below the salt from the other, hostesses had solved the embarrassing dilemma by never inviting them to the same party.

Seated at the same table with the two of them that evening, I sighed inwardly. Surely a dire error had been committed, and sparks would shortly fly. But not so! As the butlers appeared with our squabs and *paté de foie gras,* Alice Longworth, observing that Dolly was seated in an awkward corner, asked sweetly, "May I serve you, Dolly dear?"

Dolly would appreciate it very much, "darling," and the two old foes, united at last in their opposition to Democratic President Roosevelt, spun the conversational ball. After dinner Alice and I sat together for the movie in the ballroom and chatted like old friends. The witty idol of the Teddy Roosevelt years thrust out a foot clad in a gold-brocaded slipper, saying, "Look, my dress and shoes match. I wore them for my daughter Paulina's wedding, and it's the first time in my life I've owned two things that went together." The gold brocade, she further confided, had lain in a closet for nearly half a century, a wedding gift to her from an Oriental potentate, until put to its present use.

Alice Roosevelt Longworth and I have long since become good friends, and the intoxicating enchantment of that first evening's meeting has naturally been diluted by subsequent thrills, but my father was able to recapture some of the glow when, five years later, he and Mother came to Washington for my inauguration as president of the Women's National Press Club and I seated Dad next to Alice. After all, a nineteenth-century Illinois farm boy had also read and dreamed of the madcap "Princess" in the White House.

At a subsequent party in Evalyn McLean's *Friendship,* the ebullient hostess slipped off the Hope diamond and passed it around the table for us to try on and admire. Thirteen is my lucky number, and I am undaunted by ladders and black cats, but I could never bring myself to touch the jewel, which according to superstition had brought tragedy to all who wore it. Mrs. McLean's husband had already died tragically, and her only daughter was later to end her life with an overdose of sleeping pills.

In those wartime years before Madame Perle Mesta seized the party crown, weary legislators did not lack for lavish hostesses. My favorite parties, more intimate and intellectually stimulating than the extravaganzas at Friendship, were given by Mrs. Eleanor Medill "Cissy" Patterson, publisher of the Washington *Times-Herald,* whose brother published the New York *Daily News.* Their first cousin was Colonel McCormick, and their inherited fortunes were intertwined in the *Tribune* and the *News.*

Brilliant, redheaded Cissy had precipitated an international incident during the Taft administration when she kidnapped her baby daughter from Russian-ruled Poland and was hotly pursued by her fortune-hunting Polish husband, Count Josef Gizycki. President Taft finally had to appeal to the Russian czar for permission for Cissy to bring her child back to America after her marriage had collapsed.

I first met the regal Cissy in the Congressional Press Gallery the day that President Roosevelt reported on his mission to Yalta. She had asked columnist George Dixon if I were there, and when he sped me over for an introduction, she grasped my hands in her surprisingly soft ones, saying, "My dear, you write such beautiful pieces for my paper!" Because of an arrangement with Captain Patterson, Cissy's Washington paper was entitled to use any of our *News* copy that she chose, and she was giving generous play to mine.

Shortly thereafter Bob and I were invited to a formal dinner at Cissy's palatial home on Dupont Circle, which had been designed by architect Stanford White for her parents, and newspaper photographs of famous personages magically came to life for us. Supreme Court Justice Frank Murphy, seated at my left, lauded Bob's eldest brother, Henry Montgomery, who while editor of the Detroit *Times* had helped start Murphy on his dizzying climb from local judge to mayor and governor, a climb that ultimately led to the governor-generalship of the Philippines, a Cabinet post under Roosevelt as Attorney General, and the highest bench in the land.

Across the table, United Mine Workers boss John L. Lewis was wagging his beetling brows at Alice Longworth, who had recently patched up a publicized feud with her girlhood friend Cissy. In those strikeless war years the fiery labor leader was moving in the best Republican circles and dining frequently with the sophisticated widow of Speaker Longworth. John L., who had lost his wife several years previously, confided to me during a lull in the conversation that he had permitted no single piece of furniture to be disturbed in his wife's bedroom since her death.

On my other side sat Lawrence Wood "Chip" Robert, treasurer of the Democratic National Committee, who recounted to me how he had simultaneously courted his present wife, Evie Walker Robert, and Lady Lewis when both those beautiful women were in Nevada acquiring divorces. Cissy, who thrived on intrigue, had deliberately seated Chip next to Connie Lewis at our dinner table and placed Evie Robert with her back to them at an adjoining one.

Cissy also enjoyed controversy, so although columnist Westbrook Pegler was then conducting a one-man vendetta against "playboy" Frank Murphy in his Hearst column, she gaily invited both of them to her party. Murphy, a close friend of John L. Lewis, watched Pegler drop an arm across the shoulder of the labor chieftain after dinner and bristled: "Ruth, every time I look at that man, I want to vomit." The jurist was not amused when I impishly inquired, "Which one, Mr. Justice?"

Uniforms had to be worn by military men on all occasions during the war years, and male attire at Cissy's elegant soirees was about evenly divided between tuxedos and the gold-starred uniforms of generals and admirals. There were only two exceptions at the many wartime dinner parties which we attended there. Bob wore the lowly stripes of a Navy lieutenant, and Secretary of the Army James E. Forrestal sometimes came in a brown tweed suit, directly from his heavy duties at the Pentagon.

After dinner a small orchestra invariably played for dancing in the exquisite ballroom of Cissy's fan-shaped mansion, and once she gave a party in honor of Colonel McCormick and his bride which none of us guests can forget. The famed publisher, apparently feeling the effects of the wine, retired immediately after dinner, despite the fact that a hundred other guests had begun arriving to meet him and Maryland McCormick and enjoy the dancing.

Maryland, performing the social graces for her absent bridegroom, joined the rest of us in tripping the light fantastic, until suddenly the double doors of the balcony overlooking the ballroom swung open, and the colonel strode forth in his neatly pressed pajamas and commanded, "Stop that damned noise. I can't sleep." The music ceased.

Every Christmas Cissy gave a large cocktail party to which some of her less intimate friends and their families were invited. At one of these Bob and I witnessed what may well have been the beginning of the much-publicized social feud between Perle Mesta and Gwen Cafritz before either had captured the social reins. The future minister to Luxembourg was engaging us in animated conversation when Gwen suddenly swooped across to her, gushing, "Oh, Mrs. Black, how nice to see you."

Perle, drawing herself up like a battleship under full flag, hissed, "The name is *Mesta.*"

Blushing violently, Gwen dissolved into the merry throng while Perle exploded to us, "How dare that woman call me by the wrong name, and a —— at that!" Perle had had the good fortune to choose a father who struck it rich in Oklahoma oil during her youth and who sent her to a good musical school. With her marriage to George Mesta, a Pittsburgh steel magnate, her fortune expanded, and after they donated $25,000 to Calvin Coolidge's Presidential campaign, Perle was presented at the Court of St. James's. Following Mesta's death, Perle became an ardent Willkie for President booster, but on moving to Washington she switched to Roosevelt for his fourth-term campaign and had the remarkable foresight to give the first large party for the Trumans when he became Vice President. Little more than two months later her grateful friend became President, and the astute Mrs. Mesta gave a debut dance for Margaret Truman.

First Lady Bess Truman had little interest in wearing the Washington social mantle, but her friend Perle did, and she promptly began gathering the great and near great to her rented abode. In those days the Mesta parties were highly informal. Caterers moved in the food and butlers en masse, card tables were set up around the drawing rooms, and martini-imbibing guests jostled one another while servants shifted the furniture. After dinner the relaxed Congressmen and Cabinet officials broke into barbershop harmony around the piano, but promptly at 10:15 P.M. the ranking guest donned his hat and departed, a signal to others that any who wished could now leave. That custom is well established at nearly all parties in official Washington, because the men must be about their official duties early in the morning.

Perle Mesta, who by now had been dubbed Two Party Perle, once again won the undying gratitude of President Truman when, during his uphill campaign against GOP standard-bearer Thomas E. Dewey in 1948, his train would have ground to a halt had not Perle opened her own purse and solicited emergency funds for him from others. Truman, who had learned party loyalty at the knees of Boss Pendergast in Kansas City, promptly began searching for a plum with which to reward Perle.

While lunching at the Mayflower Hotel one day with Perle and our mutual friend author Louis Bromfield, I mentioned the rumors that she was to be given a diplomatic post in Belgium, Holland, or Luxembourg.

Louie, pouncing gleefully on the subject, assured Perle that she "simply must" choose Luxembourg. "It's the center of everything in Europe," he exclaimed. "Belgium and Holland are off the beaten track, but all your friends would come to see you in Luxembourg, because it's so near Paris."

"Really, Louie?" Perle began doubtfully. "But Luxembourg seems so small!"

Exploding with laughter, Bromfield bellowed, "My God, Perle, you don't think I'd trust you with anything bigger, do you?" Perle, adoring Bromfield, joined in our laughter.

By that time Evalyn Walsh McLean and Cissy Patterson were dead. The old order had passed, and when Perle departed in a blaze of farewell parties for her Luxembourg post, Gwen Cafritz at last came into her own. The Hungarian-born beauty, who was married to real estate tycoon Morris Cafritz, promptly tossed a magnificent party in her modernistic mansion on Foxhall Road, perhaps to cele-brate the absence of Madame Mesta, and managed to capture another Vice President, the party-loving Alben W. Barkley, as her guest of honor.

CHAPTER IV

Peacetime Intrigues

THE war ended in August, 1945, and the problems of peace began. From mothers across the nation arose in swelling crescendo the appeal to bring our boys back home. Republicans finally succeeded in forcing an investigation of the Pearl Harbor disaster, and General George C. Marshall's testimony that he could not recall where he was the night before Pearl Harbor launched a new parlor quiz. Over after-dinner coffee, guests prodded one another's memories about their own whereabouts on the last night of peace, and all could remember vividly.

Six months after V-J Day my husband finally became a civilian again, and we gratefully flew to the Bahamas for a month at Paradise Beach. The island had seen virtually no tourists for six long years, and the dusty stocks of cashmere sweaters and camel's hair topcoats, slightly the worse for moth holes, could be had for a song. We dined along picturesque wharves and in magnolia-scented gardens, while strolling natives, in the clipped British accent which makes all Bahama Negroes sound like Oxford dons, offered to strum "Bahama Mama" for pitched dimes.

We flew home in March, 1946, and that Sunday night Bob entrained for New York to resume his management consultant career with Stevenson, Jordan, and Harrison, Inc. For the next year, until the Republicans took over Congress and Senators Homer Ferguson and Styles Bridges tapped him for the newly created professional staff of the Senate Appropriations Committee, Bob was to spend every

Friday and Sunday evening commuting between Washington and Connecticut, where he was heading a consulting job for his firm.

Immediately after the Potsdam Conference in August, 1945, the British electorate tossed Prime Minister Churchill out of office, but he was still very much a hero when he came to Washington the following spring. Beaming across his cigar, fooling nobody by drinking brandy from a coffee cup, and lifting his inspiring voice in oratorical splendor, he seemed magnificent to those of us who heard him at a press luncheon.

Another famous Britisher, American-born Lady Astor, drew a more mixed reaction at a different luncheon that month. She accused her former countrymen of becoming anti-British and chided that "Americans should get down on their knees and thank God for Great Britain."

A year later Lady Astor came again, and this time some women arrived for her luncheon speech with the light of battle in their eyes. As soon as the peppery speaker sailed into Americans for their interest in "clothes, liquor and brassiere ads," Perle Mesta and two of her friends haughtily arose and departed. Perle, to ensure that her action did not pass unnoticed, patiently waited outside the Mayflower ballroom until the fiery British MP had reached her last exclamation point by saying that Americans should change their form of government. Then, as I emerged from the room, Perle hailed me to declare, "I've listened to that woman run down Americans for the last time. I walked out on her, and I hope you print it."

Needless to say, I did. When the next day's headlines greeted Lady Astor, she irately summoned me to her table at another luncheon to ask why I had printed such lies. "Positively nobody," she huffed, "walked out on me." I smilingly advised her to speak to Mrs. Mesta about it and added that Perle would not like being called a "nobody."

Another time I wrote in my syndicated column: "Irrepressible Lady Astor, who prides herself on her glib retorts, had her comeuppance when she met isolationist Senator Homer Capehart (R-Ind.). The Virginia-born beauty who became Britain's first woman member of Parliament is visiting her former haunts in these parts. Introduced to Capehart at a party, Lady Astor needled, 'Oh, you're the one who invented that radio-phonograph. Why don't you give me a Capehart?' The Senator replied, dead-pan, 'Be happy to, ma'am. I've always said that every woman should have a little Capehart in her home.' For once in her life, the lady was speechless."

The *Reader's Digest* reprinted the item from my column, and a few days after it reached England I received a protesting letter in Lady Astor's spidery, almost illegible handwriting. How did I dare, she expostulated, write such a story when she had never met Senator Capehart in her life? And who, she demanded, did I think I was to write about women in public life? I replied that I was the president of the Women's National Press Club and that Senator Capehart had personally told me about his humorous encounter with her at the party, which I identified. Lady Astor proved herself a good sport, as well as a politician. She apologized by return mail for her "outburst" and said that she "must have forgotten" the incident.

A few weeks after our return from Nassau in 1946, the New York *Daily News* sent me to Atlantic City for two weeks to cover the UNRRA Convention. The war-devastated world was hungry, Americans were still subject to rationing, and President Truman had just decreed one less piecrust for restaurant pies. Food was the biggest story of the day as UNRRA met to find a possible solution, but delegates cringed when some of the newsmen correctly reported on the lavish meals which were being served to them at the newly reopened Traymore Hotel.

We correspondents soon discovered that our expense accounts could be more easily stretched if we dined elsewhere, instead of on American plan at the Traymore. But when Bob came to visit me for the weekend and I afterward found that we were charged for the meals which he had not eaten at the Traymore, Associated Press correspondent Sigrid Arne and I plotted retaliation. He came again the next weekend, and Sigrid and I smuggled his suitcases in and out of the hotel so that he could room with me free.

This was our first postwar assignment away from Washington, and one of the male correspondents made the most of it by generously hitting the bottle. Deadlines were so inculcated in his muddled brain that he always filed a story on time, but since he had not bothered to attend the sessions or interview delegates, he drew on fertile imagination. As a consequence, the rest of us were queried in the middle of the night by our editors, who wondered why we had not reported the sensational developments appearing in some other papers under the wire service dateline of George's by-line. UNRRA officials finally asked that the celebrant be recalled, and after his sober replacement arrived we slept more peacefully.

Retiring Director-General Herbert H. Lehman demanded an immediate return to compulsory food rationing in America to prevent "chaos" abroad, and Assistant Secretary of State Will Clayton blasted Russia for privately negotiating to sell France 400,000 tons of wheat while ignoring UNRRA pleas for wheat to feed the Soviet's East European allies. Fiorello LaGuardia, the fiery ex-mayor of New York who was chosen to succeed Lehman, pranced and gesticulated as he told the conference, "Ticker-tape ain't spaghetti. People are crying for food, not advice. I want plows, not typewriters." Asserting that New Yorkers were wasting enough food each day to feed a city of 350,000, he screwed up his little button nose as he added, "I know. I collected that garbage for twelve years."

President Truman held another of his news-packed press conferences on July 7, 1946, to tell us that he had named Secretary of the Treasury Fred M. Vinson to be Chief Justice of the United States; Reconversion Director John W. Snyder to succeed Vinson at Treasury; and John L. Sullivan to be Navy Undersecretary. Grinning broadly, he broke into an amused chuckle when several reporters whistled at the triple appointment.

President Roosevelt had promoted Vinson from associate justice of the U.S. Court of Appeals to economic stabilization director and later named him federal loan administrator. A month later Vinson had a new job, succeeding James F. Byrnes as director of the Office of War Mobilization. Truman had named Vinson to his Cabinet in July, 1945, and now was moving him up to the nation's third-ranking job.

These rapid advances provided ammunition for Democratic Senate Leader Alben W. Barkley, who was Washington's best storyteller.

The future Veep said that he complained to the Democratic national chairman about the lack of patronage for his Kentucky constituents and was told, "Why, Alben, Kentucky has had an appeals court justice, an economic stabilization director, a federal loan administrator, a director of war mobilization, a cabinet officer and a chief justice of the Supreme Court!"

"Yes," Barkley retorted, "but they're all named Vinson."

Vinson was speedily confirmed as Chief Justice, and President Truman was so pleased that he threw open the long-closed White House grounds to the public for the swearing-in on the south portico. It was a sunny June day, and the festivities had the informality of a Missouri county fair.

In July, 1946, Pan American World Airways invited thirty New York and Washington correspondents to help inaugurate its direct-flight service to Buenos Aires, and for this first exciting venture below the equator we gladly endured throbbing vaccinations and an inundation of tropical corsages at Caribbean refueling stops. Columnist Inez Robb and I were seatmates as we roared off to Puerto Rico, Trinidad, and points south, and that evening an Argentine businessman taught us the samba up and down the aisles of the plane, as we smoothly glided 10,000 feet above the sea.

Before dawn we crossed the equator and gently settled down in Belem, Brazil, at the mouth of the Amazon for a half hour's refueling stop. A half hour? Twenty-six steaming hours later we were still cooling our impatient heels in that exotic jungle clearing, until Pan Am officials at last obtained clearance from competition-minded Brazil for another refueling stop in Rio de Janeiro.

The next afternoon, having skimmed above jungle trails which white men had never trod, we touched down at Rio and then winged on to Montevideo, where ranking Uruguayans greeted our sleepy group with cocktails, canapés, and speeches. Weary and bedraggled from our two days in transit, we listened hopefully for the all-aboard signal for Buenos Aires, which finally came twelve hours later! Juan Perón, the new dictator-president of Argentina, had decided to assert himself. Bursting with dreams of a transcontinental Argentine airline system, Perón had decreed that Pan Am could fly in as many planes as it chose, but could not fly them out again. Pan Am dared not risk the loss of its newest sky ship, so we groggily trudged off to a hotel while officialdom fought the battle of red tape.

The next noon we boarded two smaller planes and soared off across the pampas for the climax of our journey. President Perón, apparently deciding that it was a mistake to snub a planeload of correspondents from America's top publications, sent his best friend, publisher Eugenio de Sosa of Cuba, to greet us in his name and wave us through customs. The red carpet rolled out for us all over Buenos Aires, and no sooner had U.S. Ambassador George S. Messersmith received us at the embassy than Perón's top cabinet officials began competing for our company.

Perón sent word that he would grant our group a rare press conference the next day at Casa Rosada, but first his Foreign Minister gave a plush cocktail party in our honor. There, while chatting with Argentine dignitaries, Señor de Sosa politely asked what he could do to make my stay more pleasant. Inez Robb had served notice on our group that when we arrived in Argentina it was "every man for himself," because she would be staying on to write features for International News Service. Thus, I replied to De Sosa, "Thank you. I would like an exclusive interview with President Perón."

The Cuban publisher was aghast. As politely as possible, this Latin gentleman explained that the "great President" believed a woman's place to be in the home, that he would not dream of encouraging a woman reporter, and that he never granted exclusive interviews anyway. Persistence is a prime quality in any reporter's makeup, and since the gallant Cuban found it increasingly difficult to say no to a young woman, he finally said that if I would submit a few written questions, he might be able to persuade his "great friend" to reply in writing. It was better than nothing, so I agreed.

The next evening, still busily polishing my written questions, I arrived a few minutes late at the Casa Rosada for the mass press conference. I tried to slip unobtrusively into the rear of the vast salon, where Perón, at the head of a tremendous oval table, had already begun to address my traveling companions, but De Sosa had done his spadework well. The moment that he glimpsed me at the door he whispered to Perón, and the President promptly beckoned an underling to escort me to his side. Perón rose, bowed, and gallantly kissed my hand while cameras clicked. Then he directed that a chair for me be squeezed into the place of honor by his side. Brandy glasses at each of our places bespoke a conviviality which would certainly revolutionize U.S. press conferences, and after the conference Perón bowed once more over my hand, before affably escorting us around the state rooms of the palace.

Inez and I were roommates. That evening after dinner she went to the opera with some of our colleagues, but I went wearily to bed and had scarcely fallen asleep when my bedside telephone rang. De Sosa, after swearing me to secrecy, confided that Perón would grant me an exclusive interview the following morning. His Presidential limousine would call for me at 9 A.M., but none of the other reporters must know.

Early the next morning I dressed in the darkened room, to avoid awakening Inez, and slipped downstairs for breakfast. The lobby was forsaken except for an Argentinian hotel clerk, who recognized me as one of the visiting Americans and began affably, "You know about Madame Perón?"

"No," I replied guardedly, although rumors about the amours of Argentina's First Lady had already begun to encircle the globe.

"You *don't* know about Madame Perón?" he prodded.

Shrugging, I asked, "Well, what?"

At this the Latino became highly excited and, ticking off the count on his fingers, exclaimed, "I myself, six friends...all of us...tsch tsch...with her."

At that precise moment a flustered doorman bustled into the lobby, announcing, "Señora Montgomery, *El Presidente*'s car awaits." The garrulous hotel clerk paled visibly and slunk back into his cage, while I sailed grandly out of the lobby and into the bulletproof limousine for my ride to the palace. With all wheels miraculously greased, I was ushered upstairs in the President's luxuriously appointed elevator and into a palm-festooned waiting room, where steaming coffee was served to me from a sterling silver service. Unfortunately I am allergic to coffee, and when the lackey's back was turned I emptied my cup into a potted palm which looked as if it needed a stimulant.

De Sosa then emerged from the inner sanctum, hospitably announced that his "best friend" was ready to receive me, and led me to the President. Perón, bowing again over my hand, escorted me to an elaborately set coffee table, where, fortunately, tea was also to be had. For more than an hour, while De Sosa translated and Perón beamed, the dictator assured me of his hatred for Communism, his detestation of former U.S. Ambassador Spruille Braden, and his firm intention of cementing our good-neighbor relationship. Crossing his heart, the man who had refused to back us in World War II promised that the next time the United States went to war, Argentina would promptly enlist on our side. The President also—shades of Evita Perón, who was soon to emerge as leader of the Shirtless Ones —stoutly declared that women belonged at home.

"But if all *norteamericanos* were like you," he murmured flatteringly, "there would be no misunderstandings between our two continents."

At last I arose to leave, but Perón ingratiatingly delayed my departure while he sent for his largest self-portrait (bigger than my suitcase, I unhappily observed) and with a flourish wrote a flowery sentiment in white ink on the dark background. Then he snatched the blue-and-white pennant of Argentine Airlines from his wall and bestowed it as formally as an Order of the Garter.

De Sosa drove me to the cable office, where I wrote the interview and dispatched it to the New York *Daily News*. Then I joined my unsuspecting colleagues for lunch, and that evening we began our long flight back to Rio. On our arrival at dawn, I was disconcerted to find that my adventurous interview had made front pages throughout the South American continent. Brazilian newspapers were headlining long accounts of my interview, which wire services had picked up from the *Daily News* dispatch. Inez had remained behind, and I had to endure some good-natured joshing from columnist George Dixon and others, but all agreed that if they had had the opportunity, they would have done the same.

Rio de Janeiro, citadel of demonic drivers, honking horns, hairpin curves, and breathtaking scenery, opened her arms to us. In a caravan of creaking old cars driven by laughing Latinos apparently bent on their own destruction and ours, we lurched precariously to the peak of Corcovado Mountain, on which is perched the towering statue of Christ the Redeemer. Then we set out for our hotel thirty miles above Rio, in the mountains of Petropolis. Pan Am publicist Roger Wolin kept apologizing that he had been compelled by crowded conditions to lodge us in "a sort of tourist cabin" outside of town, but how he was teasing! As we rounded the last peak, shimmering before our dazzled eyes across a mountain lake rose the picturesque gables of one of the loveliest hotels in the Western Hemisphere, the fabulous Quitandinha. Within the glassed lobby coiled a kidney-shaped swimming pool, and abovestairs I found myself installed in a luxurious suite which had been decorated by Dorothy Draper for King Carol of Rumania and his mistress, Madame Lupescu. Dancing that evening in the tropical nightclub of the hotel, we spotted our Argentine flying companion who had taught us the samba above the clouds, but this time he carefully avoided the eyes of our group. His beauteous Brazilian mistress was with him, and he apparently sought no competition from U.S. newsmen.

The next day, after a press conference with Ambassador William Pawley at the U.S. Embassy, we went to the eighteenth-century palace of the last Brazilian emperor to interview President Dutra and his Foreign Minister. Then it was home to Washington, without stopovers.

Field Marshal Viscount Bernard Montgomery, chief of the British Imperial General Staff, came to Washington in September and held a press conference at the Pentagon. If he was aware of talk concerning the Presidential possibilities of General Dwight D. Eisenhower and General Douglas MacArthur, he gave no sign of it but told reporters, "The qualities required by a soldier and by a politician are at almost opposite poles," and he made plain that he thought soldiers had no business trying to seek high office. General Eisenhower unsmilingly sat through the press conference.

General Montgomery, who had first visited our neighbor to the north, was quoted in Canadian newspapers as having said that he wanted no women present at any parties for him in Washington. During the press conference I asked him why, and John O'Donnell's syndicated column reported the exchange:

> The hero of North Africa and great opponent of Rommel actually gulped as he faced the question of Montgomery (Ruth). The Field Marshal recovered promptly and, as one Montgomery to another, replied, "My dear lady, I can't think where that story ever grew up." Then he beamed at Montgomery, the reporter, and winked and grinned, and as the audience roared, pleaded, "It's really definitely unfair to attribute such a thing to me, because I'm very fond of the ladies. As a matter of fact [this to Montgomery, Ruth] I'm delighted to see you this morning. And please, will you tell the ladies that I like them?"

Bob and I gave a cocktail party that month, with other reporters and some top news sources as guests, and columnist Jane Eads of the Associated Press wrote of it:

> Some of the best parties in this party-loving town are given by newspaper people. They bat around together day after day on stories, eat lunch together at the Press Club and on Capitol Hill, meet for cocktails, and sometimes play cards together all night, but they never tire of each other's company. When they give a party, they usually invite a smattering of big names and one another. Success is assured. The big names are always happy to be on hand. They come early and stay late. That's what Senator Robert A. Taft did the other evening, but he wouldn't have known about the party if he hadn't been opening his wife's mail. Mrs. Taft was in Cincinnati. Petite and popular Ruth Montgomery of the New York *Daily News* staff, who was giving the party with her husband Bob, had addressed the invitation to Mrs. Taft. The Senator opened it, found he was included, and went, although he had to catch a train around eight o'clock. He kept pulling out his watch, but he managed to make a lot of conversation and drink a daiquiri or two. Once, when he didn't have a glass in his hand, someone thought he didn't touch the stuff and offered him a coke. "I don't think that would be very good with daiquiris, do you?" he asked.

A press agent for Henry A. Wallace, President Truman's Secretary of Commerce, dropped in to see me one day and suggested that I write a column about his boss. Delighted to have any legitimate news, I listened appreciatively and then wrote that Wallace, who had taken up flying as a hobby, "soon became so impressed with his own prowess that he inveigled some of his pals from the Department to come out to Washington airport and watch him solo.

"One of the Department's neat two-seater Ercoupes awaited the Secretary, and with a flourish he was in, up and away. After spreading his wings down Chesapeake Bay for awhile, Henry turned homeward toward his by now admiring cohorts. Determined to commit no flying faux pas for the benefit of such an audience, who had been kidding him unmercifully about his flying, he meticulously circled the field and swept in for a perfect three-point landing. Flushed with pleasure at his own skill, he stepped out to do a little ribbing of his own, but the Exponent of the Common Man stood alone. He had landed in Baltimore instead of Washington."

Wallace's press secretary also told me that Colonel Henry A. Berliner, chairman of the board of Engineering and Research Corporation which manufactured Ercoupes, had presented the Secretary with the first table model of the plane, and Wallace gave it the place of honor on his desk. Then New York's Macy's department store decided to sell airplanes over the counter, and the inexpensive, nonspinnable Ercoupe was a natural. Since Wallace had the only existing model, Berliner called at the Secretary's office and asked to borrow it back to lend to Macy's. This I reported in the same column, and as soon as Wallace scanned the paper the next morning, he personally telephoned to demand where I had received such absurd information. I let him rant for a while about the falsity of both items before purring, "But, Mr. Secretary, your own press agent gave me those humanizing items and asked me to print them."

"Haw haw haw," the Secretary unexpectedly guffawed into the telephone. "Well, I didn't know you knew it, but I guess I did make that Baltimore landing."

Shocked, I asked about the Ercoupe story and heard him ask his secretary about it. In a moment he was back on the line, saying,

"Excuse me, Miss Montgomery, but my secretary says that story was true, too. Well, nice talking to you. Good-bye." It gave me the shudders to think how nearly that strange man had come to being President!

Bab Lincoln, publicist for the Mayflower Hotel, gave a small tea for Martha Rountree that September, and I stopped in briefly on my way to a black-tie dinner with Bob. Martha and Larry Spivak had recently started a radio panel show called *Meet the Press,* and I soon became a panel member, continuing as one when it later became the most popular panel show on television as well. I was also to become a frequent TV panelist on the Rountree-Spivak *Keep Posted* show and on George Allen's *Man of the Week* and Martha's *Press Conference.* The amazing thing about television is that although I was by then a daily syndicated columnist in more than a hundred newspapers from coast to coast, strangers who had never seemed to notice my by-line suddenly began recognizing me by name, as well as face and voice, wherever I went. It is an exceedingly personal medium.

Mrs. Truman gave a charming buffet supper for women of the press in November, 1945, with candlelit tables scattered about the State Dining Room. Cissy Patterson, seated across the room with Mrs. Eugene Meyer, wife of the publisher of the rival Washington *Post,* came over to my table and sighed, "I wish I could sit here. I'm so sick of listening to that boring Agnes Meyer." Cissy fortunately could not foresee that although she had generously willed her own newspaper, the Washington *Times-Herald,* to her seven top executives, they sold it after her death to Colonel McCormick, who subsequently sold it to Eugene Meyer. Cissy's beloved newspaper was then merged with that of her archrival and quickly lost its identity.

CHAPTER V

Much Ado

In December, 1945, assigned to cover a Senatorial investigation of Senator Theodore "The Man" Bilbo in Jackson, Mississippi, I telephoned the principal hotel there to request a reservation. In no uncertain terms, the hotel clerk told me that there was no room at the inn for nosy Yankees, who had better stay up North where they belonged. I had made the mistake of telling the clerk why I needed the room, but I located another a block away. En route by train to Jackson, I had an amiable conversation with a charming Southern woman, who could not have been more agreeable until she learned that I would be covering the Bilbo investigation. Then, fairly hissing through her teeth, she read me the riot act about damnyankees and spoke to me no more.

For the next week I listened to a parade of witnesses who testified that the white supremacy Senator, while running for reelection, had accepted from war contractors a free Cadillac, a twenty-three-acre artificial lake on his farm, a swimming pool, furniture for his "dream house," a nearly $2,000 paint job on its exterior, thousands of dollars' worth of donations for a church and large parsonage which he built on his farm but kept vacant, and numerous other emoluments.

Bilbo took the stand and denied the charges that he had precipitated a reign of terror among would-be Negro voters. "I'm the best friend the niggers got in the U.S. Senate," he shouted. Asked if he had told a political rally that "Clare Boothe Luce is the greatest nigger-lover in the North except for Old Lady Eleanor Roosevelt,"

49

he grinned crookedly and retorted, "I sure did. It's true, you know." Asked if he had advised horse-whipping Negroes who tried to vote, he squirmed. "No, what I advocated was ridin' 'em out of town on a rail."

A dope addict confessed paying Senator Bilbo his life savings of $1,000 to obtain a dope permit, and a contractor said his friendship with Bilbo had cost him more than $60,000 in payoffs. When the new Senate convened in January, 1947, Bilbo was asked to step aside. Unsworn to office, he died a short time later of cancer of the jaw. My articles on the Bilbo hearings had been making front-page headlines for weeks, both in New York and Washington, but one day the Washington *Times-Herald* carried a Chicago *Tribune* story instead of mine. That was a "sister paper" also, but the next day, and thereafter, it carried my by-lined reports. Mason Peters, city editor of the Washington paper, ruefully told me why. The *Times-Herald* had been on the streets only a few minutes when Cissy Patterson called Peters to demand why he had used another reporter's story instead of mine. He correctly explained that my lead that day had a New York angle, but Cissy snapped, "I want Ruth's stories used every day, young man. Can you take orders?"

"Yes, ma'am," he meekly replied.

Early in January, 1947, I received one of the most mysterious telephone calls of my career. Eugenio de Sosa, the Cuban publisher who had arranged my interview with Juan Perón, was calling from New York. In conspiratorial tones, he asked how I would like a free trip to Havana to cover a big story. When I pressed him for details, he finally whispered that he was helping to finance a revolution to oust President Ramón Grau San Martín of Cuba, and that the invasion ships would sail toward Havana within a week. He added that he wanted me there to ensure "fair" coverage of the revolution, because he believed that President Grau was on the verge of handing over Cuba to Communist forces. I checked with my editor and on January 13 met De Sosa at LaGuardia Airport in New York for the adventuresome flight.

Two hours out over the Atlantic one of our motors caught fire.

The crew extinguished the flames, and we limped back to New York. That should have been enough adventure for one day, but my secretive traveling companion insisted that time was of the essence, so we took a taxi to Newark Airport, boarded another flight, changed planes in Miami, and flew across Caribbean waters to Havana. Just before disembarking, De Sosa warned me not to "recognize" him in the airport, and he sprinted ahead through customs. I found my own way to the Nacional Hotel, and the next day his aide appeared to advise that I should relax and enjoy myself until the action began.

Basking beside a sunbathed swimming pool in January is a not unpleasant way to earn a living, but after a few days of it I yearned for greater activity. The next time that the mysterious aide appeared, I therefore suggested that I should interview President Grau. He eagerly assented, and when I dispatched a telegram to the President requesting the interview, his answer was surprisingly prompt. No sooner had my eyes swelled almost shut from too much exposure to tropical sun than an invitation arrived to meet President Grau that evening at the palace. While a Cuban physician poured strange potions onto ice-cold poultices for my swollen eyes, I telephoned my predicament to the President's office and received a one-day reprieve.

The next evening, hiding my swollen lids behind dark glasses, I arrived at the palace and took a seat in the crowded anteroom. Shortly, guns began to boom, and my jumpy nerves telegraphed the instantaneous warning that the revolution must have begun; but after nine blasts they ceased, and I realized that the guns of Morro Castle had merely marked the time of day. By 10 P.M. the waiting room was still as crowded as when I arrived, and a lackey appeared to suggest that I return the following evening. I began an indignant protest, but a Cuban gentleman urged me not to be upset. He said that he was an ambassador to another Latin American republic, he had also had an appointment, and he had been waiting for three nights without success. The next time that I saw him, several years later, he was Cuban Ambassador to the United States and we became good friends.

Returning the next evening, I had not long to wait. Admitted to the inner office, I talked with President Grau for more than an hour about Cuban politics. Once, remarking that he feared a revolution, he led me to the broad windows overlooking the plaza and the harbor, and with a dramatic sweep of his arm, declared, "Planes will swoop down this mall and try to destroy me, but if I live I will defeat them." Recalling the booming guns the evening before, my spine tingled apprehensively.

Knowing that the Cuban constitution, which Dr. Grau had chiefly written, forbade a second term for the President, I asked whether he planned to run anyway, as some of his critics suspected. The answer that he gave me was to make eight-column banner headlines in all Cuban newspapers for nearly a week to come: "I will not seek reelection next year on one condition," he declared. "That is, if Batista or any of the old political crowd does not seek a comeback."

What a story! Inasmuch as the party of ex-President Fulgencio Batista obviously intended to try for a comeback, Grau was actually saying that he would defy the constitution. As soon as I could gracefully withdraw, I sped to the cable office to file my story. The next day United Press picked up my dispatch from the *Daily News,* and on my return to the Nacional Hotel after an evening with friends, the lobby was jammed with Cuban reporters and photographers. For once in my life I felt like Eleanor Roosevelt as they snapped my picture, bombarded me with questions about "your scoop," and pressed me for my full life story.

All of Havana's daily newspapers played my story in banner headlines, some reprinting my dispatch in full above their papers' mastheads. One daily devoted four solid pages to my story, career, and photographs, along with editorial comments about Grau's astonishing declaration. Then delegations of politicians descended on me, and Senator Eduardo Chibas, leader of President Grau's own Autentico party, whose millionaire father had fought with Teddy Roosevelt at San Juan Hill, arrived with radio engineers to record an interview with me for his daily broadcast. The president of Havana University asked for the "privilege" of giving a dinner in my honor, and others clamored for me to make speeches.

My privacy had vanished, and so had the revolutionary invasion. De Sosa and his fellow plotters, convinced that the furor surrounding

President Grau's revelation of his illegal intentions would defeat him without bloodshed, postponed their plot. Understanding at last why Greta Garbo wanted to "be alone," I flew back to Washington. I much preferred to write, rather than make headlines. I did not, however, acquire the anonymity that I sought. Cuban magazine writers flew to Washington to photograph and interview me, and the next week's issue of *Newsweek* magazine featured me in an article which began:

Ruth Montgomery of the New York *Daily News* is a vivacious and blue-eyed Washington reporter who looks like a cub, but isn't. Last July, with several fellow Washington correspondents Miss Montgomery took the inaugural postwar Pan American Airways flight to Buenos Aires. While her traveling colleagues enjoyed the pleasures accorded newsmen on a junket, Miss Montgomery got the first exclusive interview with newly elected President Juan Perón of Argentina.

Returning last week from another junket to the south, Miss Montgomery left behind her an editorial and political uproar in Havana. In an exclusive interview with President Ramón Grau San Martín, she broke a story Cuban newsmen have been trying to break for a year—whether Grau would seek reelection. She quoted him, "I will not seek reelection next year on one condition —that is, if Batista or any of the old political crowd does not seek a comeback."

Cuban editors, aware that the Batista faction plans a comeback, interpreted Grau's statement as meaning he would run again, although the constitution now bans consecutive terms for a president. Havana's seven big papers headlined the interview; Senator Eduardo (Eddy) Chibas, leader of Grau's Autentico Party, appeared with Miss Montgomery on the radio, and other government officials gleefully wined and dined her for smoking out the story. Cuban newsmen fidgeted. The *News'* Washington correspondent said she would be back soon.

Simultaneously, *Editor & Publisher* magazine carried a lengthy dispatch from Havana about "the American newswoman who caused a political sensation that landed her picture and name on the front page of nearly a score of Havana papers." After recounting the events, the magazine writer said: "Havana papers reacted to the beat in various ways. The Communist *Hoy* called the *Daily News* writer 'a Yankee adventurer who put words into the mouth of President Grau,' while the anti-Grau *Prensa Libra* ran three pictures of her on Page One and commented, 'Ruth Montgomery, the woman who succeeded in obtaining the sensational interview with Grau, is one of the best news writers in the United States.' "

The article added: "Several Cuban papers commented that the President 'should not have given such important news to a foreigner, when he had refused it so long to Cuban newsmen.' As a result of the newspapers' stories, a number of high ranking politicians called on Miss Montgomery to learn more details about the President's intentions."

After my return to Washington the Communist newspaper *Hoy,* a staunch supporter of Grau, carried a fanciful article announcing to its Red readers that I must have been drunk while obtaining the interview "because she was wearing dark glasses to hide her blood-shot eyes." My poor sunburned eyes! I did not know of the artful explanation until Frank McCarthy, head of United Press in Havana, sent me the clipping, together with the "answer" published by an anti-Grau newspaper. The latter, above its masthead on page one, carried an eight-column banner line which read YO NO BEBO, DICE MONTGOMERY. Knowing my ignorance of the Spanish language, McCarthy gleefully translated the bannerline. "I don't drink," the paper kindly had me replying to the charges, although I had not said it.

In the fall of 1946 Secretary of State Jimmy Byrnes made a trip to Moscow as President Truman's personal emissary and was widely criticized by Republicans and newspaper editorials for his mission. On his return, the Trumans gave a garden party at the White House for wounded war veterans and invited Byrnes to stand with them in the receiving line. Along with several other newswomen, I was standing just behind them to report the conversations and was intrigued to hear one of the limping veterans say to Byrnes, "Gosh, Mr. Secretary, you did a wonderful job for us in Russia."

Byrnes, happy at last to hear a kind word about his mission, beamed as he said, "Why, thank you, soldier. Where are you from?" "St. Elizabeth's," the veteran replied.

I could scarcely contain my amusement, since St. Elizabeth's is a government institution for the mentally disturbed. As soon as there was a break in the receiving line, I impishly slipped over to Mrs. Truman to tell her about the conversation, and she bent double with laughter, gasping, "I can't wait to tell Harry. This will simply make his day!"

The news of Byrnes' resignation early in January caught everyone by surprise. The question rattling the teacups was: "Did Jimmy really want to quit?" The excuse given was failing health, but that very morning the State Department had released a medical report saying that a recent checkup showed Byrnes to be in excellent physical condition. In my column that day, I quoted sources as hinting that Byrnes was being booted to ground the political kite of General Eisenhower. They reasoned that with the surprise nomination of General George C. Marshall to succeed Byrnes at the State Department, Ike would not embarrass his former chief by declaring for the Presidency in 1948.

President Truman's ninety-four-year-old mother had broken her hip early that year, and her health was failing rapidly. In late July I was assigned to cover President Truman on his flight to his mother's bedside, and we were 10,000 feet above Cincinnati when the pilot received a message: "The President's mother died at 11:09 A.M. CST." Truman had just dozed off for a nap when his personal physician awakened him to break the news. From Dr. Wallace Graham's expression the President guessed the import and sighed, "Well, now she won't have to suffer anymore."

We had been slightly delayed at takeoff while Truman signed the armed services unification bill at the airport, but he still could not have reached the bedside of the spunky old lady in time to bid her a last farewell. At her simple five-room cottage beside the railroad tracks in Grandview, Missouri, President Truman sat in a rocker on the back porch as lifelong friends gathered to pay their last respects to his mother. The friends were barred from the services for lack of space, but the First Family and her other son and daughter clustered in the kitchen while services were read in the living room. Then, with highway patrolmen blocking cross highways, the family and news reporters drove in a twelve-car procession to the wooded knoll in Forest Hills Cemetery, where she was placed to rest beside her husband, John, who had lain in an unmarked grave for thirty-one years. A towering sandstone monument identified the plot as that of Martha Truman's father, Solomon Young, a onetime millionaire who operated a flourishing express service between Independence and Salt Lake City before the Civil War.

CHAPTER VI

Out of the Jaws of Victory

THE Presidential nominating conventions of 1948 were the first that I had covered and consequently seem the most exciting. Philadelphia, the City of Brotherly Love, was a shambles by the time Thomas E. Dewey beat out Taft and Harold Stassen for the GOP nomination, Truman roused unhappy Democratic delegates to frenzy with his Turnip Day acceptance speech, and Henry A. Wallace lent himself as a willing tool to the left-wing Progressive Party which splintered from the Democratic to nominate its own slate. Television, the new baby of the airwaves, was covering its first political convention, and I appeared on some TV interviews with candidates, while working sixteen-hour days covering the news for my papers.

None in the convention hall can forget the "doves of peace" which were dramatically unleashed during the Republican conclave. While the frightened birds soared overhead, we members of the press corps frantically dived beneath newspapers and benches to escape the pelted droppings, which reminded us less of peace than of the indignities of war. On the first two ballots, Governor Dewey held more votes than Taft and Stassen combined, and my story of June 24, 1948, read: "A shirt-sleeved, self-confident Tom Dewey emerged grinning late today from his Bellevue-Stratford hotel suite and predicted victory on the third ballot. His tie was definitely awry." Victory was soon his, and the scramble for the Vice Presidential nomination began. With a close friend of California Governor Earl Warren, I called on him at his hotel suite to determine whether he would be available.

Warren's reply was unequivocal. Under absolutely no circumstances, he assured us gravely, would he accept the nomination. Meanwhile, Congressman Charles Halleck had thrown the Indiana delegation to Dewey to put him over the top, with the understanding (he thought) that he would receive the Vice Presidential nod. The next evening, I covered Governor Warren's acceptance speech as the running mate for Dewey and began to learn that anything a politician says is not to be confused with what he does.

Democrats are invariably more fun than Republicans when politics is afoot. They play harder, scrap better, and seem to have more zest for living. With barely time to sleep the clock around, I began covering the arrival in Philadelphia of the dispirited donkey party boys. Defeat was in the air, and the more honest of them conceded that 1948 would be a Republican year. The Dixie Democrats wanted no part of their incumbent President, although tradition decreed that he should be entitled to nomination for a second term and Harry definitely wanted the job.

Gloom heavily festooned the rafters of Convention Hall until, as party keynoter, Barkley took the podium. Then the sad-eyed Democratic Convention came alive and shouted itself hoarse, as the Kentucky Senator pulled out all the stops in a lengthy diatribe against the Republican Party and the GOP-controlled Eightieth Congress. In the hour-and-ten-minute keynote address, the Senate Democratic leader mentioned President Truman only once. When he did, every person in the flag-draped auditorium sat on his hands. Barkley ended his speech with a prayer. At its conclusion, every delegate leaped to his feet in rousing ovation, while hundreds clutched their party placards and paraded around the hall. The Barkley boom for Vice President was on.

Harris G. Sims, editor of the Leland (Florida) *Ledger,* wrote in his convention report that day:

> What a gallant southern gentleman Senator Barkley is. About a dozen of us newspaper men surrounded him on the speakers' platform and asked him whether he had heard from President Truman in regard to having him for a running mate. He said the President had telephoned to congratulate him on his keynote

speech, and as the sleepy-eyed Kentuckian said that, he recognized a charming young woman who had come up back of us to see what was going on.

The Senator threw her a kiss and said, "Hello. Where have you been all my recent life?" "I've been busy, writing about you," she replied. "Don't write *about* me," he said, smiling broadly, "write *to* me." The girl, blushing as the group laughed, continued, "I'll send you a copy of what I wrote about you." To which the Senator from Old Kentucky responded, "Don't *send* it to me. *Bring* it to me." We asked the girl to write down her name and newspaper so that we could write a sidelight about the Senator's public romance with her. She turned out to be Ruth Montgomery, Washington correspondent for the New York *Daily News*.

Everyone thought that Barkley had the nomination in the bag; everyone except President Truman. Four Southern delegations had already walked out in protest against Truman's renomination, so the Chief Executive sought desperately to keep the liberals in line by getting Supreme Court Justice William O. Douglas for his running mate. But the Justice, convinced that Democrats were doomed to defeat in 1948, kept out of range of telephones in the mountains of Washington State to avoid the Presidential draft and the loss of his court seat.

During the long wait I slipped backstage at Convention Hall, where Barkley and Senate Secretary Leslie Biffle were angrily pacing the floor, and when I asked Alben if he would still accept if chosen, he muttered the now-famed words, later to be repeated at a press conference, "I don't want any warmed-over biscuits." He said Truman had better be quick with his offer, or he wouldn't take it, but I knew that my old friend was longing for the chance to be Vice President.

Truman, in a railroad car parked at a nearby siding, eventually gave up hope of reaching Douglas and handed the prize to Barkley. Then, at 1:30 A.M., House Speaker Sam Rayburn introduced Truman as "our leader and the next President of the United States," and the weary delegates managed a rising ovation. Truman thereupon launched into a slashing attack on the GOP and declared that he would call Congress back into special session on Turnip Day, July 24, to finish its business. Dubbing the Republican Eightieth Congress the "do-nothing Congress," despite its loyal backing of his Marshall Plan, foreign aid, and Greece-Turkey aid bills, he said he would keep it in session until it passed an "adequate" housing bill, a civil rights program, anti-inflation legislation, and an expanded Social Security program.

Democratic delegates, finding a new lease on political life, roared their approval, and I whispered to my editor, Richard E. Clarke, "The little man had better be careful with that kind of talk, or he'll find himself reelected." Later, Clarke dictated an editorial quoting my prophetic utterance and warning Dewey to fight, or else.

Bob had joined me in Philadelphia for the Democratic Convention, and after our return to Washington we stayed only a few days before leaving for vacation in Bermuda. On July 12, 1948, *Newsweek* magazine headed its business section with a story which began: "Bound for a week's vacation after a strenuous tour of duty at the Conventions, a New York *Daily News* Washington correspondent, Ruth Montgomery, stopped in at a Sunday night cocktail party. She sniffed out a tip. The next day, instead of idling in a hammock, the pert newspaperwoman was hammering out the financial scoop of the week —the Federal Reserve Board had quietly filed an anti-trust complaint against A. P. Giannini's Bank of America and its holding network, the Transamerican Corporation." It then reprinted my article.

The last evening before our departure for Bermuda, Bob and I attended a dinner party given by Evie Robert in honor of Cissy Patterson. We had grown exceedingly fond of Cissy, who had invited us to so many parties at her Du Pont Circle mansion and her country estate in the nearby Maryland countryside, and we felt rather concerned about her that evening. Having just returned from a board meeting of the *Tribune* in Chicago, she seemed overly tired, but she did a hilarious imitation of "Cousin Bertie" McCormick imitating Alicia Patterson, Cissy's niece, when Cissy proposed her for membership on the *Tribune* board. Alicia, then editing her own highly successful paper, *Newsday,* was considered too liberal by the archconservative McCormick, even though Alicia's late father had been co-owner Joseph Medill Patterson.

As Bob and I prepared to leave the party, Evie Robert whispered to us to delay Cissy's departure as long as possible, because a process server was hiding in wait for her outside. We did our best, but Cissy was so tired that eventually Evie had to tell her why she was being detained, whereupon Cissy's eyes lighted and she exclaimed, "Good! That will be the best excitement I've had all day." Firmly taking Bob's arm, she started toward her waiting limousine, and as the man leaped from the bushes to serve the summons, Cissy haughtily cast it to the ground, snorting disdainfully, "How dare you?" We later learned that a rug-cleaning establishment was suing Cissy for non-payment, despite her allegation that in cleaning some of her Oriental rugs, the nap and fringe had been ruined. We gave Cissy a fond kiss of farewell, and early the next morning left for Bermuda. While there, we learned that Cissy had died in her bed the night after Evie's party. We felt overcome with sadness.

A month later Mary King Patterson, widow of Cissy's beloved brother Joe, sent me a copy of the *Women Lawyers' Journal* which reported an interview its writer had had with Cissy the day of Evie's party. One question asked of her had been: "Who are the outstanding Washington newspaperwomen?" Tears filled my eyes as I read Cissy's gracious response, "In my opinion, Ruth Montgomery is tops."

I can only say of Cissy Patterson that she was the most colorful newspaperwoman I have ever known, and probably the best. She had her foibles and eccentricities, but I never saw the side of her which others have criticized and berated. To us she was always the embodiment of kindness, charm, and graciousness. We have never ceased to miss her radiant personality.

Shortly after the Turnip Day session of Congress reconvened, I began covering the exciting Hiss-Chambers hearings before the House Un-American Activities Committee on Capitol Hill. Chambers, an admitted ex-Communist who was then a senior editor of *Time* magazine, charged Hiss with having been a member of an elite guard in the prewar Communist underground. Hiss, a former high-ranking State Department official who had stood at President Roosevelt's elbow during the Yalta Conference, where the U.S. sold out so much of the free world to Joseph Stalin, vigorously denied any Red affiliation—ever—and questioned Chambers' sanity. We knew that one of the men had to be lying, but which? The suave Hiss, at that time president of the Carnegie Peace Foundation, certainly presented a better appearance to us than plump, badly rumpled Chambers, and sympathy at first was with him.

During Congressional questioning, Hiss claimed to have given a 1929 Model A Ford roadster to Chambers in an apartment-subletting deal because he had bought a new Plymouth, but Chambers said that Hiss gave the car to a Communist Party organizer. The next day the committee produced an official District of Columbia transfer of title showing that Hiss had signed over the car to the Turner Motor Company, which assigned it to a mysterious William Rosen the same day. Hiss conceded that it was his signature, notarized by a personal friend, but professed to have no recollection of the deal.

At this point Representative Richard M. Nixon, a California Republican, broke in to ask disgustedly, "How many cars did you give away while working for the government, if you can't remember the details of this gift?" Hiss had claimed a sentimental attachment to this particular car, and since my own first automobile was also a 1929 Model A Ford, as I sat there I began to doubt the honesty of the polished, well-groomed man. I knew exactly how I had disposed of mine. Louis Budenz, an ex-Communist editor, testified that Alger Hiss was known by Communist Party leaders to be a member in 1940, and Elizabeth Bentley added her damning testimony against Hiss. The committee was making daily headlines, as was freshman Congressman Nixon with his new leads and sharp questioning. Because of the anti-Red fame which accrued to him through these hearings, Nixon was later to be elected Senator and then to be tapped by General Dwight D. Eisenhower as his running mate. Those Hiss-Chambers hearings were the rung of the ladder that ultimately led to the Presidency for Richard Milhous Nixon.

But the nation was by no means united behind the committee in those skittish postwar years. The Justice Department accused the committee of "trying to tear down the American system of government," and Truman called the charges against Hiss "a red herring." Chairman J. Parnell Thomas replied with a blast at President Truman and Attorney General Tom Clark for attempting to "obstruct and thwart" the unit's investigation of Communist espionage.

Hiss eventually was convicted by the courts of perjury but was out on appeal when, on January 25, 1950, I attended a memorable press conference at the State Department. Dean Acheson had by then succeeded General Marshall as Secretary of State, and the conference that day was held in an upstairs room, where I was seated next to Acheson at a large oval table. When a newsman asked him for comment on the appeal, the Secretary, tense with emotion, said that it would be highly improper for him to discuss the legal aspects of the case "or anything to do with the case" while it was before the courts. I believe that he should have left it at that. Instead, he took a long breath and blushed to the roots of his graying hair as he continued, "I should like to make it clear to you that whatever the outcome of any appeal which Mr. Hiss or his lawyers may take in this case I do not intend to turn my back on Alger Hiss."

Several legislators had already demanded Acheson's resignation because of his close association with Hiss and his brother Donald, a member of Acheson's law firm who had been his former State Department assistant. Acheson, suave, debonair, and witty, had always seemed the master of any situation, but as he plunged ahead, I had the feeling that he had rehearsed before the mirror what he was about to say: "I think every person who has known Alger Hiss or has served with him at any time has upon his conscience the very serious task of deciding what his attitude is and what his conduct should be. That must be done by each person in the light of his own standards and his own principles. For me, there is very little doubt about those standards or those principles. I think they were stated for us a very long time ago. They were stated on the Mount of Olives and if you are interested in seeing them you will find them in the 25th chapter of the Gospel According to St. Matthew beginning with verse 34." It was a beautiful sentiment, but I could not help but remember that the Master had also angrily thrown the money changers out of the Temple, without speaking a word in their defense. The charges against Alger Hiss were that while in a position of highest governmental trust, he had passed on secret papers of state to our enemy, Russia. Was this less culpable?

Back in 1948, at the height of the Hiss exposé, the U.S. Atomic Energy Commission took the unprecedented action of blacklisting two CIO unions because of the alleged Communist affiliation of some of their officers, while Truman adamantly declared that there was no danger from Communism.

By then the Presidential campaigns had begun in earnest, and I rode all that fall on the Dewey campaign special. My editors, convinced that Truman would lose, wanted me to become acquainted with the new group that would soon take over the White House. As our train pulled into Owosso, Michigan, in October, Governor Dewey's boyhood neighbors gave him a hero's welcome. Some 20,000 people cheered while his caravan rolled along the treelined streets to William Field, where another 15,000 awaited—in a town whose total population was only 18,000.

Owing to lack of hotel accommodations, we reporters slept on the train, which was parked on a siding during Dewey's two-day visit with his mother. Humor columnist George Dixon had previously written a story about the lack of bathing facilities aboard the train and kidded the "dirty reporters," although actually we each had a compartment with a lavatory, and we occasionally sprinted into hotel rooms long enough to line up for a shower at brief stopovers.

That Sunday morning in Owosso the reporters attended church with Governor Dewey, and while seated in the quaint Episcopal church where Dewey had sung as a choirboy, a sweet-faced old lady tapped me gently on the shoulder, whispering, "Dear, we live right next door to Mrs. Dewey. Wouldn't you like to come home with us and take a bath?" I must have looked rather startled, because she hastily assured me that she had been "reading about your lack of bathing accommodations." At least she hadn't been smelling us!

The Washington press corps is largely Democratic, and numerous stories which emanated from the Dewey train were harshly critical because of the writers' personal dislike of the GOP nominee. Typical was the way many reporters handled the story at a stop where Dewey was to address a large crowd from the rear platform at a railroad station. Just as the nominee started speaking, the train suddenly began backing into the throng massed together on the tracks, and Dewey exclaimed, "What's the matter with that engineer? Is he crazy or something?" Frankly, I could not imagine a more normal reaction. The engineer well knew that at each depot stop, the tracks were always crowded with Dewey well-wishers, but some reporters gleefully played it up as an insult to railway trainmen by the Republican nominee.

At Mrs. Dewey's hometown, Sapulpa, Oklahoma, a large crowd of townfolk turned out to greet that state's favorite son-in-law, and Dewey was in fine humor as he stood beside his sparkling wife on the train's rear platform. Noting the many youngsters in the forefront of the crowd, Dewey smilingly declared, "I'll bet you like me because I got you out of school this morning."

The youngsters, with one accord, yelled back, "Yaaaahhhh, it's Saturday." The hardworking candidate had forgotten the day of the week.

The rival Truman train was meanwhile chugging around the country, and as the President would "pour it on" Dewey and the Eightieth Congress, partisans shouted, "Give 'em hell, Harry." Truman was even convincing normally Republican farmers that they lacked silos for crop storage because of GOP Congressional inaction, and Dewey was disappointing his followers by refusing to retaliate in kind. Dewey, believing that he had the election in the bag, did not want to divide the country by a low-level campaign, but we reporters were growing increasingly restive with his repetitive speeches about "sweeping with a new broom."

A week before election I received a letter from Mother which declared, "All of us out here are disgusted with Tom Dewey's namby-pamby campaign, and all this talk about unity. A lot of my Republican friends say they are not going to vote. They think Dewey will win anyway, but they don't want to give him a landslide."

I hastily sought out James F. Hagerty, Dewey's press secretary, and said, "Jim, better tell Mr. Dewey that unless he starts fighting and putting some punch into his speeches, he's going to lose my Midwest relatives. And if he loses dyed-in-the-wool Republicans like that, he'll lose the election."

I liked Governor and Mrs. Dewey and had had several interviews with them, but if Jim delivered my amateurish advice, it was ignored. The high-flown speeches continued. At the request of my editor I talked with all the top Dewey advisers aboard the train for a lengthy article about what Dewey would do as President. Winding up the campaign trail in New York, I covered Dewey's final rally at Madison Square Garden, which was jammed to the rafters, and the next day watched the Deweys vote. After dinner that night, we reporters gathered at press headquarters to listen to the returns, and it soon became apparent that something was amiss. In my story for the evening edition I wrote, "An air of gloom settled over Dewey headquarters at the Roosevelt Hotel tonight as nip and tuck election returns failed to produce the anticipated Republican landslide."

Campaign manager Herbert Brownell, Jr., continued to release encouraging messages for party faithful in the crowded ballroom, but news tickers were telling a different story. At midnight, when Brownell made another victory-in-the-offing statement, I asked, "Herb, do you really think that Dewey still has a chance?" His shoulders sagged as he responded wearily, "I hope so." Herb Brownell was too astute a politician to believe his own pep talks.

The next morning, having conceded defeat, Governor Dewey called a press conference and told us that he would never again run for President. It was his second rejection, and GOP leader Hugh Scott was to coin the phrase "Dewey snatched defeat out of the jaws of victory." Dewey was in fine fettle at the conference, and when asked if hindsight would have changed his campaign strategy, he declared, "Governor Warren and I are both happy that we waged a clean and constructive campaign, and I have no regrets whatsoever." Meanwhile, newsmen were gleefully exhibiting an early morning edition of the Chicago *Tribune* whose eight-column headline read DEWEY WINS. At least the disappointed candidate had that for his scrapbook.

CHAPTER VII

Truman Rides Again

CHINESE nationalists had also assumed a Republican victory in 1948, and when Madame Chiang Kai-shek made an 11,000-mile flight to Washington to plead for U.S. aid for her Communist-threatened homeland, she received a chilly reception, which contrasted sharply with the tumultuous ovation given her on a similar mission in 1942. Not a single top-ranking U.S. official met her plane, although she was the wife of an allied head of state. Madame Chiang had intended to request the advisory services of General Douglas MacArthur for her country, but Truman jumped the gun on her by telling an overflow press conference that MacArthur would not be sent to China.

A few days after the election upset, our Women's National Press Club held a reception for Mrs. Truman and Margaret, and when I shook hands with the First Lady, I smilingly remarked, "As you know, I'm a Republican, but I want to congratulate you anyway."

Her face lighting with high good humor, she chuckled. "Ruth, I can't tell you how pleasant it is to meet an honest person. Margaret and I are pretty sick of Wednesday Democrats." She meant, of course, the people who loudly sang Dewey's praises until the Tuesday election, but were now pretending that they had been for Truman all along.

Among our good friends were Mr. and Mrs. William P. Hunt, at whose beautiful estate in Greenwich, Connecticut, we often attended house parties. Together with Senate Secretary and Mrs. Leslie Biffle, *Diplomat* magazine editor Hope Ridings Miller, Governor and Mrs. James K. Vardaman of the Federal Reserve Board, and others, we went to New York for the debut dance of their pretty daughter, June Hunt, in the Plaza grand ballroom. At Bill Hunt's dinner party beforehand, I was seated next to Dr. H. H. Kung, a former Premier of China whose sister-in-law was Madame Chiang Kai-shek.

The next week we went to a party which Perle Mesta gave for Dr. Kung, and when the Hunts came to Washington, Bob and I hosted a dinner party for Vera and Bill. Margaret Truman was among our guests, as were Vice President-elect Barkley, Senator and Mrs. Leverett Saltonstall, Senator and Mrs. Brien McMahon, Senator and Mrs. Burton K. Wheeler, Senator Robert M. La Follette, Representative and Mrs. John Davis Lodge, Perle Mesta, Alice Roosevelt Longworth, the George Allens, and Senators Robert Taft, William Knowland, Homer Ferguson, Styles Bridges, C. Wayland Brooks, and their wives.

Bill Hunt presented Barkley with an oil portrait which he had commissioned of the future Veep and the *Reader's Digest* subsequently carried an anecdote about the party, which said in part: "At a buffet supper in Washington, a careless waiter spilled something on Senator Leverett Saltonstall's knee. As the Massachusetts Senator rubbed the trouser leg vigorously, his supper partner commented, 'That's good material. It won't spot badly.' 'It should be good material,' confided the Senator. 'These pants belonged to my father.'"

The Hunts were "old China hands," and Bill had made a fortune selling banknotes to the inflationary Chinese government, before he was imprisoned by the conquering Japanese and eventually repatriated on the *Gripsholm*. He maintained excellent connections with the Nationalist government after World War II, so when he gave me a tip to investigate a man named Michael J. Lee, who was chief of the Commerce Department's Far Eastern division, I hastened to comply.

Contacting friends in the Commerce Department, FBI, and CIA,

I learned the astonishing fact that Lee had been turned down three times for U.S. citizenship on the grounds "Not good character, not attached to principles of the Constitution, incompetent witnesses" before marrying an American and finally becoming a citizen. Lee had been brought into the Commerce Department by Henry A. Wallace, after both the Army and the Navy had rejected his application for commissions. I further learned that he had been born Ephraim Zinovi Liberman in Harbin, Manchuria, and had made a trip to Soviet Russia before coming to America. Now he was head of the strategic Far Eastern division, which controlled shipments to China, and no real material had begun reaching China until eight months after Congress authorized such aid.

My revelations created a furor in government circles, and as soon as Congress reconvened in January, Chairman Edwin Johnson of the Senate Commerce Committee launched a full-dress investigation of Lee and his division. The committee, leaning heavily on my research, also subpoenaed Commerce files and discovered that Lee had falsified his job application, claiming to have bachelor's, master's, and doctorate degrees from a nonexistent university in Manchuria.

I had put Commerce Secretary Charles Sawyer on the hot seat, but he granted me an interview about Lee and invited Bob and me to dinner with him at his apartment. Several years later, when Neil McElroy came to Washington as Eisenhower's Secretary of Defense, Sawyer told his fellow Cincinnatian, "Be sure to look up Ruth Montgomery in Washington. She's a darned good newspaperwoman, who will never double-cross you, so don't be afraid to level with her." McElroy later told me of the conversation, and I was glad that Sawyer bore me no ill will, because my stories had forced his hand and he had discharged Lee from government as a security risk.

Shortly after Truman's election Governor Dewey came to Washington and gave a party for the reporters who had accompanied him during the campaign. Before my arrival, he told John O'Donnell and several other correspondents that if he had won he had intended to appoint Ruth Montgomery as the first woman White House press secretary. Having had no previous inkling of his intent, I was astonished and flattered to hear the news.

During the Congressional recess before his swearing in as Vice President, I sent Alben Barkley an invitation to a party that Bob and I were planning in honor of William Randolph Hearst, Jr., and his bride, Austine Cassini. From his home in Paducah, Kentucky, Barkley sent me a gay letter which said, "If I get to Washington in time and can attend the cocktail party, before being compelled to go to the Gridiron dinner to roam around there with a lot of stags, without benefit of femininity, I will make a desperate effort to do so. Let me thank you also for your congratulations upon my election, which you did not remotely expect." How right he was!

Our party had to be postponed until January 15, and after I wrote Barkley to that effect, he responded: "Dear Ruth, your invitation to the delayed, postponed and otherwise mismanaged Hearst celebration was promptly received. I am hoping that I will be able to come, although I am sure you realize that as the twentieth of January approaches, I am becoming more nervous, frustrated, discombobulated, postponed and mismanaged myself. I do not know what I will be required to do as much as 24 hours ahead of any given time. At any rate, I remember your attractions, I remember your charm and all the things you are, if you know what I mean. Thanking you and hoping to rejoice with you, I am affectionately and devotedly, Alben."

Among the society page write-ups about our party was one which declared, "The Kentucky Man of the Hour, Vice President-elect Alben W. Barkley, was among the guests, as were Senators Burnett Maybank, Homer Ferguson, Styles Bridges, William Knowland, Lister Hill and their wives, Perle Mesta, Justice Frank Murphy, and Congresswomen Clare Boothe Luce and Margaret Chase Smith."

Two weeks before Truman was to take his second inaugural oath, he accepted General Marshall's resignation and appointed Dean Acheson to succeed him as Secretary of State. Senator Tom Connally of Texas, who had recaptured his chairmanship of the Senate Foreign Relations Committee when Congress went Democratic, grumbled that Truman had not informed him of the appointment until a half hour before telling our press conference, and outgoing Chairman Arthur H. Vandenberg had been ignored. This put a severe strain on the already taut bipartisanship of our foreign policy. Tall, cultured Acheson was subjected to public hearings about his relationship with the Hiss brothers, during which he said, "My friendship is not easily given and not easily withdrawn." He was then confirmed.

On January 20, 1949, the thirty-five-degree temperature provided crisp marching weather for the seven-mile extravaganza, as Harry S. Truman led the biggest inaugural parade thus far in the century. General Eisenhower and Secretary of the Army Kenneth Royall shared an open touring car in the parade, and that evening Bob and I went to a party for Ike and Mamie Eisenhower at the Wardman Park apartment of George (*Presidents Who Have Known Me*) Allen. The Eisenhowers, in sparkling humor, stayed as long as possible before leaving to attend Truman's inaugural ball.

Eight years later, when Harry S. Truman of Independence gruffly told newsmen that he would not attend Eisenhower's second presidential inauguration "because he didn't come to mine," Ike was asked about it at a press conference. He replied that he could not recall offhand whether he had been there, but he grinned delightedly when I rose to remind him that he had ridden in the parade and gone to the ball.

The week of Truman's inauguration a jury was selected to decide the fate of Axis Sally, the nickname given to forty-eight-year-old Mildred E. Gillars, an American woman who had broadcast Nazi propaganda to American GI's from Germany during the war. At her treason trial, which I covered daily for several weeks, the prosecution played taped broadcasts in which she called our pilots "American murderers" and proclaimed, "This is a war of Gentiles against the Jews." In the broadcasts beamed to America, she had told U.S. mothers that their soldier sons "know now that they are simply cannon fodder to aid and abet Jewish interests."

Axis Sally's defense lawyer, realizing that he had little chance to free his client, made a motion for mistrial based on a newspaper column written by Mrs. William Randolph Hearst, Jr., and he flatteringly filed a $100,000 suit against me for a column that I had written about the trial, but Federal Judge Edward M. Curran threw both claims out of court. Axis Sally was convicted of treason, sentenced to ten to thirty years in prison, and fined $10,000.

Shortly afterward I returned to federal courthouse to cover the espionage trial of a suspended Justice Department employee named Judith Coplon. The tiny twenty-seven-year-old Barnard College honor graduate was charged with stealing secret Justice Department papers for transmission to Russia through her boyfriend, Valentine Gubitchev, a Russian engineer employed by the United Nations. One of the more than twenty confidential FBI data slips which Miss Coplon was charged with stealing stated that Ruth Gruber, a confidential aide to former Secretary of the Interior Harold L. Ickes, was "reported to have been a contact of a man at the Soviet Embassy." Twelve other FBI slips seized from Judy's purse at her arrest proved so hot that the government withheld them from evidence for fear of jeopardizing our national security. Judy's subsequent conviction was later reversed, and for reasons unknown she was not retried.

James Forrestal had become our first Secretary of Defense, but he resigned in early 1949 and Truman speedily nominated Louis Johnson to succeed him. After covering the Senate hearings on his nomination, Bob and I spent the weekend with the Hunts in Connecticut, where Bill gave me photostatic copies of an exchange of letters between David and Lewis Kung, the so-called Kung kids, who had given White House servants a headache when they visited there with their aunt, Madame Chiang Kai-shek, during the Roosevelt era. The correspondence indicated that the two Chinese had had considerable business dealings with Louis Johnson in connection with the Yangtze Trading Corporation.

Returning to Washington on March 24, I telephoned Johnson to ask why he had told the Senate hearing nothing about those dealings, while supposedly listing all his business associations. The connection seemed dead, but after a moment he stammered, "Wha—wha—what's that again?" He finally said that he didn't believe I knew what I was talking about and huffily rang off.

That afternoon I went to President Truman's press conference and as usual was standing beside his desk waiting for the "all in" signal, when Truman glared at me and muttered sarcastically, "I see you've been having some fun for yourself." Surprised, I asked what he meant, and he replied, "You know very well. You've been up to your favorite game of needling someone."

I hadn't the foggiest notion what he meant, but after telling Ted Lewis about it at the office, we hit upon the logical answer. Even as we were talking about it, a bulletin sounded on the news ticker stating that the Senate, in a surprise vote without previous notification to Senators, had confirmed Johnson's nomination as Secretary of Defense. Apparently Johnson had called the President about my disturbing telephone call, and Truman, fearing that the information might affect the Senate vote if I wrote it, had requested immediate confirmation.

It was unsavory action, but the deed was done, so Ted and I decided not to break the story. This must have been a tremendous relief to the administration, for at Truman's next press conference, as soon as he entered the room, he deliberately caught my eye and, beaming broadly, said, "Good morning, Miss Ruth."

Louis Johnson appointed our mutual friend, Stephen T. Early, as his Undersecretary of Defense, and after Steve's prompt confirmation he invited me to lunch in his Pentagon suite with Johnson. We never mentioned my telephone call again, and in March while I was covering war maneuvers on Vieques Island off Puerto Rico (the only time that women were permitted to cover war games) Johnson tramped halfway across the island to look me up and convey greetings from Steve.

Washington also had its lighter side in those early postwar years. Leslie Biffle, disguised as a chicken farmer to sample rural political sentiment during the 1948 campaign, had won fame by predicting that Truman would win. Almost as unique as his prognostication was his chubby spouse, Glade, who was also making column footnotes with her droll witticisms, now that the Biffles were White House intimates. Some of us were sitting with Glade under an umbrella at the British Embassy's garden party in honor of the queen's birthday, when Leslie sauntered over to ask if he could bring her some strawberries. "Why, that would be real nice," she drawled, but when he wanted to know if she would like Devonshire cream on them, she firmly replied in the negative. "I do hate milk in any form," she said in her West Virginia accent. "It tastes too personal."

At a party in the modern mansion of Morris and Gwen Cafritz, Treasury Secretary John Snyder spilled a glass of wine and was abjectly apologizing, but when a butler came running with a mop, Glade soothed Snyder, saying, "Now don't you worry. They were expecting it. That's a brand-new mop."

Her dry wit reached its peak, however, when she recounted the aftermath of a stag party attended by President Truman in the Biffles' Westchester apartment. Leslie was still asleep the next morning when Glade, surveying the empty liquor bottles in the dining room, decided that she had better get rid of them before the maid came.

"I slipped into my kimono," she drawled, "and loaded up my arms with bottles. I carried them down the hall, and as I was dropping them one by one down the incinerator, I noticed that one of them still had a little liquor left in it. Well, it was too much to throw away and too little to save, so I was downing it just as a woman opened her door across the hall to get the Sunday paper. She took one look at me and said, 'Why, Mrs. Biffle!' I said to her, 'I do hate waste in any form,' and finished the bottle."

Another time, when Glade accompanied Vice President Barkley to the launching of a new passenger ship, the sun beat down relentlessly, and Glade sighed, "I'm soaking wet. I feel like I've been to a lynching instead of a launching."

Senator Lyndon B. Johnson was having a dinner party one evening, and as the hour approached, Lady Bird became increasingly distressed. The butler engaged for the evening had failed to arrive, and a dozen telephone calls failed to produce a substitute. In desperation she called fellow Texan Mary Clark, wife of the Supreme Court Justice, and said she simply had to get a butler to turn the ice-cream freezer.

"If that's all you need," Mary Clark said, "I'll send Ramsey over to turn it." The Clarks' son, Ramsey, did his good deed for the day, and fifteen years later President Johnson appointed him Attorney General of the United States.

CHAPTER VIII

Barkley Takes Center Stage

Few thrills can exceed one's first trip to Europe, and on a glorious day in May, 1949, I flew over for a five weeks' work-and-play excursion through occupied Germany and Austria, Paris, London, and Rome. I flew in a coal plane in the Berlin Airlift, at ceiling zero, clutching a card printed in Russian, which in the event of a crash would identify me to unfriendly Soviet ground troops as a reporter instead of a spy. During a tour of West Berlin my heart ached for the German children who groveled with their mothers in the rat-infested cellars of bombed-out dwellings, and in the Soviet eastern sector I saw the mounds of rubble which were all that remained of the building and bomb shelter where Adolf Hitler met his death.

Near Munich I went to Dachau, where unnatural heaps of swollen earth bespoke the mass burials of thousands of innocent Jews who died in gas chambers to satisfy the bloody housepainter's lust for power, and at Berchtesgaden I picked my way through the shambles of a once-imposing mansion where Hitler had frolicked with Eva Braun. Then I pressed on to the somewhat happier capitals of war-torn Europe.

Shortly after my return home, Senate Majority Leader Scott W. Lucas sought me out and asked whether I was happily married. Puzzled, I assured him that I was. He then asked if there was any possibility of my leaving Bob, and I emphatically replied in the negative. I was totally bewildered by the odd conversation, until I later learned that Lucas was acting in behalf of his close friend Veep Barkley, who had recently met an attractive St. Louis widow named Jane Hadley. A few days following my encounter with Lucas, Barkley paid a second visit to Jane in St. Louis, and rumors of possible matrimony began to fly. No one had yet been able to pin down the Veep on his intentions, but my news editor asked me to try, and *Time* magazine reported in its August 22 issue as follows:

A Washington newswoman bustled up to Vice President Alben Barkley and asked coyly, "Veep, my editor would like to know what Mrs. Hadley has that we don't have—except maybe you?" Barkley promptly seized good-looking, thirty-ish Ruth Montgomery and bussed her smack on the lips. "There is your answer, kid," cried the Veep. Chortling, he added, "I'll tell you something you've got that she hasn't got. A husband."

The New York *Daily News'* Montgomery was talking about Mrs. Carleton Hadley, the comely 37-year-old St. Louis widow whom Barkley has managed of late to see almost every weekend. But the nation's tabloid readers needed no explanation. Last week they were following the sedate capers of 71-year-old widower Alben Barkley with the interest usually reserved for limber-loined starlets bound for the Riviera. Barkley was a mite stiff in the joints, but his eagerness to kiss a pretty girl was as well known as his homespun quips.

The day that the story about Alben's kiss appeared, I was walking along the corridor outside the Senate when Barkley came around the corner, gave one look, and to a crowd of reporters shouted happily, "There's my kiss-and-tell girl. I'm going to give her something really to tell about." I laughingly began to sprint toward the press gallery, with the Veep in hot pursuit, and as I darted into a telephone booth, he grabbed and bussed me soundly, before the whistling press corps.

All that fall the Senate was meeting in the old Supreme Court chambers while its own chamber was being renovated, and the Veep, who had become increasingly nearsighted, spent much of his time in the presiding officer's chair writing letters, with his kindly face pressed almost against the paper. To tease my old friend, I sent a note up to him, asking if he was writing a love letter to Jane. With his delightful sense of humor, he summoned a page boy and sent me two pages of the letter that he was writing to her.

The October announcement of their approaching nuptials was reacted to like a shot in the arm by frustrated society hostesses, because the White House was undergoing its most extensive renovation since the British burned it and the formal entertaining season had been canceled. Pretty Jane Hadley was full of social graces, the Trumans rarely went to private parties, and the party-loving Veep would soon be showing off his bride.

The New York *Daily News* dispatched me to cover the St. Louis wedding, whose details were being handled by Jane's closest friend, Mrs. Richmond Coburn, who was also a friend of mine. Thus, while other newswomen camped on Ruth Coburn's doorstep hoping for tidbits, I was talking frequently to her by telephone, and she invited me to a small family party for Alben and Jane the evening before the nuptials. Jane met Alben's plane and brought him to the home of Mrs. T. M. Saymon, where the rest of us waited, and as they entered the door, Mrs. Coburn called out, "Alben, I have a surprise for you."

The nearsighted Veep peered around, caught sight of me, and grabbed me in his arms. Then, leading me to his future mother-in-law, he said, "Mrs. Rucker, I want you to meet the girl who would have been Mrs. Alben W. Barkley if she didn't already have a husband."

Jane, standing alongside, smilingly exclaimed, "Don't think I don't know it!" Startled by his lack of tact, I quickly responded that if that were the case, he would probably have divorced me when he met Jane, and we laughed together.

The next morning we assembled in a quaint Gothic chapel to hear Jane and Alben pledge their troth. Afterward, when Jane caught sight of some 2,000 people massed outside the church steps, she groaned, "Alben, I can't go out there and face that mob."

The Veep, firmly taking her arm, replied, "That's not a mob, Jane. That's the great American people."

No one from Washington had been invited to the wedding festivi-

ties for lack of space, but as an old friend I was asked to join the
Rucker-Barkley relatives and a few St. Louis friends for the bridal
luncheon after the wedding. When it was nearly time for the newlyweds to leave, Jane took me upstairs with her while she changed
into her going-away costume. Alben was having too much fun to
leave the party, and in desperation his younger daughter, Mrs.
Douglas MacArthur II, whispered to me, "Ruth, you're the only one
here with enough influence on Daddy to get him moving. Will you
persuade him to go upstairs and change clothes?"

I headed for the Veep, firmly grasped his arm, and said, "Come
on, Alben. You'll be the life of the party at plenty of others when
you get back to Washington, but now it's time for you to go." With
a few more tugs at his sleeve, he finally went upstairs, and soon they
were on their way, with Jane at the wheel of her new car, to Paducah.

A week after the Barkley wedding, I covered Margaret Truman's
first professional singing appearance in Washington in two years.
The President and Mrs. Truman, acting like proud parents the world
over, wiped away tears of joy as the packed house at Constitution
Hall tumultuously cheered their daughter through encores and curtain calls. Subsequently, when music critic Paul Hume wrote an
unfavorable review of her performance, Truman angrily dashed off
a handwritten letter which was replete with unprintable phrases.
Other newsmen, learning of the President's undignified letter, broke
the story, and Mrs. Truman reportedly gave her husband a worse
dressing down than he had given the music critic.

Two days before Christmas Bob and I moved into our newly purchased Georgetown house, a section of Evalyn Walsh McLean's
Friendship which was being divided into four separate townhouses,
and when the Barkleys returned from their honeymoon for the opening session of Congress, we gave a party for them. The Veep was
never in better form. As soon as the receiving line disbanded he
found himself irresistibly drawn to the first landing of our open
staircase, which he used as a stage from which to recount one hilarious story after another to the explosively laughing guests below.

I had invited two other staff members from my Washington

bureau, chief correspondent John O'Donnell and war correspondent Frank Holeman, who had just returned from Korea. Even Frank admits that I gave him the correct address, but he mistakenly went to the house next door, where a different party was in progress, and he had been imbibing for more than an hour when O'Donnell glimpsed Frank's unmistakable six-foot-six-inch frame through the doorway. Whistling him outside, he began tentatively, "I thought you were coming to Ruth's party."

Frank, fixing him with a wary eye, asked, "You mean I'm not here?"

John guided him next door, and as they mounted my front steps he prodded curiously, "Didn't it ever occur to you that you hadn't seen Ruth there?"

"Well, sure," Frank drawled in his North Carolina accent, "but I don't know about these fancy shindigs. I thought maybe it was the custom for the hostess to swing down the stairs to the accompaniment of a Marine band when it was time for us to leave."

Frank is a unique and delightful character. When the Korean War broke out, our wire desk ordered him to catch the first plane there, and our sartorial giant took his tuxedo along. For all those dirty, weary months in foxholes and press camps on that embattled peninsula, Frank slept with his rumpled dinner jacket under his head. GI's came to regard the tux as their last link with civilization. The war continued, but Frank eventually came home to discover that his superb judgment had been vindicated. Every suit and overcoat that he had left in the closet of his rooming house was dissected by moths. All that the tuxedo needed was a good cleaning and pressing.

Life for a gay young bachelor like Frank was a thing of beauty. Some of the soiled laundry which he brought back from Korea was still in a suitcase beside his desk many years later, but it had become indistinguishable from the soiled laundry in four or five other suitcases and airline overnight bags—mementos of other junkets that Frank's presence had brightened. Each time that he drew another out-of-town assignment, he bought a new suitcase and more shorts and shirts. Frank's desktop overflowed with years of unanswered mail, a four-year-old birthday cake from his aunt, several samples of dripless coffee cups which he had patented but failed to sell, nine boxes of unworn ties and socks presented to him at Christmas, and a robot plane propeller. He also kept unmatched shoes, some moldy cigars, and stale candy in an overflowing cardboard box under his desk. Life may have changed for Frank since he married our office receptionist and became an assistant to the editor in New York, but we remember him with fond nostalgia.

Colonel McCormick had meanwhile bought the Washington *Times-Herald* from the seven heirs of Cissy Patterson and installed his niece, Bazy Miller, as editor. I had also begun my own column for the New York *Daily News* syndicate, and the *Times-Herald* carried a number of "puff" articles about it, with quotes from Senators Taft, Bridges, Wherry, and Margaret Chase Smith, and one from Veep Barkley which began, "Anyone as smart and sweet as Ruth is bound to produce a column of intense interest to Washington. She is one of the most intelligent persons I know, and I wish her every success in her new undertaking."

Although society reporting is not my dish of tea, I was the only newspaper writer who managed to cover another wedding which had greater security protection than a U.S. President's visit to an off-the-record council of state. Romaine Dahlgren Pierce Simpson—the second divorced "Mrs. Simpson" to wed a descendant of Britain's strait-laced Queen Victoria—became the Marchioness of Milford-Haven in a celebrity-studded wedding in Washington. All press representatives were barred from the scene, and admission to the church was by invitation only. Among those who received engraved bids were Archduke Franz Joseph and Archduchess Martha of Austria and Mary Van Rensselaer Thayer of the old New York Van Rensselaers. The former two attended. The latter, better known as Molly Thayer, did not.

Molly had been writing a society column for the Washington *Post* but had been fired shortly before the wedding. Then she received a telephone call from Mrs. Clark McIlwaine, mother of the bride, telling her that she simply could not come to the wedding because she was a "professional person" and adding, "The children know so many people who write and they can't have them all, so they are not having any. You were my only slip. Be sure to tear up the invitation in little pieces, and don't come."

That was all that Molly needed! She telephoned me, told me what had happened, and asked if I'd like her invitation. Indeed I would, and at the appointed hour I was graciously ushered to a seat at the wedding, while my newspaper friends who jammed the sidewalks outside looked on in envious mystification. Meanwhile, another newspaper had asked Molly to cover the wedding, so she drove Alice Roosevelt Longworth to the church and parked outside until the services were over, when "Princess Alice" would give her a fill-in.

After the "I do's" were said, Mrs. Longworth hurried down the steps and into Molly's car. The bride's mother, seeing them together, assumed that they both had attended the ceremony and sprinted out to the curb, screaming, "Molly, how could you? You promised you wouldn't come."

Molly gave her a haughty stare, and Mrs. McIlwaine turned her indignation on Mrs. Longworth, shrieking, "And you, Alice! What are you doing here with Molly?"

Mrs. Longworth poked her head out of the car window and replied blandly, "Oh, I'm Molly's leg woman." Then they sped from the scene.

In June, 1950, a Washington newspaper reported: "Ruth Montgomery, whose life has been marked by eight-column banner story by-lines, made news of her own last night as she was inaugurated president of the Women's National Press Club. The occasion was as politically charged as any that the beautiful and sprightly columnist has encountered on her news gathering chores. For half an hour on 'Meet the Press,' Ruth, Austine Hearst, Doris Fleeson and May Craig climaxed the inauguration dinner by firing depth-charged queries at Vice President Barkley." Martha Rountree was the moderator, and Larry Spivak sat in the audience to watch the first all-female panel in the history of *Meet the Press*.

Vice President Barkley was hilarious, as usual. After completing the installation of officers, with a half hour to spare before air time,

I called on the Veep to take over, and the Washington *Star* reported: "Rising to the occasion, the Veep spotted several members of the Senate in the audience and called on them to speak on subjects ranging from the fourth dimension to why Dick Russell, the senator from Georgia, had remained a bachelor. There were no filibusters, and the program started on time."

Our press club had long hoped for its own clubhouse, so that became my first order of business as president. Hope Ridings Miller, who was then doing publicity for Ted Mack and his *Original Amateur Hour,* suggested that we have Ted broadcast a VIP amateur hour under club sponsorship so that we could reap the proceeds for the clubhouse fund. We knew that we could fill Constitution Hall for such a celebrity-studded event, and visions of a $100,000 profit danced in our heads. We spent astronomical hours that fall enlisting talent from the three branches of government and the diplomatic corps, arranging for ticket sales, and assigning members to solicit ads for our slick-paper souvenir program. Everything was going swimmingly, and a clubhouse seemed in the bag. Then came the Korean War, and our high hopes went aglimmering.

Swallowing hard, we drastically reduced the admission fee and decided that all proceeds from the ticket sale would be donated to the USO, which Harvey Firestone, Jr., hastily reactivated in time for our show. President Truman announced that because of the war, he would attend no press functions that year, including the Gridiron Club, but because ours would benefit the war effort, he accepted my invitation, and Ted Mack and I personally presented him with tickets for the Presidential box. Constitution Hall was a complete sellout, and with trembling knees I strode to center stage that night to welcome the Trumans, the vast audience of VIP's, and the listening radio audience. Then the show was on!

Speaker Sam Rayburn, as impresario, presented skits featuring Mrs. Alben W. Barkley, Secretary of State Acheson, Supreme Court Justices William O. Douglas and Tom Clark, Treasury Secretary Snyder, Postmaster General Jesse Donaldson, Interior Secretary Oscar Chapman, Agriculture Secretary Charles Brannon, Labor Secretary Maurice Tobin, Navy Secretary Francis P. Matthews, and a bevy of other top-ranking officials and their wives. A Senate chorus consisting of Senators Hubert Humphrey, John Sparkman, John McClellan, Homer Ferguson, Herbert H. Lehman, Homer Capehart, Lister Hill, Russell Long, Warren Magnuson, and a dozen others vocalized at the top of their voices, and a House chorus also performed.

Philippine Ambassador J. M. Elizalde and Senator Guy M. Gillette played piano solos, Representative (now Senator) Albert Gore gave a violin solo, and Madame Henri Bonnet, wife of the French ambassador, staged a style show with Parisian gowns flown over from the House of Dior. Her models were the wives of Cabinet officers, Senators and ambassadors. Cuban Ambassador Luis Machado gave a guitar solo, the wife of Peruvian Ambassador Fernando Berckemeyer offered a vocal rendition, and Mrs. Joseph E. Davies (now Marjorie Merriweather Post) led a square dance which featured future Secretary of Defense Clark Clifford, Madame Bonnet, Mrs. J. Borden Harriman, and several generals and admirals.

At a dramatic moment Second Lady Jane Barkley wheeled a legless veteran of the Korean War onto center stage, while the audience of four thousand people joined in singing the "Battle Hymn of the Republic," and Secretary Acheson paid high tribute to the veteran.

A few days after the show I presented a check for $10,368.18 to USO chairman Firestone in the presence of General Omar Bradley, Chairman of the Joint Chiefs of Staff, in his Pentagon office. Newspapers throughout the country carried our pictures, and the write-ups duly reported that the club's expenses in producing the show were only $56.39, after paying federal admission taxes of $2,380. As a result, numerous government officials kidded that they wanted me to handle the government budget if I could practice that kind of economy. The only funds that the club retained were $6,000 in proceeds from the advertising in our souvenir program.

On April 18, 1951, I inaugurated our club's first Editors' Dinner, which thereafter became an annual event. It coincided with the convention of the American Society of Newspaper Editors in Washington, and some of the editors, along with Vice President Barkley, Madame Pandit, the ambassador of India, Chief Justice Fred Vinson, and Ambassador and Madame Bonnet of France graced the head table.

More than six months had elapsed since Secretary of State Acheson had given a major speech, but I persuaded him to make a major foreign policy address for us. As I introduced him and he stepped to the podium to begin his speech, several right-wing Senators and their wives, seated at a table immediately in front of us, whipped out corncob pipes and began puffing at them, in silent protest against the administration's abrupt recall of General Douglas MacArthur from Korea. The next day MacArthur arrived in Washington for a tumultuous reception, despite his firing by President Truman, and I covered the parade and his speeches in Congress and at the Monument grounds.

Our press club held a number of other events that year, including a reception for Margaret Truman, and when we learned that the all-male National Press Club had lined up Madame Perle Mesta for her first speech when she returned from Luxembourg for consultations, I persuaded her to address our club the day before. The revenge was sweet, since the men would not let us attend their club events.

Princess Elizabeth and Prince Philip came to Washington in October, 1951, and although red-coated, starry-eyed Elizabeth had the show to herself at the airport ceremonies, Philip stole the spotlight along the parade route lined with more than a half million onlookers. After tea at the White House the royal couple hurried to the Statler Hotel for a press reception, where I had a pleasant chat with Philip about our mutual friend Cobina Wright. The next day I attended the reception hosted by Princess Elizabeth at the British Embassy and covered the royal couple on their visits to Mount Vernon, Arlington Cemetery, the Capitol, the Supreme Court Building, and other official edifices.

At the House of Representatives, doorkeeper William G. "Fishbait" Miller persisted in gripping Elizabeth's arm, although royalty is not touched in Britain, and physically propelling her around to see the sights. While showing her the Speaker's podium, he pompously shouted across the chamber, "Send me the Prince." The affable Duke of Edinburgh obliged. At the Library of Congress, Elizabeth indicated polite interest in the Declaration of Independence, but the duke grinningly asked, "Does it really say 'taxation without representation'?"

Hap and Tania Seitz invited us to the theater to see a play starring Sarah Churchill, but at the box office Hap was informed that two of our seats had to be changed. We had just started to protest, when a Secret Service man beckoned me from an alcove of the lobby and whispered, "Ruth, we had to separate your four seats because President and Mrs. Truman are coming, but yours are directly behind them." We were mollified, to say the least, and throughout the performance we had ringside observation of Bess and Harry Truman and Justice and Mrs. Tom Clark.

These were rather relaxed years in the nation's capital, despite the problems of war. Mrs. Guy Innes, a spirited British visitor, found herself face to face with First Lady Bess Truman at a White House reception and bubbled, "Oh, dear, I have to watch myself. I almost curtsied." To which Bess matter-of-factly replied, "If you had, I'd probably have curtsied right back." While reception line guests tittered, the President remarked, "And that's just about what Bess would have done, too."

Madame Wellington Koo, wife of the Chinese ambassador, gave a luncheon party and hired a hypnotist to entertain us. After putting a young woman into light trance, he told her that she would no longer be able to see Madame Koo. Then he brought her out from under hypnosis, and a short time later she let loose a piercing scream. Madame Koo had offered her a glass of orange juice, but the frightened girl thought that it was floating in the air toward her. The stunt was so effective that in my column I suggested a similar solution for Secretary Acheson's biggest headache—to have the China Lobby blotted from his own view.

Jo Jo Black, daughter of the Supreme Court Justice, gave a slumber party for two dozen teen-agers, and Justice Black surprised the girls by producing President Truman to play the piano for them, while the eight other Justices looked on.

The Senate was also inadvertently providing rich comedy. GOP leader Kenneth Wherry took the floor and solemnly told his colleagues, "It is my unanimous opinion that..." and another day intoned, "We're sending aid to Burma, India and Indigo China."

Senator Tom Connally said of a Senate action, "We're just cutting off our noses to spite somebody else's face," and, turning to Saltonstall, asked, "Would the Senator from Massachusetts ask the Senator from Texas that again? The question went through the mind and out the rear."

Another time, Wherry blamed Democrats for killing their own civil rights legislation, and shaking his finger at presiding officer Barkley, demanded, "Who killed Cock Robin?" Deadpan, Barkley replied, "The chair does not know."

Senator William E. Jenner, on another issue, declared, "The economic basis of the Western world was cut in half three different ways." Jenner was as famed for his irrepressible wit as for his right-wing philosophy. One day millionaire Senator Robert Kerr, while solemnly filibustering against a tax bill that would affect his own oil interests, intoned, "I was baptized not once, not twice, but three times." Quickly, Jenner stage-whispered to a fellow Republican, "I always said the SOB was waterlogged."

Rumors were circulating that Senator Margaret Chase Smith would make a bid for the Presidency in 1952, and a reporter asked her what she would do if she woke up and found herself in the White House. With a trace of a smile, the only woman Senator replied, "I would apologize to Mrs. Truman and go home."

Madame Perle Mesta was busily earning the title of Mrs. Malaprop. Hearing that a Republican had been appointed to UNESCO, she exclaimed airily, "I know all about that organization. I attended a meeting of ESCROW in Paris last fall." In Luxembourg she was winning plaudits for her hospitality to GI's who were with our occupation forces. One day she received a delegation of touring Four-H Club farm youngsters and, flashing her winning Oklahoma smile, effused, "It's always a pleasure to entertain you 4-F's."

In the write-up of a party which we attended, a society reporter mentioned the ambassadors and Cabinet officers there, "and also Ruth Montgomery, wearing the same eye-catching white straw hat with a bunch of red and white flowers which caused Secretary of State Acheson, at a recent press conference, to pause and inquire, 'Have you watered those recently, Ruth?'"

One day a photographer new to Washington snapped a picture of a group of dignitaries and then went, pencil in hand, to ask each his name. All gave correct answers except the smiling man in the middle. When the novice poked his pencil at him and asked what's yer name, Harry S. Truman deadpanned, "Merriman Smith of United Press."

CHAPTER IX

The Eisenhower Crusade

I TRAVELED across the continent by train in September, 1951, to cover the Japanese Peace Conference in San Francisco, where Anne O'Hare McCormick and I were the only women correspondents. As the sole representative of the New York *Daily News,* I was working eighteen-hour days to stay abreast of the competition, and at the end of one of my dispatches I wired my editor, "Pity poor me, all alone covering this conference while the New York *Times* has ten reporters here, and the New York *Herald Tribune* seven." Within a half hour came his return message, "Our sympathies are all with the *Times* and *Herald Tribune,* having to compete with you." I had to continue my overtime.

One evening, having just filed a story for the first edition and returned to the Conference Hall, where a Western delegate was rebuking the Soviets for intransigence, I noticed that dour-faced Russian delegate Andrei Gromyko suddenly arose and stalked from the room. The Czech and Polish delegates exchanged uneasy glances, then followed Gromyko outside. So did we correspondents who, as we began trailing him down the corridor, were mentally rewriting our leads: "Gromyko walks out on peace conference." Gromyko went down a flight of stairs, and we followed in hot pursuit, until he abruptly turned into the men's room. That was one place I couldn't follow him, but neither did the male reporters. While we stood outside in a worried huddle, wondering what to do next, Gromyko emerged and stiffly retraced his steps to the Conference Hall. In a few minutes, the two Red satellite delegates also slunk back into the hall and resumed their seats. That call of nature was more embarrassing for them than for us.

During the conference, Mrs. Ambrose Diehl and soprano Lily Pons gave a party in my honor, and afterward I joined Charles "Chip" Bohlen and John Allison of the State Department for a drink. Within a few years they would become ambassadors to Russia and Japan respectively.

President Truman's address to the conference was the first ever televised coast to coast, and after the treaty was at last signed, I flew down for a visit with Cobina Wright at her home in Beverly Hills. While there, she gave a party for Philippine Ambassador Carlos Romulo, at which I renewed acquaintance with multimillionairess Doris Duke and met such legendary screen stars as Norma Shearer, Douglas Fairbanks, Jr., Jane Wyman, Janet Gaynor, Tyrone Power, and Edgar Bergen. The next day we went to tea at Pickfair with Mary Pickford and Buddy Rogers and to a later party at the home of Edward G. Robinson.

Doris Duke gave a party for me at the Bel-Air, and afterward we went to Ciro's to hear Pearl Bailey sing. On our way home we stopped off awhile to see Marion Davies, at whose home publisher William Randolph Hearst had died a few weeks earlier. Stacks of Hearst newspapers, gathering dust on a table in the front hall, bore mute testimony to reports that the Hearst Empire had abruptly stopped delivery of papers there the day that he died. Marion looked ghastly. Dark circles underscored her hollow eyes, her bleached hair hung unkempt, and she was the epitome of despair, but she married within the year.

Back in Washington I broke a story about Daniel J. Flood, a New Deal Congressman from Wilkes-Barre, Pennsylvania, who had enjoyed more than a hundred free commuting trips to his home district on Colonial Airlines, the most subsidized of all U.S. carriers, in violation of Civil Aeronautics Board regulations. Flood, a lawyer by profession, was a member of the appropriations subcommittee which controlled the purse strings of the Commerce Department and the

Civil Aeronautics Board, and I noted in the story that he had harassed the CAB chairman for not granting Colonial's request for several highly lucrative new routes. Also riding Colonial, he had taken a free honeymoon trip to Bermuda, listed as "company business" on the records, but his trips abruptly ceased just before the CAB fined Colonial president Sigmund Janas $75,000 and turned over eighty criminal counts to the U.S. Attorney's office for prosecution of the airline. Records showed that in less than four years, tax-subsidized Colonial Airlines had paid nearly $500,000 to the legal firms of such influential Democrats as William Boyle, Truman's handpicked chairman of the Democratic National Committee, former Defense Secretary Louis Johnson, former Ambassador to Moscow Joseph E. Davies, and former Navy Secretary John L. Sullivan, in addition to fees for its own staff of attorneys.

My story made front-page headlines, and I followed it with another disclosing that Flood's new wife was drawing a top salary on her husband's tax-supported payroll, although she did no work there and was spending the summer at a vacation cottage in Pocono Pines, Pennsylvania, while Congress was in session. As a result, Flood was defeated for reelection, but the coal miners of his district returned him to office two years hence.

The wife of Senator Robert A. Taft suffered a stroke shortly before the Presidential primaries of 1952, and her speech was greatly impaired, but not her sense of humor. Bob and I went to a small dinner party in their Georgetown home, where a butler took our coats, and after Senator John Butler of Maryland arrived, Martha stammered, "My aren't we grand! Two butlers tonight."

In March, 1952, I accompanied President Truman and his entourage to Key West for his work-and-play vacation. Truman's name had been entered in the New Hampshire primary, scheduled for a few days hence, and neither the President nor his staff was in a good humor, because they felt he would not win it. In fact, Presidential press secretary Joseph Short curtly announced that any photographer who snapped a picture of the President would "be thrown off the base."

My editors had decided that I needed a rest and this would be a good place to get it, but I had just daubed myself with suntan oil when the inevitable wire arrived from my New York desk: "Revolution broken out in Cuba. All incoming planes and ships being turned back from island, but get there anyway."

Wiring back that "Gertrude Ederle is on her way," I secured passage on an antiquated two-motor Cuban plane and landed in Havana without incident. The downtown mall was lined with beardless lads holding submachine guns and rifles, and a strange silence enwrapped the once-vibrant capital. Strong man Fulgencio Batista took over Cuba in a seventy-seven-minute almost-bloodless coup and proclaimed himself dictator, saying, "We are the law." He suspended constitutional guarantees, canceled the Presidential election, installed his own chief of police, and sent President Carlos Prío Socarrás fleeing from the country. Batista, who had been living in exile in Florida since he lost the Presidency in 1944, was once again the undisputed ruler, and after a couple of days I flew back to Key West to resume my coverage of Truman's loud sport shirts and daily swims.

We were still at Key West when Estes Kefauver defeated President Truman in the New Hampshire primary and General Eisenhower won a landslide victory over Senator Taft, although Ike was still at his NATO post near Paris. Joe Short said we could quote the President as saying that his defeat would have absolutely no effect on his decision whether to seek reelection.

What everyone wanted to know was whether Truman would run, and on returning to Washington I began my syndicated column of March 26, 1952, this way:

> The biggest political guessing game of the season should be all over by Sunday morning. At least, that's the dope from one of President Truman's shrewdest political advisers. This source confides that the President's political address at the Jefferson-Jackson Day dinner here Saturday evening will tip his hand on whether he plans to run for reelection, even if he doesn't mention the

subject. If Truman should decide to take himself out of the running, this electrifying announcement would be carefully omitted from the prepared text of Truman's speech released in advance to radio and press reporters.

On Sunday, March 30, the New York *Daily News* reprinted my column with this editorial comment: "Ruth Montgomery correctly foretold in her column last Thursday the procedure which Truman followed last night. She wrote that if Truman decided to quit the running, he would omit that statement from his prepared text. That's exactly what he did." The headline was: HST WON'T RUN, STUNS JEFF DAY DINERS WITH UNSCHEDULED ANNOUNCEMENT. Oddly enough, another Democratic President named Lyndon B. Johnson was later to follow that procedure in a television speech to the nation a generation later, and he, too, had finished an unexpired term of a predecessor who died in office.

Democrats were becoming increasingly worried about scandals involving some highly placed officials in the Truman administration as the 1952 elections approached, and, on April 3, I went to interview Newbold Morris, who had been brought from New York by Truman and the Justice Department to investigate charges of corruption. We had a pleasant discussion about his plans to force income disclosures, and I had just returned to the office when news tickers flashed a bulletin. Newbold Morris had been fired by Attorney General J. Howard McGrath.

Picking up the telephone, I called Morris and asked if he had heard the news. He hadn't, and I read him the bulletin. After a moment of dead silence, he said explosively, "Well, the bum could at least have fired me himself, instead of by news ticker!" Another pause, and he added, "Say, it would be something, wouldn't it, if McGrath fired Morris and then Truman fired McGrath." That is exactly what happened within a few hours.

In my interview with Morris that morning, he had said that he was going to quit unless President Truman either discharged Mc-Grath or forced him to fill out a financial questionnaire that he had prepared. But if Truman backed him, he had arranged a new batch of questionnaires for ambassadorial and governmental officials "aimed at people like Ambassador to Mexico William O'Dwyer," who had been accused of financial skulduggery.

McGrath, instead of answering the questionnaire, fired Morris, and Truman then fired the Attorney General. Morris, taking it philosophically, charged that he had been brought to Washington to "whitewash" the administration but added, "If we haven't done anything else, we've gotten rid of Howard McGrath in only two months. I don't think official Washington wants to be investigated."

Publisher F. M. Flynn, delighted with my exclusive on Morris, told John O'Donnell that I was responsible, more than any other factor, for the tremendous jump in circulation which the New York *Daily News* had enjoyed that year. My paychecks, however, reflected no improvement.

A week later, I broke the story that Supreme Court Justice William O. Douglas and Mercedes Davidson, wife of a former assistant Secretary of the Interior, were asking their respective spouses for divorces so that they could wed. I reported that Douglas and Mrs. Davidson had spent two weeks together at an isolated dude ranch called Rancha de la Osa on the Mexican border and that she had now slipped away to seek a divorce. My story sent shock waves reverberating through Washington and was quoted in newspapers throughout the country. No personal scandal had previously touched a Supreme Court Justice, but of course, there is only one Douglas. He did indeed get a divorce and marry Mercedes. Since then he has had two more divorces and remarriages, picking younger brides each time. Amusingly, my story broke simultaneously with an issue of the *New Republic* magazine, which on its front cover plugged a major piece entitled "Justice William O. Douglas on the Power of Righteousness."

The Republican Convention of 1952 unfurled its banners in Chicago, and the rival Eisenhower and Taft factions found fleeting harmony as former President Herbert Hoover walked to the podium. The spontaneous twelve-minute ovation brought tears to the old man's eyes, and later he told radio commentator Ray Henle, "Do you know what Ruth Montgomery called me in her column? A living doll."

This was the ugly era of McCarthyism, and the next day a wild demonstration greeted Senator Joseph R. McCarthy as he charged that the same men who delivered half the world to Communist Russia by treason or stupidity "are still in control in Washington and Moscow." Vigorously defending himself against charges of being too rough, the ex-marine sneered. "We can't fight Communists in the Acheson-Lattimore fashion of hitting them with a perfumed silk handkerchief at the front door, while they batter our friends with brass knuckles and blackjacks at the back door. One Communist among the American advisers at Yalta was one Communist too many."

General Eisenhower captured the nomination and, eager to heal the partisan wounds, paid a drama-charged visit to loser Taft a few minutes after his victory became official. Crossing the street from his Blackstone Hotel suite to the Conrad Hilton, Ike stepped out of the elevator into a Taft camp filled with sobbing women volunteers and stunned diehards. A group of students from Northwestern University hailed him with derisive cries of "We want Taft." With Taft it was a different story. He was closeted for ten minutes with the victor. Then the Senator and the general came out and posed for photographs, shaking hands. Ike beamed. Taft tried hard to smile. He did it, but it wasn't easy. It was the end of a twelve-year dream for the Ohio Senator, who had been a favorite son candidate for President since 1940. True to his preconvention pledge, however, he stood valiantly beside the winner and told his red-eyed followers, "I want to congratulate General Eisenhower and say I'll do everything possible to assist him in his campaign, and in his administration when he is elected." To Ike he added, "Oh, you'll win in November." His hands visibly shaking, Ike told the crowd that he had come to make "a call of friendship on a very great American."

The next day I attended Mamie Eisenhower's first press conference, and looking as cool as a Paris spring despite the ninety-five-degree temperature, she said "Oh, definitely," when asked if she thought Ike would win.

The Democratic Convention opened at the same stomping ground in Chicago's stockyards a week later, with women vying for the early headlines. Perle Mesta held a press conference to announce that her only candidate was Harry S. Truman, and when reminded that he might not be available for a draft, she said confidently, "He will be. You just wait and see. He'll get it." Marie Harriman, Jane Barkley, and the wives of Senators Robert Kerr and Estes Kefauver also called press conferences to promote the candidacies of their husbands. The only possible contender without a wife to root for him was Adlai Stevenson, whose ex-wife announced that she would vote Republican.

Alben Barkley, to demonstrate that he was hale and hearty despite his seventy-four winters, arrived in Chicago by train and walked the two miles to his headquarters, at the head of a cheering throng of supporters. The Veep felt that he had earned the right to the nomination, but the day after his arrival the labor leaders for whom he had so often gone to bat turned him down as "too old." It nearly broke Barkley's heart. Infuriated by their perfidy, he announced he was quitting Chicago before the convention opened, but he was persuaded to remain, and cheering delegates demonstrated for twenty-four minutes as he began the address to take himself out of the race.

Stevenson eventually won the nomination and made a delightful acceptance speech which charmed most of the nation. But a month later, when he visited the White House at Truman's invitation, it was a day of hilarious snafus. Determined to stay as far removed from the not-so-popular President as possible, Stevenson had declined Truman's offer of the Presidential plane. His commercial flight was late, and he had to keep the President and other high officials waiting for a White House luncheon in his honor. The most eloquent chair was the vacant one. Vice President Barkley had pleaded a previous speaking engagement in Illinois, but his top aide told reporters that the speaking date was actually two days hence.

After the luncheon, Truman listened tight-lipped while Stevenson muffed one for the TV and radio mikes. Housewives throughout the

Ruth Montgomery with her poodle Pepe le Moco in her drawing room, showing a few of her personally autographed Presidential pictures.

Left: Ruth's husband, Robert H. Montgomery, in his Navy lieutenant's uniform as he left for World War II in 1943.

Right: Ruth covering war maneuvers, April, 1944.

With Eleanor Roosevelt.

Covering a Presidential nominating convention in Chicago.

Being interviewed in Havana by Señor Pascual, star reporter of *El Mundo*, after her scoop about President Grau.

President Perón of Argentina personally greeting Ruth in Buenos Aires.

Ruth, as president of the Women's National Press Club, in ceremony presenting tickets to President Truman for the club's VIP Original Amateur Hour show. Ted Mack holds the poster.

Ted Mack, General Omar Bradley, and Ruth. Ruth is presenting proceeds of the Women's National Press Club VIP show to General Omar Bradley, chairman of the Joint Chiefs of Staff, for the USO during the Korean War.

country were groaning about the increasingly high cost of food, but Stevenson told the listening millions, "I've had a very pleasant opportunity to lunch with the President and members of the Cabinet. Another such lunch and I'll be so fat I won't be able to campaign, I'm afraid."

Adlai's next stop was the Democratic National Committee headquarters, where he had little opportunity to meet party workers because Vice-Chairman India Edwards had packed the building with wives of Truman-appointed officials. Stevenson looked trapped as photographers snapped pictures of him with Madame Perle Mesta and Cabinet wives, and when they asked him to make a gesture for the cameras, the Presidential candidate made another unfortunate remark: "The only one I can think of, I don't dare use."

A few blocks away, top Democrats of the District of Columbia and six hundred partisans were impatiently awaiting their first date with the new standard-bearer, but the hour came and went. Finally, forty minutes later, loudspeakers brought word that he was on his way to the airport. Adlai had stood up the party faithful, and a number of women exclaimed that under no circumstances would they now vote for him.

I learned that during the White House luncheon, Truman had confidently shown Stevenson his own travel itinerary and passenger list for a Presidential campaign train which he would mount in support of Stevenson's candidacy, but the Illinois governor firmly told him that there could be no campaign train for Truman. He said that the President could deliver a handful of speeches in big-city industrial areas and that Stevenson, not Truman, would decide where and when. Except for that, the Chief Executive was to be kept carefully under wraps, and Truman was understandably furious.

White House intimates were indignant that Truman even had to fight for the right to deliver a Labor Day address in Milwaukee and were angrier still when Stevenson requested that an advance draft of his speech be submitted to Stevenson headquarters in Springfield. They were already doing a slow burn because, with no advance notice to the White House, Stevenson had replaced Democratic Chairman Frank McKinney with Stephen Mitchell.

President Truman had a short temper all that summer. At an August press conference icicles figuratively dripped from Truman's normally hot tongue as the Stevenson campaign came under discussion. Asked for comment on an exchange of letters in which Stevenson had told an editor that he would do his best to "clean up the mess in Washington," Truman snapped that he knew of no "mess." A reporter remarked that Stevenson had told a news conference that crime and corruption in Washington had been proved by the fact that some had been indicted, and another reporter declared, "Mr. President, Vice Presidential nominee John Sparkman said the steel strike had been mishandled by the administration. What is your comment?"

"No comment," Truman angrily retorted. Then, in no uncertain terms he served notice on Stevenson and Sparkman that they would have to run on his record and Roosevelt's, "and that's all they can run on." The boss of the White House only two weeks previously had modestly described himself as "just a private in the ranks awaiting orders," but he had apparently had enough of that nonsense.

Senator Taft had meanwhile held a breakfast meeting with candidate Eisenhower, during which he reportedly exacted some promises on what Ike's Presidential policies would be if he were elected. A Republican wag promptly invented the slogan "Fight, hell! We've just begun to surrender."

The story about Vice Presidential nominee Dick Nixon's expense account broke in the headlines, he delivered his nationally televised "Checkers" speech, and Ike afterward greeted him with "He's my boy!" Then Democrats decided that they had "another Nixon scandal" to spring on the voters. Eager to combat the "white supremacy" voting record of rival Vice Presidential candidate Sparkman of Alabama, a Democrat dug up the fact that Nixon had signed a covenant agreeing not to resell his $41,000 house in Spring Valley to Negroes or Jews.

In my column, I pointed out that Sparkman had also signed the covenant for his Spring Valley home, as had liberal Democratic Senators Estes Kefauver, Blair Moody, and Harley Kilgore. Walter Winchell, supporting Eisenhower, gleefully praised my sleuthing in his Sunday evening broadcast, but little resourcefulness had been needed. It was a standard contract in those days for anyone buying in the Spring Valley subdivision of Washington.

Throughout October, I traveled with the Eisenhower campaign train, sometimes chatting with Mamie and her mother, Mrs. John Doud, in the general's private car. Mamie viewed her major problem as seeing that her hungry husband was properly fed, but she would plan a piping hot leg of lamb dinner to be consumed in a twenty-minute interval between his rear platform stops, only to have the train run behind schedule and pick up speed, so that the general would have to wolf his meal in five or ten minutes.

Another problem was the prominent politicians who would board the train for lunch in the rear car, and Mamie never knew how many there would be. Sighing softly, she said it was like running a cafeteria in a kitchenette apartment. Both Mamie and Ike were cooperative with cameramen on board. Early one morning an AP photographer scooped his rivals by snapping Mamie and Ike in their dressing gowns waving to village rubbernecks at an unscheduled stop. An hour later, when the others worried out loud about missing the picture, the Eisenhowers obligingly posed for the same shot, with Mamie's hair again done up in ribbons.

Huge and enthusiastic crowds greeted the Eisenhowers wherever we went. Following the Presidential car in a motorcade, we heard a wildly waving woman exclaim, "Hell's bells, I missed Mamie." A Minnesota farmwife, recovered from the first shock of having the Eisenhowers wave directly at her, said to her husband, "And I didn't even put on my Sunday dress." At a rear platform stop Mamie had been signing autographs, and as the train started to pull away, she was handing over the pen with the paper when Ike inadvertently yelled into the microphone, "Hell, Mamie, that's my fountain pen."

After touring the West and Southwest, we spent several days in Denver, Mamie's hometown; then on to New Orleans, San Antonio, and Houston. When we reached Waco, Texas, I stopped off for twelve hours to visit old friends at Baylor University, my alma mater, and the Waco *News-Tribune,* where I had begun my newspaper career while still in college. In the lobby of my hotel that evening I ran into Speaker Sam Rayburn, who had arrived to address a Democratic rally at the courthouse. Mr. Sam threw his arms around me and asked if I was attending the hotel dinner in his honor, but before I could reply in the negative, the chairman hastily said that it was an all-stag affair.

"I won't go unless Ruth can come, too," Speaker Rayburn snapped, and the chairman unhappily invited me inside for dinner. Then I flew on to Kansas City to write a story about President Truman. Judge Bundschu again hosted a dinner for me, after which I rejoined the Eisenhower train for the remainder of the campaign.

Comics were meanwhile having fun with the campaign. Edgar Bergen enlisted the help of his dummy, Charlie McCarthy, to stage a skit at an Eisenhower rally in Los Angeles, which went like this: Bergen: "What do you think our farm policy needs?" McCarthy: "Fertilizer. That reminds me. Have you heard Truman's speeches lately?" Bergen: "I hear Adlai Stevenson plays golf. What's his handicap?" McCarthy: "Truman." Bergen: "What do you think of the Democratic Party?" McCarthy: "It's the best party money can buy."

Anecdotes about Adlai Stevenson and his unorthodox campaign will probably embellish future political textbooks. When politicos broke the news to him that his sixteen-year-old son, John, had fallen asleep during his father's acceptance speech at the convention, Adlai quipped, "The only civilized man in the hall." His ad libs and wise-cracking speeches were a delight to the ear, but his advisers morosely begged him to desist. The American people, they insisted, did not like humor from Presidential candidates.

We wound up our 51,000-mile Eisenhower campaign in Boston on November 3, where Ike again pledged that if elected, he would go to Korea. After his victory, Truman sarcastically told him that he could use a government plane for the trip to Korea, "if you still want to go." Ike went.

During the campaign we often spoke of "Eisenhower weather," because wherever we went, the sun was shining brightly, even if the local stop had previously been inundated by sleet, rain, or snow.

Inauguration day was also Ike weather all the way, with the sun beaming like a Republican. Three-quarters of a million people shed their coats to cheer lustily as Ike and Mamie set a precedent by riding together in the massive inaugural parade. Congress speedily confirmed Eisenhower's newly appointed Cabinet the next day, except for Defense Secretary Charles E. Wilson, whose confirmation was held up five days until he agreed to rid himself of $2,700,000 in General Motors stock. A wag promptly dubbed the Cabinet "Eight millionaires and a plumber," the latter being Secretary of Labor Martin P. Durkin, who huffily quit after a few months and went back to his presidency of a plumbers' union. Later, when Ike appointed Oveta Culp Hobby to the newly created post of Secretary of Health, Education, and Welfare, Labor Secretary James P. Mitchell proposed that the Cabinet be called "Nine men with a Hobby." After Wilson was confirmed, an alert photographer at the White House overheard this exchange between the President and the Secretary of Defense: Ike: "Hey, Charlie, have you heard why Molotov didn't get to be Premier of Russia?" Wilson: "Yeah, I've heard it. He wouldn't sell his GM stock."

In early March, Mamie Eisenhower held her first press conference in the White House and laughingly let it be known that the legislation in which she was most interested was tax reduction.

CHAPTER X

Living Out of Suitcases

BY now I was becoming a fairly regular commuter to Europe, combining writing assignments with vacations. My second trip, in 1950, covered much the same ground as the previous one but was considerably more luxurious. A group of newspaper correspondents were guests of Trans World Airlines on its inaugural flight, so instead of paying our own way at press camps and left-bank hotels, we were housed like royalty at the finest hotels in Paris, London, Germany, Switzerland, Athens, and Rome. We dined at epicurean restaurants, embassies, and nightclubs and hobnobbed with high officials.

In London I shared a BBC television program with Gracie Fields and met with Parliament leader Herbert Morrison at No. 11 Downing Street. We were entertained by John McCloy in Berlin, Ambassador James Dunn in Rome, Chip Bohlen in Paris, and King Paul and Queen Frederica at their palace in Athens. As we deplaned in Athens, I was greeted with a friendly embrace by our old friend Ambassador John F. Peurifoy, and the resulting picture made the front pages of Greek newspapers. Jack and Betty Jane Peurifoy gave a party for our group at the U.S. Embassy and afterward took me upstairs to confide their high hopes and current woes.

With their consent, I cabled a column which told of the snub administered to Betty Jane by wives of the British and French ambassadors, who had declined to attend a welcoming party for the Peurifoys the previous week because Betty Jane had not first called on them. They must have known, however, that she had arrived from America only the day before, with her four-year-old son in tow, and their stuffy protocol seemed high-handed, since we were upholding their countries' economies with Marshall Plan aid. Thus, my column was picked up by the newspapers of two continents.

In Rome, I had my second audience with Pope Pius XII, who blessed the hastily acquired rosaries and medals which overflowed our outstretched hands. And we visited with Robert Taylor and director Mervyn LeRoy on the film set of *Quo Vadis*.

During my next trip to Europe in 1952 I interviewed Ingrid Bergman, who had eloped with Roberto Rosselini and given birth to their much-publicized baby the previous week. Then I flew on to Egypt, where anti-British rioters had recently burned Shepheards Hotel to the ground. A night curfew was being rigidly enforced, and after arriving at the airport at 3 A.M., I reached Cairo's Semiramis Hotel by riding a bus which was guarded by four Egyptian officers, who grimly aimed their rifles into the desert night.

Dropped at my hotel at 4:30 A.M., I shivered apprehensively as galabia-clad Arabs swooped up my luggage and disappeared around the corner; but it magically appeared again in my beautiful room overlooking the Nile, and as dawn broke I stared in awe at the majestic pyramids in the distance. At noon I interviewed Foreign Minister Hassouna Pasha, wrote the story, and then warred with Fawzi Bey, Egypt's UN ambassador, who imposed censorship over most of the quotes from his superior.

Princess Tawhida Halim Rediker, a Washington friend, had written her former husband of my impending arrival, and when I returned to my hotel that evening, Prince Abbas Halim was awaiting me in the lobby. The next evening I dined with him and his two daughters, whose debuts I had attended in Washington, at the Royal Automobile Club. Prince Abbas, a cousin of King Farouk, entertained me frequently during my stay, and fate was later to give me a rich opportunity to reward his kindness.

Maher Doss, a member of Egypt's Foreign Office, arranged my interviews with officialdom, hosted a luncheon for me at his mother's beautiful villa on the Nile, and took me sight-seeing to the pyramids,

the Sphinx, and the Antiquity Museum. Ramadan, the Moslem
month of fasting, began shortly after my arrival and marked the
end of the curfew.

One pitilessly hot Sunday morning I drove into the desert for a
rare interview with the Grand Mufti, stormy petrel of the Mideast,
who was living in political asylum in Heliopolis. The sun beat relentlessly against his massive sandstone house. It glittered off the
rifles of Egyptian police who guarded the entry, and it wilted my
cotton frock. Inside, in an airless room shuttered against the sun,
the Grand Mufti looked as cool as his green, appraising eyes. Despite
the intense heat, a thick white turban encircled his head and a black
wool robe enveloped him to his shoetops. A stainless-steel wristwatch,
peeping from one sleeve, seemed to afford his one link with Western
civilization.

The Grand Mufti bowed low, apologized for his limited English,
and asked how the interview should begin. Knowing of his pro-
Hitler tactics during the war, I asked where he and his Moslem followers stood in the cold war, but he smiled benignly at my American
impetuosity. Gently chiding that that should be the climax, not the
beginning of the story, he said, "We Moslems naturally do not like
Communism, which is against our religion, but we are suffering now
the effects of British capitalism backed by American dollars more
than we could possibly expect to suffer under Communism." Green
eyes flashing, he demanded, "Why should Egypt fight the enemies
of Britain, when Britain is her chief enemy? How can Arab refugees
from Palestine, slowly starving and morally disintegrating in DP
camps, possibly be afraid of Russia, when the worst that could possibly happen to them has already happened? Why should America
pay the price of British mistakes? By backing colonialism she has
lost the affection of the very people who want to be her friends. We
don't ask for American aid, and we don't even ask America to stop
aiding the Jews with millions of dollars. All we ask is that America
and Britain be neutral in our Palestinian dispute. But if America and
Britain fail to adopt neutrality, we Arabs must take a position of
neutrality in the cold war, and in any hot war which may come."

He had spoken for ninety minutes before he finally reached that climax which he had promised. America had her answer from the Grand Mufti, and as I traveled around Egypt, it became increasingly apparent that America was indeed squandering the vast reservoir of goodwill which she had once enjoyed in the Land of the Nile. Moslems could not forget that a quick stroke of President Truman's pen had granted U.S. recognition of the new state of Israel before Britain or any other country had acted.

I paid return visits to Rome and Zurich and flew on to Paris, where I dined with Doug and Wahwee MacArthur, whom I had last seen at her father's wedding in St. Louis. The next day I covered General Eisenhower's farewell press conference at SHAPE headquarters and the ceremony in which Ike turned over NATO command to General Matthew Ridgway. During my night flight home, our MATS plane stopped for several hours for refueling in Iceland, and we gazed at the midnight sun gliding sideways along the horizon as the snow-capped mountains changed from azure to purple to gold.

The remainder of 1952 was a hectic period, with the nominating conventions and the Presidential campaigns. After covering Ike's inaugural festivities, I flew with the wife of Congressman Ken Regan to California for a vacation in the desert oasis of La Quinta, where we had a delightful time with George and Mary Allen, Sid Richardson, the Bennett Cerfs, Jerry Devines, John Balabans, and Mike Cowles'. Jerry Devine, author of the *This Is Your FBI* television series, came to visit Bob and me in Washington shortly thereafter, and at our dinner party for him Veep Barkley upset the gravy on our damask tablecloth but had a dozen funny new stories to tell.

The next day I went to New York to be on the CBS *Man of the Week* TV show and accompanied the Cerfs to *What's My Line?*, and to Toots Shor's for a late dinner. I was virtually commuting to New York for television shows and frequent parties with such luminaries as playwrights Howard Lindsay and Russell Crouse, publisher Walter Annenberg (now ambassador to Great Britain) and his wife, Mrs. Joseph Medill Patterson, editor Richard E. Clarke, Perle Mesta, and many others.

Bob and I went to Indianapolis in May, where I addressed the

Indiana Press Club, and Mother and Dad rode back to Washington with us. Bob was ailing with a sore throat, and on reaching home, I asked our family doctor to give him an injection of the new wonder drug penicillin. Bob has yet to thank me for my thoughtfulness. His tongue promptly turned black and hairy, and his throat swelled so nearly shut that the allergist whom we hastily summoned warned that Bob would die if he ever had penicillin again.

Meanwhile, Dad had discovered the loss of his wallet, and we vainly sought to trace it, but after my parents returned home, Dad wrote that he had found it in the pocket of a suit he had last worn just before they left with us for Washington. "Please don't tell your Mother, or I'll never hear the last of it," he wrote. "I've never done such a thing before." I treasure it as the last note I ever had from Dad.

He and Mother went to southern Illinois for a family reunion, and while there, Dad contracted pneumonia. As soon as he was able to be moved, they returned to Indianapolis, and he was convalescing nicely when I telephoned him in mid-July to say good-bye, before leaving with a group of correspondents for Egypt to cover the first anniversay of King Farouk's ouster by a military junta.

The pyramids, the bazaars, and the natives seemed unchanged, but some of my friends from the previous Egyptian visit thirteen months before were sadly missing. Maher Doss was living in self-imposed exile in Switzerland, and Prince Abbas Halim had been languishing in jail for nearly a year, a political prisoner of the new regime, which ousted his cousin the king. The attractive swashbuckler who flew with Hermann Göring in World War I had stayed on in Germany after the Armistice long enough to become enchanted with the Olympic Games and to wonder why his own land had no competing athletes. Returning home, the rich young nobleman soon learned the reason. Hopeless Egyptians, working from dawn to dark to earn a meager subsistence, obviously had no time for sports.

Prince Abbas thereupon appointed himself a one-man committee to try to rectify the situation. After organizing the Arab workmen into unions, he led their fight for shorter hours and more pay. King Fuad, his kinsman and father of Farouk, jailed the prince for a time in the 1930's, but laborers did not forget their benefactor. During the riots in which Shepheards Hotel and so many other haunts of the British were burned, Prince Abbas was president of the Royal Automobile Club. Throughout that long night, rioters repeatedly carried their torches to the club where Farouk loved to gamble the hours away, but each time the doorman spoke the magic words "Prince Abbas is inside," and the lavish building was spared. After the *coup d'état* in 1952 which installed General Mohammed Naguib as President, Prince Abbas and numerous others were arrested as possible enemies of the new regime and were still imprisoned when we arrived.

President Naguib and Colonel Gamal Abdel Nasser, the real strongman of the military junta, held a joint press conference for visiting foreign correspondents to extol the virtues of the new regime. Naguib, a kindly-looking, grandfatherly type, answered our questions adroitly, but when I asked why his government was still holding such political prisoners as Abbas Halim, Naguib for the first time went into hasty consultation with Nasser and three other colonels before replying, "There are two hundred of them, all agents of foreign powers."

"Is Halim an agent of a foreign power?" I prodded.

Again the five ranking heads of Egypt huddled together. Finally Naguib replied blandly, "Abbas and three others, no. All the rest, yes."

The next day columnist Dorothy Thompson and I shared a taxi to the railroad station, where we were to accompany Naguib and the scores of other foreign correspondents on a train trip down the Nile to inaugurate Egypt's first land redistribution program. A tumultuous crowd of Arabs hailed Naguib as he entered his private car, and the long train had barely pulled out of the depot before an Egyptian official sought me out to say that President Naguib wished me to ride with him. Puzzled, I said good-bye to my newspaper colleagues and followed him through several press cars to the

Presidential one, where Naguib bowed and indicated that I was to sit beside him.

His English was excellent, his manner charming, and we were enjoying such an affable conversation that I finally ventured to ask, "Mr. President, what about Abbas Halim? When do you think that your government will be stable enough to free its political prisoners?"

"Oh, it's stable now," he responded. "A very stable government."

"Then why not let them out?" I pressed.

Shrugging his shoulders, he demurred. "But Abbas is a trouble-maker, Miss Montgomery. For a year now, since he's been in jail, we've had no strikes. When Abbas is out, we have strikes."

I softly pointed out that in America we have strikes, too, when conditions warrant them, and that we do not jail labor leaders for seeking shorter hours or better wages for the workmen. This furrowed his brow, and we rode silently for several minutes. At last a smile erased the frown, as he exclaimed, "Miss Montgomery, for you I will let him out."

True to his promise, Prince Abbas was freed within a week. By then I had returned home, but he wrote me a profuse letter of appreciation. Years later, when Bob and I visited Egypt and Abbas was living at the one villa that he had been allowed to retain, in Alexandria, we chuckled over the timing of my request to Naguib. What I had not realized when I spoke to the President was that the vast estate which the government was distributing that day to the peasants had been expropriated from Abbas Halim.

As our train pulled into the station of Etay-El-Tarus that July day in 1953, mobs of grateful peasants shouting "Naguib, Naguib" were brutally clubbed by police to make way for the President and his entourage. We walked through the wretched native village, wincing at the sight of babies with bleeding eyes, to a vast tent whose inner walls and dirt floors were paved with exquisite Oriental rugs. There the ceremony was held which transferred ownership of the rich delta land to hundreds of ragged tillers of the soil. Hopefully, they could pay off their indebtedness to the government during the next half century and somehow better their lot.

After returning to Cairo, we went for dinner to Mena House, where President Roosevelt had held a wartime conference with Winston Churchill; then to the Giza pyramids and the Sphinx, where we had our fortunes told by a sand reader who squatted in the moonlit sands. My room at the Heliopolis Palace was unscreened and so miserably hot that the next morning I moved to the Semiramis Hotel, where I again had a lovely balcony overlooking the windswept Nile. The remainder of our press group would be leaving in a day or so, but I planned to stay for another week of news reporting, before joining Bob for a holiday in Rome.

We were guests of Ambassador and Mrs. Jefferson Caffery for dinner at the U.S. Embassy our last night, after which my colleagues departed for the airport and I returned to the Semiramis. The next morning I slept late, washed my hair, and was preparing to write a column in my room, when a cable arrived from my husband. Dad had died of his first and only heart attack. Too stunned to think, I threw myself across the bed in the most violent weeping attack of my life. Never to see Dad again! Bob's cable, delayed in transit because it had gone first to the Heliopolis Palace Hotel, relayed word that my family said I should not return for the funeral, but I was determined to go.

It was the height of the tourist season, TWA was on strike, and I soon learned that other airlines were solidly booked for a week. I tried to telephone Bob in Washington, but the lines were out of order and many other calls were ahead of mine on the waiting list. In desperation I appealed to the American Embassy, and wheels began to turn. Shortly, the embassy called to say that my call would be first when telephone service resumed and that I could have a seat on an all-coach flight to Rome, which would arrive from Saudi Arabia at midnight. Meanwhile, I was frantically packing, and when my plane eventually departed Cairo at 2:30 A.M., I wept the night through, while babies cried in hammocks which swung above our heads.

I changed planes in Rome, in Paris, and in New York before reaching Indianapolis, where some of my family and Bob were awaiting me for the drive to Sumner, Illinois. Mother and the other relatives had gone on ahead, and the next day my father was lovingly laid to rest in the beautiful Sumner Cemetery with our ancestors.

Six months later I accompanied members of the House Agriculture Committee to Cuba, and this time we were entertained at the palace by President Batista, after Congressmen had inspected the sugar fields and refineries to determine Cuba's sugar quota for the coming year.

After another three months, Bob and I visited Cuba and also toured Haiti, the Dominican Republic, and Jamaica. And in the fall of the year I flew with a Sabena Airlines junket to Brussels, for a tour of Belgium; then Roberta Regan and I pressed on to Milan, Venice, Florence, Naples, Ravello, and Pompeii. Arriving in Rome, I found a message from Ambassador Clare Boothe Luce that she had arranged a party for me that evening, and after cocktails at our palatial American Embassy, Clare took us for dinner and dancing to Osteria dell'Orso, a quaint thirteenth-century inn which had been frequented by Dante. Among her other guests were the Austrian ambassador, Princess Johannes Schwarzenberg, Dr. Giovanni Fummi, banker to the Pope, Wells Stabler of the embassy staff, Joseph Bryan III, and Clare's brother-in-law, Maurice Moore of New York.

CHAPTER XI

Guns and Games

THE brand-new Eisenhower administration proved a boon for the Gridiron Club and the Women's National Press Club, because after twenty Democratic years we had a whole new cast of governmental characters to spoof in our skits. At the annual WNPC Stunt Party in the spring of 1953, society columnist Betty Beale played Ike, complete with golf clubs and cap. Cast in the role of Mamie, I wore a frothy, ankle-length frock (unearthed from the attics of our members) which bore a striking resemblance to one worn by Mamie in her courting days, a picture of which had recently been reproduced in a national magazine. In that photograph the gay Denver belle had bewitchingly held a fringed parasol behind her back, and with my hair set in "Mamie bangs" I did the same as I walked onstage to speak my assigned lines.

During the thunderous applause, President Eisenhower leaned over to our club president and opined, "Ruth looks so exactly like Mamie used to that it makes me feel downright nostalgic." Ike was obviously enjoying himself, and when he later took the podium to make some complimentary remarks, he said, "I kiss your hands, Mesdames." Then, grinning down the head table at Oveta Culp Hobby, who only a few days previously had told newsmen that she did not wish to be addressed as Madame, he kidded, "Perhaps I shouldn't say that in front of Mrs. Hobby, but it sounds kind of silly to say, 'I kiss your hands, Misses.' "

A few days later Mamie gave a tea at the White House, and when she spotted my arrival, she whooped, "Here comes my double!" Throwing her arm around my shoulder, she led me to the receiving line while confiding, "Ike simply loved your takeoff of me. He said you looked so young and pretty and so exactly like I did when we were married that it made him feel downright sad."

To our astonishment, May Craig and I were invited by the all-male National Press Club to costar with Larry Spivak and humor columnist Fred Othman in a reverse twist of *Meet the Press*. Senators Wayne Morse and Robert Kerr and Representatives Kenneth Keating and Clarence Brown were to shoot the questions at us for a change, with former Vice President Barkley serving as moderator. The show received wide coverage in newspapers, and one story recounted this tongue-in-cheek exchange:

> SENATOR KERR: Mrs. Montgomery, do you think the Washington press corps is after scoops or scalps?
>
> MRS. MONTGOMERY: I'll answer that as you once answered a question of mine on "Meet the Press." You are stupider than I thought to ask a stupid question like that.

Maverick Senator Morse asked Spivak, "I wonder when you ten percenters are going to pay Congressmen what they are worth for appearing on your television program," to which Larry replied, "According to our audience reaction, you are being paid what you are worth." (Which, of course, was nothing.)

All reporters who regularly covered the Presidential press conferences were dues-paying members of the White House Correspondents' Association, which annually held a dinner for the President, but the handful of women members was always banned. We could pay our dues, but we could not attend the only event of the year. In those days the organization was almost as democratic as a secret meeting of the Soviet Politburo. An election of officers was held once a year on whatever spring day four or five regular members of the White House press corps could be found lounging around the press room, and there was a standing gag that the election was decided in a telephone booth to ensure that the boys could vote for each other. Not only were women members disenfranchised, but several hundred male correspondents as well.

Through some horrible oversight, an invitation to the annual dinner in May, 1953, went to Mrs. Oveta Hobby along with the nine male members of the Eisenhower Cabinet. Oveta, a longtime newspaperwoman, let the boys stew for a while, but finally called White House press secretary Jim Hagerty to ask if he thought she should be out of town the night of the dinner. This created a crisis. Jim could scarcely take the initiative of telling the highest-ranking woman in government that she could not go to an event that would be attended by her Cabinet colleagues, so he dumped the problem in the lap of the little clique which ran the organization. Soon word came back to Mrs. Hobby that she was not to come to the dinner, and although the lads were importing some women singers from out of town, Mrs. Hobby spent the evening alone with her husband, who owned the Houston *Post*.

President Eisenhower appointed a number of other women to high posts, including witty Ivy Baker Priest as Treasurer of the United States. During hearings on her nomination, a Senator quipped that Ivy's face would look better than George Washington's on a dollar bill. Standing in the receiving line at the Republican Women's Club, the president, Mrs. Lillis Lord, introduced Ivy to Congresswoman Marguerite Church, and Ivy exclaimed, "Now we've got everything. Mrs. Lord presents Mrs. Church to Mrs. Priest." Ivy confessed that as a child she had always wanted to name her first baby Judith, but after she married Roy Priest she could hardly name their daughter Judith Priest, as it would sound like a swearword.

Richard Wilson, chief Washington correspondent for Cowles Publications, asked me to write a cover story about First Lady Mamie Eisenhower for *Look* magazine, and *Look* bought a full-page advertisement in the New York *Times* to promote that issue. It also published a highly flattering plug for the author, which read:

> Ruth Montgomery, one of the best looking and best dressed of Washington correspondents, has known her subject, Mamie, for

eight years. They first met at a party given by the George Allens at Washington's Wardman Park Hotel, shortly after General Eisenhower got back from Europe. Allen was then a confidante of both President Truman and the General. From that time on, mutual friends kept bringing Ruth and Mamie together socially. Their propinquity led to real gabfests during the presidential campaign, when Ruth was the only lady reporter who stuck with Eisenhower from beginning to election. She spent a lot of that time sitting in the rear car of the campaign train with Mamie and Mamie's mother, and she came to believe that Mrs. Ike was a lot more interested in woman-talk than in politics.

For instance, one day Ruth turned up in the rear car wearing one of her stunning costumes. Mamie took a look, felt the material, and advised her, "Now you go right back and take that nice suit off. There's no use ruining anything that good-looking while you're working on this train, and cashmere doesn't wear well." It sounds as though it's a thoroughly economy-minded woman who's bossing the White House help today.

In my *Look* article, I pointed out that Mamie was unusually well qualified to be First Lady because "Visiting royalty and Prime Ministers hold no terrors for the girl from Boone, Iowa, who already has dined with them in Europe. Once she pressed Queen Juliana of the Netherlands and Ike into a three-handed game of canasta at the Royal Palace." I also quoted Mamie as saying, "I'm a one-man woman. When Ike was in Europe during the war, I kept one of his old tweed suits hanging in my closet, just so that I could handle it and luxuriate in that wonderful tobacco smell."

My article continued:

Rumor-mongers who tried to link General Eisenhower's name romantically with that of his British secretary-chauffeur during the war failed to ruffle Mamie's faith in her husband. To a monseigneur who knew the Eisenhowers well while he was a chaplain at West Point, Mamie commented serenely, "Of course I don't believe it. I know Ike."

Once a slip of the tongue linked Mamie's name with General George C. Marshall. Attending a ceremony in which General

Marshall was being honored for his work as president of the American Red Cross, she joined in the roar of laughter that came when the toastmaster said, "All General Marshall wants to do is retire to his Leesburg home with Mrs. Eisenhower." The speaker, red-faced, quickly tendered "my apology to the General," and Mamie brought down the house with her quip, "Which General?"

As the wife of the Allied Supreme Commander in Europe during the war, Mamie was a popular volunteer waitress in USO Clubs. Once, however, she almost lost the admiration of a Wardman Park janitor. Ike had flown back to Washington for a hush-hush conference with President Roosevelt, and for security reasons Mamie could tell no one of his visit. The next morning, while her bathrobed husband was preparing breakfast in the apartment kitchen, the janitor unceremoniously popped his head in the door. His expression told them exactly what he thought of wives who played around while their husbands were at war.

Mamie also told me her favorite story about inauguration day. She had been First Lady only a few hours, and at the close of the longest inaugural parade in memory the Eisenhowers trudged wearily into their new home for the first time to dress for two inaugural balls. Mamie's maid had just begun to zip her into a sparkling Mamie-pink ballgown when an outraged shout came from her husband.

"Hey, Mamie," he bellowed from the adjoining room, "where in the hell is my monkey suit?" The wheels stood still while Mamie and the President's valet frantically searched the closets for the white tie and tails which the President was scheduled to wear. Mamie, limp from laughing, finally suggested that they might have left it on the train which brought them to Washington. And that's where they eventually found it.

In September of that year, another magazine article of mine appeared under the heading "The Ten Sweetest Senators." The headline was not my idea. I had been asked to do one on the ten handsomest senators, and high among my selections was John F. Kennedy of Massachusetts, about whom I kiddingly wrote:

If you're a motherly type, how can you resist his little-boy charm? He is frequently mistaken for a page boy, because of his tousled hair and wiry frame. His blue cashmere overcoat is threadbare from being returned so frequently from planes, trains, committee rooms, and parties where he has left it. The winsome young Irishman's hazel eyes, pearly teeth, resort-tan complexion and unruly mop of hair have made a legend of his appeal to women.

Bob and I took over La Fonda restaurant for a Sunday evening dinner party that spring, and *Diplomat* magazine gave a two-page picture spread to it, saying:

Mellowed, atmosphered La Fonda, exuding Spanish music from its quaint interior, recently was the scene of a blue-ribbon party hosted by the nationally known news columnist, Ruth Montgomery, and her husband, Robert, Deputy Administrator of the Small Business Administration. Iberian motifs were carried into the realm of hors d'oeuvres, tacos and tiny tamales. Two high-geared cocktail bars, one on each floor, kept producing pre-dinner drinks to the over one hundred guests.

Almost stealing the show from the select list of ambassadors, members of Congress, White House executives and their wives was the rarely seen personality these days, Perle Mesta. For excellence and consistency in cuisine, for the graciously smooth piloting of a dinner party (seventeen tables), it's recorded as one of the best parties of the season. With their good-party stars in their crowns, the Montgomerys left a few days later for a trip around the blue Caribbean.

In September, 1953, during Eisenhower's first Presidential year, Chief Justice Fred Vinson died and California Governor Earl Warren was named to replace him. Shortly thereafter, with permission from Roberta Vinson, I wrote a column which began:

The widow of Chief Justice Fred M. Vinson is sadly preparing to move next month to cheaper quarters, because legislators have failed to provide her with a pension, while voting substantial ones for themselves and their own potential widows. The ailing wife of the incorruptible Kentuckian, who amassed an estate of only $8,000 in a lifetime of public service, must leave the apartment which was home to the Vinsons for twenty-one years. Roberta, greatly beloved on both sides of this capital's political aisle, is philosophical about her reduced position. Her Kentucky father, when she came here as a young Congressman's wife in the mid-1920's, cautioned, "Be nice to people on your way up, because you may be meeting them again on your way down." The gay Southern belle accepted that as the maxim of her life, and it has paid off. She was forced to sell the family Cadillac, but her former chauffeur now comes to see her on his days off, and volunteers to do odd jobs.

The column noted that none of Roberta's old friends from her high protocol days was more loyal than her former neighbor at the Wardman Park. Mamie Eisenhower, talking on the telephone with a mutual friend, declared firmly, "We must do something about getting Roberta down here to the White House. She's been around Washington so long that if I ask her, she'll regard it as a command performance and think she has to come. You fix it up for some day when you and Roberta are free, and I'm not receiving scads of club groups, and bring her with you. Then we'll have a real old-fashioned visit." My column concluded:

Mrs. Vinson has been ailing for several years, and after her husband's death she began suffering with a painful arthritic condition of the back. A sheltered Kentucky blue blood, she has never worked and is now unable to take a job. A pension for the widow of a man who served his country well for thirty years as Congressman, Federal Judge, wartime Economic Stabilizer, Federal Loan Administrator, Director of War Mobilization, Secretary of the Treasury, and Chief Justice of the United States would not be amiss for a wealthy country such as ours.

Several legislators inserted my column in the *Congressional Record,* and Congress promptly voted Roberta Vinson a lifetime pension. She has always been warmly grateful to me, as has her son Fred, Jr., who later became an Assistant Attorney General under LBJ.

That fall the White House announced the resumption of a glittering, full-scale social season for the first time in seven years. The eagerly awaited disclosure proved a godsend for Washington society dowagers, who began busily dropping their calling cards at the Executive Mansion, in the prayerful hope of a party bid. President Eisenhower, true to his campaign promise, had negotiated an armistice in the Korean War, and the nation was once again enjoying a tenuous peace.

On March 1, 1954, a small band of disgruntled Puerto Ricans started firing into the crowded House of Representatives as the House was voting on whether to take up the farm labor or "wetback" bill. Speaker Joseph W. Martin had just asked for the opposition vote, after counting the affirmatives, when he saw four or five people in a corner of the public gallery begin shooting. The House dissolved into utter confusion, with some Congressmen dropping to the floor and others crawling or sprinting to the cloakrooms.

I hastily interviewed Representative Edna F. Kelly, a New York Democrat, who exclaimed:

> This is the luckiest day of my life. The leather seat in which
> I was sitting now boasts a bullet hole. Fortunately for me, when
> the bullet hit I was squatting on the floor behind my chair. Sam
> Rayburn and several other legislators were squatting on the floor
> behind me. After a moment one of them said shakily, "Edna,
> it's clear. You can get up now." I started to rise, but when I saw
> that the would-be assassins were still standing in the gallery, and
> not a soul interfering with them, I shouted, "No no no. They're
> loading again." And sure enough, they were. The shots rang
> again. The moment the firing ceased, I could hear shouts of
> "Bentley's hit, Jensen's hit, Davis, Allen, Roberts." I screamed,
> "Where are the doctors? Where are the priests? Who can pray
> over them?" I kept blessing myself as I crawled on the floor to
> the Democratic cloakroom in the rear.

I wanted to telephone my mother, who has had a heart attack and spends all her time in front of the television set, and when I rushed back into the House Chamber, five of my colleagues were stretched out in the aisles, with blood spurting from their wounds. Talk about Korea! By this time doctors were all over the place, and priests and ministers too.

It reminded me of the day, three and a half years earlier, when I had rushed to Blair House after two Puerto Rican fanatics tried to shoot their way inside, where President Truman was taking a siesta. That time a White House guard was killed, and two other guards were seriously wounded. Fortunately, the wounded House members survived.

Three former first ladies, Bess Truman, Eleanor Roosevelt, and Edith Wilson, stood elbow to elbow in May, 1954, to pay tribute to a self-effacing capital dowager who had served all of them as social secretary. The Washington party celebrated publication of the memoirs of Mrs. Edith Helm, and even former President Truman, who was addicted to stag parties, braved the feminine receiving line to shake the hand of the author of *The Captains and the Kings*.

The Trumans took center stage on the cocktail circuit that week. At one of the parties, when someone tried to introduce us, Truman grabbed my hand and said with a chuckle, "You don't have to introduce me to Miss Ruth. She's been writing all the mean things she could think of about me for years."

Returning his grin, I replied, "That's right, Mr. President, and for that reason we certainly do miss you around here."

All smiles, he quipped, "Why, sure. You don't have anything to write about now. But it wasn't your fault you were born a Republican, so you're not to blame for that."

I asked if there was a chance of his returning to Washington to live, and with a nostalgic gesture around the gay salon, he said, "This is the way I love Washington; the parties and friends. But I can't come back to stay. Missouri is my home, and the Boss wants to live there."

But Mrs. Truman had crossed him up. Across the room, the "Boss" was confiding, "I'm terribly lonesome back in Independence. I thought I wanted to return there, but Washington has been my home for the past nineteen years, and I just can't tell you how badly I miss it out there."

Autograph seekers surrounded the former President, and one young man boasted that he had a letter written by him. The man from Missouri, grinning broadly, asked whether it had any dirty words in it, and when the startled chap assured him that it did not, Truman said, "Oh, well, it's not worth much then. If it had some dirty words in it, you could probably sell it for a pretty good price."

First Lady Mamie Eisenhower invited Bess Truman to a luncheon for Senate wives at the White House, but Eisenhower ignored Truman, who was angry over his "neglect" by Ike. With a touch of bitterness, he recalled that after becoming President, he had "lifted Herbert Hoover out of obscurity, tapped his storehouse of knowledge, and even sent a White House aide in a chauffeured limousine to Union Station to meet Hoover when he came to Washington on business." Some of us felt that Ike was carrying his feud with Truman too far!

Another thing rankled the peppery ex-President, and one day Dean Acheson told me about it at a party. Sizzling because Eisenhower and Secretary of State John Foster Dulles were being praised for ending the fighting in Korea, Truman scornfully told Acheson, "That's the same truce terms we were offered, and we rejected them."

"No," Acheson gently reminded. "They were the truce terms that we tried to get and couldn't."

On his next visit to Washington, Truman made the same boast to Acheson and received the same quiet correction. The third time that he came, he said it again, and his former Secretary of State sadly shook his head. Truman apparently enjoyed having a faulty memory.

CHAPTER XII

Love-Ins and Laugh-Ins

A FRIEND gave me a tip on June 24, 1954, that John F. Kennedy, the Senate's most eligible bachelor, was planning to marry Jacqueline Bouvier. I immediately telephoned Jack, who readily confirmed the report and gave me details of the forthcoming nuptials to be held in Newport, Rhode Island. The invitations, he said, would be mailed out the following Friday. I had just finished writing the exclusive report when Jack called back. This time he sounded like a small boy whose hand had been caught in a cookie jar, as he began apologetically, "Gee, Ruth, I guess I've ruined your scoop. I mentioned to Jackie that I'd told you about the engagement, and I guess I'm pretty dumb about these things, but it seems that the mother of the bride is supposed to make the announcement. Because I told you, her mother has decided to move up the announcement to today. I'm awfully sorry, but I hope I've at least given you a head start on the other reporters."

He had indeed, and my story in the early edition began:

> Come September, the Senate's gay young bachelor will be no more. Hopeful debutantes from Washington to Boston, from Palm Beach to Hollywood can begin unpacking their hope chests. Those thousands of Boston teen-agers who squeal like Sinatra fans every time young millionaire John Kennedy campaigned at their high school will get the bad news officially this week.
>
> The lean, tousle-haired, 36-year-old Senator from Massachusetts will take as his bride, in an elaborate ceremony at Newport in

September, a pretty former camera girl from the Washington *Times-Herald*. She's 23-year-old Jacqueline Bouvier, a debutante of the 1947 season who studied at Vassar, graduated from George Washington University in 1951, and won *Vogue* magazine's "Prix de Paris" which would have permitted her to study art at the Sorbonne in Paris. The ceremony may rival, but cannot surpass, the fabulous nuptials of John's sister, Eunice, to Robert Sargent Shriver Jr. last month in Manhattan's St. Patrick's Cathedral, at which Cardinal Spellman officiated, assisted by several bishops, monseigneurs and nine priests. After the Apostolic blessings were bestowed, seventeen hundred distinguished guests attended a lavish luncheon at the Starlight Roof of the Waldorf-Astoria. Incidentally, during Eunice's ceremony a distinguished guest who was slightly deaf asked the person next to him what was going on now. Told that the bishop was reading a message from the Pope, the man shouted, "The Pope? You mean the Pope's not here?"

My story duly identified Jackie's parents, and added: "John and Jacqueline are already house-hunting in Washington, and money should be no object. The Senator's father, former Ambassador to Britain Joseph P. Kennedy, gave each of his nine offspring a million dollars, so that they need not be hampered by earning a living."

The announcement of Jack's engagement had been deliberately delayed until publication in the *Saturday Evening Post* of an article about Jack by newspaperman Paul Healy entitled "The Senate's Gay Young Bachelor." Kennedy considered it unsporting to spoil Paul's piece until it had appeared on newsstands.

On the day that Jacqueline went to work for the *Times-Herald,* in January, 1952, she had announced her engagement to John G. W. Husted, Jr., of Bedford Hills, New York, a Yale graduate and Wall Street broker. In the nick of time she met the dashing young Senator, and her June nuptials were canceled. Two years later, when rumors of her frequent dates with Jack Kennedy came to the attention of the newspaper, a reporter asked Jackie's boss if he thought Kennedy would marry her.

Having observed her stubborn streak at first hand, he peered over his glasses and replied, "I'll just tell you one thing. If she's made up her mind that he's going to marry her, he sure will!"

Shortly after Jack became a Senator, I wrote a column about his absentmindedness. On a trip to England with other Senatorial pals, he had requested an appointment with British Foreign Secretary Anthony Eden, which was granted to the very junior Senator because his father had been an ambassador to Great Britain. Senator George Smathers and the others were not so fortunate, but they were eager to hear about it, and when they rejoined Jack that afternoon, they asked how the session had gone. "Oh!" he exclaimed, a stricken look crossing his face. "I forgot to go."

After my story appeared, I received a hand-scrawled letter from Jack, the gist of which was "How could you do such a thing to me?" I immediately telephoned to say that I was sorry but had thought the item was true. "True? Of course it's true," he replied, "but I didn't want anyone to know about it."

Having once been a reporter himself, he quickly forgave me for what he recognized to be a legitimate news story, and Bob and I received engraved invitations to his wedding. We dispatched a wedding present to the bride, and within a few days received a mimeographed acknowledgment from Jackie's mother, saying that the bride-to-be would write a personal note of thanks. She never did, and most of the other guests also had only the mimeographed form to show for their trouble.

Bob and I had to miss the wedding, as did a number of Democratic bigwigs. The date unfortunately coincided with a highly newsworthy conclave in Chicago which was billed as a Mid-Term Party Convention.

I was assigned to cover the session, at which titular leader Adlai Stevenson donned political gloves to blast the Eisenhower administration as "government by postponement" and jeered, "When in doubt, the administration appoints a commission." Former President Truman also came out swinging and charged that the administration was "moving the money changers back into the temples of government."

The day that the Democrats moved out of Chicago, the Republicans moved in, and Postmaster General Arthur E. Summerfield chided Stevenson for returning from his five-month tour "from Burma to Bloomington with camera and cliché, without finding a single new thought or fresh understanding of the great problems besetting the world." President Eisenhower also made an unscheduled appearance on his way back to Washington from Denver and mildly declared that the moral standards of the world were in the hands of women.

Republicans lost control of Congress in November, and Eisenhower, after viewing the long faces at a Cabinet meeting, said, "Boys, do you know the definition of an atheist?" His appointees snapped to attention. Obviously the boss had some important new information about Soviet intentions, but Ike, flashing his lopsided grin, declared, "An atheist is a guy who watches a Notre Dame-SMU football game and doesn't care who wins." Some Republicans privately grumbled that Eisenhower also hadn't cared enough about which political party won the Congressional elections.

Congress reconvened in January, with Sam Rayburn once more restored to the House speakership, and Lyndon B. Johnson became Senate majority leader. Texans were riding high in the saddle. Mr. Sam, now only two heartbeats removed from the Presidency, despised Vice President Nixon, the heartbeat ahead of his, and although he had once been an outspoken admirer of Eisenhower's, he turned on him when Ike had the temerity to run for President on the Republican ticket. "Ruth," he explained to me, "that general don't know a damn bit more about running the country than I'd know about running the Army."

Now Mr. Sam was leading the party revolt in Congress against the Eisenhower administration, and when he was invited in March, 1955, to a White House luncheon for a foreign head of state, he sent his regrets only minutes before guests were to be seated by elaborate protocol. Since he was the third-highest-ranking official in America, he must have known the frantic rescrambling of placecards that this would entail, but his only excuse was a laconic "I'm busy with some visiting constituents."

A few evenings later, when President Eisenhower strode to the place of honor at a bipartisan dinner, everyone applauded except Speaker Rayburn, who was also seated at the head table. Shortly thereafter Mr. Sam addressed our Women's National Press Club, and during the question-and-answer period I teased, "Mr. Speaker, why are you so hard on President Eisenhower, since you're always kind to constituents and he was born in your Texas district?"

Without a moment's hesitation, he shot back, "I've always said Ike was a beautiful baby."

Truman came back to Washington to testify before the Senate Foreign Relations Committee on the United Nations Charter, but was still being ignored by the White House. When a friend asked how he felt about the snub, the man who had offered to support Eisenhower for President on the Democratic ticket replied condescendingly, "Oh, I don't think Ike knows any better. After all, he's just one of those Army fellows."

In those days, Alice Roosevelt Longworth was attending more Congressional hearings than most Congressmen. She and a small coterie of Senators' wives customarily occupied front row seats for virtually every kleig-lighted hearing, looking for all the world like Madame La Farges knitting while heads fell, and after covering the morning sessions, I frequently lunched with them in the Senate dining room. Alice had been practicing yoga since the days when her father took jujitsu lessons at the White House, and she seldom wasted a moment. Chatting with friends on the telephone, the septuagenarian crossed one leg behind her head and rested the phone against her foot, while catching up on the latest gossip. Riding in her chauffeur-driven limousine around Washington, she sat cross-legged in the lotus position on the rear seat. One night a friend, crossing the Potomac River, recognized Mrs. Longworth's car parked on the bridge, with only her chauffeur in attendance. Fearful of foul play, he stopped and asked for an explanation. Replied the chauffeur,

"Miss Alice heard the shad was runnin', so she's gone down the bank to snag some."

Britain's Lady Astor again invaded our shores in early 1955, and the lash of her tongue was as sharp as ever. Attending a party at the home of Senator and Mrs. Taft, with Mamie Eisenhower as guest of honor, Lady Astor shook her finger at several Senators and Cabinet members, while lecturing them on "those terrible appointments of President Eisenhower's." Then she wheeled on me, expostulating, "Ruth, how dare you women put up with Eisenhower's appointment of that dreadful Fleur Cowles to represent you at Queen Elizabeth's coronation? Why didn't you do something about it? You women shouldn't stand for it a minute." I said I liked Fleur.

At this point Senator Joseph R. McCarthy, who had been wrangling with the administration over Red China trade, barged into the Taft party. Observing a drink in my hand, he grabbed it, saying, "I need this worse than you do, Ruthie."

Commented the acid-tongued Lady Astor, "A pity it isn't poison, for that disgraceful Senator."

Tallulah Bankhead was currently starring in *Dear Charles* at the National Theater, and a national women's organization thought it would be nice to have Lady Astor and Tallulah appear as guests of honor on the same platform. That is, until Lady Astor was approached. The Virginia-born woman promptly set the club delegation straight, snapping, "I will definitely not appear anywhere with that perfectly horrible woman. I'm repelled by her."

Tallulah, informed of Nancy Astor's snub, retorted, "She probably disapproves of me as much as I do of her, the bitchy old hypocrite." A friend urged Tallulah to delete the colorful adjective, but in her best tragedienne manner she dramatically repeated it for my benefit, and coaxed, "Say that I called her a bitch, dahlin'. Born in Virginia, was she? Huh, just another carpetbagger."

The Alabama-born daughter of former House Speaker William Bankhead, pouring another cocktail, continued. "And look at Oveta Culp Hobby. Another South'n girl, dahlin', but voting Republican. Just a turncoat carpetbagger." Merrily gabbing away about her next opening at the Hanna Theater in Cleveland, named for the late GOP kingmaker, Mark Hanna, she grinned. "Do you know how I fixed the Hannas once, dahlin'? They have a fabulous book with the autographs and comments of every famous visitor from Abraham Lincoln to Helen Hayes. They asked me to sign it, too, and after carefully selecting a page where they'd have to tear out John Barrymore's autograph if they wanted to remove mine, I wrote, 'Tallulah Bankhead, Huntsville, Alabama. Vote for Roosevelt.'"

Rhapsodizing about Speaker Sam Rayburn of Texas, she chortled, "My sister calls him Sam. I always call him Mr. Sam, but then she's a year older than I am."

The McCarthy era was still casting a long shadow over Washington, although Republicans had replaced Democrats in the White House and State Department, and the brash Senator from Wisconsin was still striking terror in the hearts of officialdom. When Bob and I attended the wedding of Joe McCarthy to beauteous Jean Kerr, St. Matthew's Cathedral was jammed with government dignitaries, as was the reception afterward at Cissy Patterson's former mansion, which had been turned into a club.

The newlyweds bought a townhouse on Capitol Hill, where I went to interview them for a magazine article. After the article appeared, Joe liked it because it was complimentary to Jean, but she was unhappy with it because I had criticized Joe's boorish manners and sledgehammer approach to governmental policy. Joe's sweeping charges about homegrown Communists were still evoking such widespread hysteria among voters that when the Senate eventually voted to censure him, hospitalized Senator John F. Kennedy dodged taking a stand by failing to provide a "pair" for another absent Senator.

Bob and I were seeing Jack and Jackie Kennedy frequently at parties, and from time to time I reported about them in my column. Jacqueline had not been married into the Kennedy family very long before she discovered that if she were ever to win at "Categories," the clan's favorite parlor game, she would have to learn more about American history. She consequently enrolled at Georgetown University's Foreign Service School for a course, and passed her final exam with a grade of 89.

One evening, at a dinner party given by Marguerite Higgins and her husband, General William E. Hall, Jacqueline Kennedy arrived on time, as did an assortment of Senators, but dinner cooled on the back burners while we waited for Jack to appear. Jackie became increasingly agitated, as she tried vainly to telephone him at his office, but he finally arrived with the casual explanation that he had been detained. Being the bride of a man accustomed to carefree bachelorhood was not all tea and crumpets. The handsome millionaire never bothered to carry money, and his less wealthy friends like Senator Smathers privately complained that they were always having to pick up the check for him. On a trip together to Europe, Smathers became so irritated that he finally exploded, "Jack, I'll pay all your damn bills, but I'm keeping track of every one of them, and when we return home, I'll present you with the bill." Jack amiably agreed.

Painting had become the rage in Washington, now that Ike Eisenhower and Winston Churchill were the world's two most famous amateur artists, and when portrait painter Guido Fulignot came to Washington from Trieste, Jacqueline was one of his first subjects. I was another, and when my portrait was completed, I became so fascinated by his technique with pastels that I tried to imitate his deft strokes. Although I had never before painted, I boldly began producing portraits of my friends, which they framed on their walls; but when Fulignot returned to Washington, he screamed, "No, no! You don't start with portraits; start with oranges." But who wants to paint oranges? I learned how to mix oils, and copied two Rembrandts and the "Mona Lisa," which still hang in our drawing room.

Friends who spent weekends at Camp David with Eisenhower reported to me that their hero lacked the proper temperament for an artist. He would set up his easel on the rolling lawn and go happily to work, while kibitzers told him that he had the shadows wrong or a tree a little crooked. Instead of flying into a temperamental rage, as befits artists, Ike would furrow his brow, peer at the scenery, study his canvas, and remark, "By golly, I believe you're right." Then he would change the painting.

Tom Stephens, the President's appointments secretary, decided to assemble a private collection of original paintings by top administration officials, and after Cabinet officers dutifully contributed their works (some of them frankly traced), they were hung outside Ike's office. When Ambassador Clare Boothe Luce came home for consultations, Eisenhower proudly showed them to her, adding, "And I want one by you hanging there." I wrote a column about Clare's dilemma, and when Sir Winston Churchill read it, he cabled Clare, "Come to Sicily and I'll teach you to paint." She subsequently took him up on the offer, and he gave her an elaborate box of oils and some firm instructions on how to "set to with a right royal will." Clare decided that if President Eisenhower would also give her a few lessons, she could become the most distinguished amateur in the world, "started by Churchill and finished by Eisenhower."

My column reported on another anecdote about Sir Winston. A traveler who shared the same floor of a Riviera hotel with the Churchills told me that when he opened his door one morning, there was the rotund statesman wandering down the hall in his birthday suit. At that moment Lady Clementine thrust her head from the Churchill suite, surveyed her famed spouse's nude figure, and chided, "Winston, where are your slippers?"

Betty Beale and I again portrayed Ike and Mamie in our WNPC annual Stunt Party in 1955, and we led onstage an eight-month-old Aberdeen Angus heifer as a surprise gift for the President from Rayburn and LBJ. President Eisenhower, in a thank-you note after the party, wrote, "For me, of course, the highlight of the evening was the presentation of Amandale Bosta Blackbird VI. Although I don't dare qualify as an expert on appearance and blood-lines, I can see that she is a fine animal and one of which I shall be very proud. I assure you nothing could have pleased me more." A newspaper columnist interpreted the gift as a plot by Johnson and Rayburn to persuade Ike to retire to Gettysburg the next year. If so, it didn't work.

CHAPTER XIII

Around the World in Thirty Days

IT was clearly time to see the rest of the world. President Eisenhower had fortuitously appointed some of our favorite friends to ambassadorships in faraway places, and their welcome mat was out. On June 4, 1955, Bob bade me good-bye at National Airport, and in San Francisco I changed to a Pan American Clipper which sped me toward my rendezvous with the mysterious Orient. Hawaiian delegate to Congress Betty Farrington had alerted her editor, Riley Allen, who met my plane in Honolulu at the indecent hour of 5 A.M. and took me on a complete tour of the island, before I again became airborne that night. The next day is one that I have never regained. We crossed the international dateline, refueled at Wake Island, and arrived at Tokyo Airport. There I unexpectedly ran into Senator Earle Clements of Kentucky, who was on his maiden trek outside the continental United States. We shared a car to the Imperial Hotel, designed by Frank Lloyd Wright to withstand earthquakes and offend the eye, where Ambassador John Allison's invitation awaited us to dine at the embassy that evening.

The spectacular embassy, nicknamed Hoover's Folly when President Herbert Hoover expended more than $1,000,000 for the construction of the residence, gardens, chancery, and two apartment buildings in 1931, was by then worth $10,000,000, and its value is still soaring today. In the VIP guest room Mrs. Allison had playfully posted a sign reading "General MacArthur, Adlai Stevenson, Secretary Dulles, General Mark Clark, Vice President Nixon, and Senator

Knowland slept here, but not at the same time." At dinner I sat on the ambassador's right and arranged to interview him the next morning.

During the remainder of my stay in Japan I went shopping, lunched with newspaper colleagues, attended the Kabuki Theater where all female roles are played by men, had tea at a geisha house where we removed our shoes before entering, and went to a GI nightclub and to a dinner party at United Press correspondent Rod Poats' house.

The next stop was Hong Kong, where I had a cashmere coat made to order overnight, shopped, lunched with John Osborne of *Time* magazine, and toured the beautiful countryside to see Aberdeen fishing village, Repulse Bay, and Tiger Balm Park. I rode a rickshaw to dinner at the Correspondents' Club and dined with George and Paula Bell at their beautiful home on the Peak.

John Osborne of *Time* took me to British headquarters to arrange for a trip to the bamboo curtain and generously lent me his chauffeured car for the adventure. On a beautiful June morning we drove through the Free Territory to Tai Po, where we changed to the car of Superintendent Lundy Gordon, a redheaded Scotsman who strapped a holster and pistol over his British walking shorts before we proceeded. Parking a few rods from the frontier, we set out on foot down the railroad tracks from the village depot, which was once a peaceful stop on the Canton-Hong Kong run. That day it was a madhouse. A train from Canton had just chugged to the border bearing six carloads of water buffalo to provide food for Hong Kong despite the Red Chinese famine.

At the barbed-wire border I stood so close that I could have touched the grim-faced helmeted Communist Guards on the other side, who held rifles at the ready. Another train from Hong Kong stood puffing in the depot, while Chinese coolies bustled back and forth across the border to make the exchange of cargo. The free and Red Chinese were indistinguishable except for their caps: the Reds wore blue and the free, red. My British escort explained that to a Chinese red means happiness and blue is for mourning.

We drove next to the Mankanto border and strolled out onto a rickety wooden bridge which marked the demarcation line between the free and captive worlds. This was a highway frontier, but since no automobiles were permitted to cross, dozens of Red Chinese coolies wearing blue sashes and free ones with red sashes scurried back and forth pushing wheelbarrows loaded with produce. En route back to Hong Kong we watched Hakka girls tending cattle in the rice paddies and saw noodles drying on clotheslines behind barbed-wire entanglements.

My flight to the Philippines was delayed for several hours by a tropical storm, but as we taxied toward the Manila airport at 8 P.M., the first thing that caught my eye was the fluttering white hair and immaculate white suit of Homer Ferguson, our ambassador to the Philippines, who was waiting to rush me through customs and into his official limousine. Without waiting for my suitcases, we sped to the embassy, where Myrtle Ferguson and twenty guests caroled "Happy Birthday!" In the excitement I had forgotten that this was June 11, but the beloved Fergusons had not. Piled high at my place of honor at the table were exquisite Filipino fabrics, blouses, and slippers and a birthday cable from Ambassador Clare Boothe Luce in Rome.

The next morning was hot and steamy when we arose at 7 A.M. to drive to the home of General Emilio Aguinaldo for the fifty-seventh reunion of veterans of the Philippine revolution which brought freedom from Spain. Aguinaldo, despite his eighty-six years, was as straight as a ramrod, but the scraggly old veterans who limped past the reviewing stand looked every hour of their years. Ambassador Ferguson stood beside Aguinaldo to review the once-proud troops, and as some of the old soldiers tearfully lifted rustic straw hats to their former leader, Aguinaldo turned stiffly to Homer, muttering, "No discipline!" Afterward, with Myrtle Ferguson and me seated on either side of him, the aging general regaled us with tales of the revolution while we partook of a sumptuous luncheon.

Leaving Manila, I flew above Corregidor and Bataan to Saigon, where I had an embassy briefing on the situation in troubled Vietnam; then to Singapore and the Raffles Hotel. Chip Robert had alerted friends of my arrival, and while in Singapore I attended a birthday party for wealthy, Cambridge-educated Loke Won Tho. The two hundred guests included British High Commissioner Malcolm McDonald, and thousands of colorful streamers, balloons, and paper dragons festooned the room as we dined with chopsticks on sharks' fins, Peking duck, and ten other courses.

My next stop was Thailand, where Ambassador and Mrs. John F. Peurifoy whisked me to their embassy guest room and then took me to a supper party at the exotic home of Prince Bhanabandh, where delicate, costumed women performed native dances to the oddly melodious Thai music. Several of the highborn Siamese complained bitterly to me of the "false picture" of Thailand presented by the recent movie of *Anna and the King of Siam*. Since Thailand's kings had each fathered from fifty to seventy children, practically every Thai at the party could claim kinship to the royal family.

One prince who had lived in the king's harem as a small boy seemed particularly incensed by the celebrated book, musical, and movie, so I asked him, "You mean that you did not have to crawl on your elbows and knees into the royal presence?"

"Only until I went away to college in London," he replied defensively. "Now my joints are too stiff."

"And how do you conduct yourself today in the presence of the king and queen?" I prompted.

"Now I can sit on the floor, if they graciously take a chair," he said proudly.

Hmmmm. Such progress! The next day, while having tea with the Peurifoys at the home of a Thai prince who had recently served as ambassador to a European nation, his princess complained, "Siamese servants are not what they used to be. They have entirely too many modern ways." At that moment, slithering across the polished floor on their elbows and knees came two lovely Siamese housemaids, each precariously balancing trays stacked with cups, saucers, and a tea service. It was right out of *Anna and the King of Siam*.

The Peurifoys escorted me on a tour of the exotic palace where the grandson of Anna's king still reigned, and my eyes feasted on the gold-roofed pagodas and palaces in the royal enclosure. Betty Jane and I went shopping and to see Jimmy Thompson, the fabulous

American who had revived the Thai silk industry following his military service there during World War II. We had tea with Jimmy at his exquisite new Thai house and listened rapturously to his stories of Oriental intrigue during the war. Since then Thompson has disappeared, and despite a widespread search, no trace of him has come to public light, although it is rumored that Red Chinese saboteurs who considered him a secret CIA agent have imprisoned him behind the bamboo curtain. Shortly after his disappearance, his sister met death mysteriously in the United States.

The Peurifoys, although they could not accompany me because of their official position, arranged for a guide to take me to one of the many opium dens which blot the streets of Bangkok. At 11 A.M. the den was jammed with some five hundred men, clad only in undershorts, who lay on wooden benches heating opium pipes, puffing the fumes, and dreaming their fanciful dreams while in a glazed stupor. Even more horrifying was the sight of numerous little boys who lolled beside their fathers' benches, staring vacantly into space. Thousands of lizards clung listlessly to the ceilings, and my guide said that inevitably the children would become addicts from breathing the pungent fumes, just as the lizards would die if removed to fresh air. And all of these opium dens were officially licensed by the Thai government!

Senator Earle Clements and Senator Everett Dirksen arrived at the embassy on my last day in Thailand, and we had a joyful reunion. During luncheon Dirksen said, "I can prove that I'm a fan of Ruth's because I've been carrying one of her by-lined articles in my wallet for eight months." The clipping, dated October 21, 1954, turned out to be a prognostication by Washington seeress Jeane Dixon, and Dirksen read us these lines from my column: "After January of 1957, Jeane says that Ike will no longer be president. Instead, she sees him associated with a big business and another blue-eyed president will take over the White House."

While we eyed Dirksen expectantly, he grinningly said, "Stu Symington and I are the only blue-eyed candidates I can think of, and it's bound to be a Republican year." Ev probably discarded the clipping before long, because in August I wrote of Jeane's changed prediction: "President Eisenhower will run for reelection next year and will win."

The two Senators shared my admiration for Jack Peurifoy as a trouble-shooting envoy. In Greece he became a hero for his magnificent work in ridding the shaky Greek government of Communist infiltration. Then President Eisenhower shifted him to Guatemala, where Communists for the first time in history had won control of a Western Hemisphere nation but had reckoned without Peurifoy. For several sleepless days and nights Jack negotiated; soon Guatemala had a new government as sturdily anti-Communist as our ambassador. His next post was Thailand, where he was succeeding so well that Thailand alone, of all Southeast Asia, had refused to recognize its towering Red Chinese neighbor across the border.

It was with real sadness that I bade Betty Jane, Jack, and their two sons good-bye that July day in 1955. I had grown extremely fond of brilliant nine-year-old Danny Peurifoy, who on one of my evenings at the embassy had played Prince Charming to a little Cinderella in a play that he had staged with his schoolmates. And I was saddened by the cruel fate of fourteen-year-old Clinton Peurifoy, a victim of cerebral palsy since birth, who could not even feed himself, but had recently been brought by his loving parents to Bangkok from a Kansas school for retarded children.

As I kissed them good-bye, Ambassador Peurifoy said, "Ruth, before you leave I want to show you the most foolish purchase I ever made." Leading the way to the garage, he pointed to a sleek Thunderbird, saying, "I wish I'd never spent the money for this car. I need it like a hole in the head, because I have to use the official limousine for business, and I've been so snowed under with work that there's little time for private life. It only has five hundred miles on it." Then, cheering up, he said, "But we're getting a vacation in a couple of weeks. We're going to a resort on the Gulf of Siam, and since the roads are not crowded there, I plan to open up the Thunderbird and see how fast it will go."

It was the last time that I saw him alive. On my return home a letter from Jack and Betty Jane awaited me, telling happily of their plans for the first family vacation in many years. The next day,

somber headlines in newspapers told the rest of the story. The Peurifoys had no sooner arrived at the Bay of Siam than Jack invited his
two sons for a ride in the Thunderbird. He must, indeed, have been
trying to "see how fast it will go," because on a virtually untraveled
road he met a truck head on in the middle of a one-lane bridge. Jack
and bright little Danny died instantly. Clinton, the helpless one, was
limply thrown from the car, and survived with minor injuries. It was
a cruel climax to the career of one of our ablest diplomats, and I
have never known a more courageous woman than lovely Betty Jane,
whom I talked with again at the burial services in Arlington Cemetery.

Senator Dirksen, Senator Clements, and I flew from Bangkok to
Rangoon, where Ambassador Howley Satterwaithe and his staff
briefed us on conditions in Burma. Then we pressed on, and I deplaned alone in Calcutta. On the drive to the Great Eastern Hotel
through a maze of crowded streets, our path was frequently blocked
by sacred but recalcitrant cows that refused to budge until it suited
their regal fancy, and there wasn't a thing we could do to hurry them.
The hotel manager, alerted by Chip Robert, gave a small dinner party
for me that evening, and afterward, because I was making only a
one-night stop in Calcutta, I insisted on going outside to see something of the teeming city on foot. The other guests were horrified
that I should think of venturing forth after dark, but when our host
saw that I was determined to go alone, if necessary, he gingerly
escorted me. Then I could understand his reluctance.

At ten o'clock at night the sidewalks in every direction were paved
with the sleeping bodies of ragged peasants and sacred cows. We had
to step over them by the hundreds to walk half a block, after which
I gladly agreed to return to the hotel. These homeless Indians, living
less well than the privileged cattle beside which they fitfully tossed
and dreamed, seemed the living embodiment of the British nickname
for that accursed place, "The black hole of Calcutta."

The next morning I boarded a plane for New Delhi, and after
checking into the Imperial Hotel, I had no sooner washed my hair
and rolled it on curlers than the wife of Ambassador John Sherman
Cooper telephoned. Could I come for luncheon right away? I ex-

plained about my wet hair and my desperate need for a nap, so she asked me for cocktails that evening. In the middle of my siesta, the telephone rang again. This time it was Ambassador Cooper, whom I had known as a Senator, asking plaintively, "Ruth, aren't you caught up on your sleep yet? I'm just dying to hear all the news of the Senate." I laughingly agreed, and after he sent his car for me, I filled in the homesick ambassador and his lovely bride on Washington gossip, while we sat in the exquisite U.S. embassy halfway around the world.

The next morning Cooper again sent his car, and he and his advisers returned my favor by telling me about India. The Coopers invited me to several dinner parties, and since I had packed only one evening dress, I bought a green-and-gold silk sari which was transformed overnight for me into a dancing frock. The wife of Cooper's press aide took me sight-seeing to the Jumna Mosque, the Red Fort, Gandhi's tomb, the Birla Temple, and the burning ghats along the river. Never shall I forget the ghats! All were in use, consuming bodies of the recently deceased in the open air, on what looked like homemade bonfires. We talked with a grieving family who patiently waited their turn, the squatting father holding a little baby whose dead body was swathed in cloth except for its tiny brown feet, which protruded from the mummylike wrappings.

By contrast, we danced that night under the stars at the lovely Nepalese embassy, and the next morning I arose at 5 A.M. for an exciting trip by embassy car to Agra and the Taj Mahal. As we headed into the desert, we seemed transported to another place and time. We drove through native mud-hut villages, past thousands of Brahma cattle, goats, and water buffalo, and paused for a half hour while a caravan of several hundred camels crossed our trail. We reached Agra at 9 A.M., and there, framed in the arch of its surrounding wall, was the mystical Taj Mahal, surely the most exquisite building in the world. Shedding our shoes, we walked barefoot through the cool oasis of its vaulted chambers, too awed to speak except in whispers. Small wonder that a few years later the natives were visibly shocked when visiting Vice President Lyndon B. Johnson emitted a "rebel yell" inside those sacred portals and gave his wife a smacking kiss!

Lorraine Cooper had thoughtfully arranged for the embassy chef to pack us a picnic lunch, and before returning to New Delhi, we feasted at a nearby park on iced tea and delicious chicken sandwiches. That evening the Coopers gave a dinner party in my honor, and we bravely forsook the air-conditioned embassy to dine at candlelit tables on the patio.

Leaving by plane the next morning, we made stops at Jaipur and Jodhpur, and I nearly had my camera confiscated when I innocently snapped a picture from the air of the palace of the Maharaja of Jodhpur. Two officials of our Pakistani embassy met my plane in Karachi, and after cooling off with a rum collins and a siesta, I went with them and their wives to an embassy reception, where I met Ambassador and Mrs. Horace A. Hildreth and their pretty daughter and new Pakistani son-in-law.

The next day was blistering, with a hot, dry wind blowing in from the desert. After writing and filing a column at the cable office, I drove with public relations officer Robert Pfeifle into the steaming desert to witness a colorful display by the Bengal Lancers, who staged jumps, races, and tent pegging on horseback for our benefit. We lunched at the embassy, and after interviewing Ambassador Hildreth, we walked through the crowded refugee camps, through the filthy Juno bazaar, and along Karachi's famed Black Beach where the sand is mica.

I began the next lap of my journey at 2 A.M. and fell asleep in my seat on the Pan American plane. Awakening several hours later, I discovered that Senator Dirksen had boarded the plane sometime during the night. He was sound asleep, his mouth wide open to the resounding snores which sounded less dulcet than his sonorous speaking voice. We enjoyed a two-hour stopover in beautiful Beirut, after which I deplaned in Istanbul, and Dirksen pressed on to Spain. At the beautiful new Istanbul Hilton I slept the clock around. Then I visited the old bazaar of Constantinople, the Blue Mosque, Hagia Sophia, and the Mosque of Suleiman the Magnificent. At the Seraglio Palace of the Ottoman emperor I saw the crown jewels and thrones.

Later we took a ferry to Asia Minor and drove along the Bosporus to Emirgan, where we dined on sea bass *en papier* and grape leaves with rice, while watching the hubble-bubble smokers.

En route home I stopped off again in Rome and then in Madrid for a visit with Ambassador and Mrs. John Davis Lodge. Francesca Lodge, Cobina Wright, and I lunched at Club Puerta de Hierro and dined at the Jockey Club. Cobina and I went with friends to a bull-fight, but I was so sickened by the blood and gore that I could not stay. Then on to Lisbon, and home by way of the Azores.

It had been an ideal time for the far-flung journey. Thanks to my friendships with so many ambassadors, who opened doors for me and spoke frankly, I was able to write a series of comprehensive articles on our diplomatic alliances and the state of our own missions. Some of the articles even influenced future legislation. I pointed out that penny-wise, pound-foolish Uncle Sam was frequently getting more for his money than he had a right to expect in our overseas establishments. At that time the yearly entertainment allowance for ambassadors in the Far East averaged only $3,500, scarcely sufficient to cover the required Fourth of July reception. From his own pocket, our envoy had to finance the countless dinner parties which must be arranged for visiting legislators, local bigwigs, and the diplomatic corps.

Several U.S. military and foreign aid officials in each world capital were receiving higher entertainment allowances than our official ambassador and could therefore top his hospitality. An antiquated law limited the expenditure for an ambassador's limousine to $3,500 a year. This penny-pinching forced Uncle Sam's top envoy to ride to official functions in a third-rate car, while ambassadors from poorer nations who were receiving U.S. foreign aid rode in Rolls-Royces or Cadillacs.

When Ambassador and Mrs. John Allison arrived at their new post in Japan, they found the embassy almost devoid of usable furniture. General Douglas MacArthur, during the occupation of Japan, had generously lent scarce items to members of his staff, who could not otherwise have set up housekeeping there, and when President Truman abruptly recalled the war hero, without even permitting him to bid his troops farewell, MacArthur also had no time to take house-hold inventory and recall the loans. As a consequence, many of his subordinates failed to return the beautiful chests, cabinets, sofas, and beds, and when they eventually came home, they shipped the furniture to their wives at taxpayers' expense.

Our embassy in Manila at that time was disgracefully inadequate. Our previous ambassadors had occupied a beautiful embassy situated on built-up land in the bay, but with World War II office space became so essential that it was converted into the consulate, and Uncle Sam rented a house for the ambassador's residence. This was the dowdy dwelling occupied by the Fergusons, where creature comforts were so limited that when U.S. officials or friends slept there, either the ambassador or the housekeeper had to relinquish a scarce bathroom to the houseguest.

Fortunately Senator Clements had returned home before I did, because on the Fourth of July weekend Senate Majority Leader Lyndon B. Johnson suffered a massive heart attack, while visiting a friend's estate in nearby Virginia, and even as his life hung in the balance, he arranged for Majority Whip Earle Clements to take over the leadership role.

I wrote a column about the jinx which seemed to haunt the Senate leadership of both parties. On the Republican side, death struck down Senators Robert A. Taft and Kenneth Wherry at the peak of their Senatorial careers in the early 1950's. The voters eliminated Scott Lucas and Ernest McFarland while each held the Democratic leadership post. Alben W. Barkley had willingly relinquished the leadership in 1948 to be Vice President but failed to win the Presidential nomination in 1952 and was out of a job for two years until he returned to the Senate as the lowliest freshman on the back row. Now LBJ hovered near death, and Earle Clements and William F. Knowland held the Democratic and Republican leadership posts respectively.

A year later, Barkley died of a heart attack, Earle Clements was defeated for reelection, and when Knowland ran for the California governorship instead of Senatorial reelection, he was soundly defeated. Johnson recovered and subsequently advanced to Vice President and President, but by 1968 he was so unpopular that he sadly relinquished the reins of power. Shortly thereafter, Senate Republican Leader Everett Dirksen died in office.

CHAPTER XIV

Faint Hearts and Gentle People

PRESIDENT EISENHOWER was genuinely fond of Senator Lyndon B. Johnson, despite their political differences. He sent flowers ten times during LBJ's convalescence from a heart attack and took time to visit him at the hospital on the day that he flew to the Geneva Conference. On September 23, 1955, during a work-and-play vacation in Denver, Eisenhower dictated a letter to Johnson, saying, "Dear Lyndon, I am delighted to have your encouraging report on your recovery. I most earnestly hope for your own sake that you will not let your natural bent for living life to the hilt make you try to do too much too quickly."

It was excellent advice, which Ike himself should have heeded. Instead, he immediately went out for a round of golf with George Allen and two other friends, playing not eighteen but thirty-six holes in mile-high Denver's thin air. Afterward, the golfers wolfed hamburgers with onions, and during the evening George Allen developed indigestion. Ike, ever the solicitous host, showered him with sympathy and advice and cut short the evening so that George could go to bed.

During the night the President also suffered pangs of indigestion, which became so acute that he was rushed to the nearby Army hospital. There it was learned that he, like Lyndon Johnson, had had a heart attack, and a shocked nation prayed for his life.

Allen, on learning of Ike's severe illness, grieved for his close friend. Being human, he also feared for his own health, and the busy director of a dozen large corporations lost no time in checking himself into

142

a doctor's office in Denver. After submitting to every known test to determine whether his heart was up to par, George sat back dejectedly to await the bad news. It was not long in coming. Accompanying the astronomical bill for examinations was the terse report "Mr. Allen is greatly overweight."

George, a renowned wit, promptly exploded, "Any taxi driver in the country could have told me that for the price of a forty-cent cab ride."

Newsmen set up a day-and-night vigil outside President Eisenhower's hospital suite, while other reporters kept a round-the-clock watch over the Vice President, who was now indeed only a heartbeat removed from the Presidency. No man ever conducted himself with more dignity than did Nixon during those trying days and weeks. Equally dignified was Second Lady Pat Nixon, who despite her official social schedule and heavy correspondence was still doing her own grocery shopping at the supermarket, besides the cooking and mending for an active family of four.

Bright and early each morning, nine-year-old Tricia and seven-year-old Julie climbed aboard the school bus to attend classes at Horace Mann school. Although practically all other officials and Washington newspapermen sent their youngsters to private schools, the Nixon girls went to a public one. Mrs. Nixon managed the household with one maid, and because the maid had agreed to work during the weekend of Eisenhower's heart attack, Pat thoughtfully gave her the next four days off. The Nixons then invited newspaper reporters to use that room during the all-night vigils, and Pat herself often took hot coffee to them.

On Sunday, when the Vice President tried to back his Oldsmobile out of the garage, the battery was dead, so the family rode in a Secret Service car to services at the Congregational Church. Afterward, Nixon told newsmen that he was looking forward to watching the World Series on television, but three women have a way with a man. A few minutes later, he sheepishly corrected himself. His wife and daughters wanted to go to the Congressional Country Club for Sunday dinner, and at the club Nixon invited accompanying reporters to "eat on me."

In October, 1955, I wrote a column about the Barkley family, which began:

> The fun-loving Barkley clan, presided over by the merriest of all patriarchs, is playing a fascinating new game called "relations." Mrs. Alben W. Barkley of Paducah, Kentucky, who used to be our Second Lady, recently wrote to Mrs. Max O. Truitt in Washington, saying, "How nice that my daughter will be my daughter's mother-in-law."
>
> Marion Truitt, eldest daughter of the "Veep," replied in kind: "When my son Tommy has children, they will be my nieces and nephews as well as my grandchildren." The "Veep" also had a contribution. "Those same children will be my grandchildren and also my great grandchildren."

What they meant was that Mrs. Barkley's namesake daughter Jane had become engaged to the Veep's grandson, Tom Truitt. But by reason of the May-December marriage of the Vice President and Jane, young Jane was already Tom's stepaunt, and his mother was her stepsister. The youngsters met at the Barkley-Hadley nuptials in St. Louis, when they were fourteen years old. Now they were twenty, and their marriage took place as scheduled, but later ended in divorce.

I had picked up a strep throat on my trip around the world, and throughout the late summer and fall I spent much of my time sitting in Dr. Allen Walker's outer office, awaiting my turn to be treated. When I at last recovered sufficiently to risk an operation, Dr. Walker removed my tonsils, and my recovery was so complete that thereafter, whenever I saw him at Chevy Chase Club dances, he would waltz over to say, "Ruth, what a fool I was to take out your tonsils. Business has fallen off considerably."

The October afternoon that I was to check into the hospital for the next day's tonsillectomy, I returned to the office from Capitol Hill and found a mysterious message awaiting me. Our receptionist said the man had left no name but insisted that I telephone a certain room number at the Mayflower Hotel. In a rush to clear my desk, after writing a column, I would have forgotten the message except for the receptionist's reminder. Calling the number, I recognized the voice of Frank Conniff, an old friend who was a Hearst official in New York. He asked me to come over and have a drink with him, Austine and Bill Hearst, and Kingsbury Smith, but I told him that I had to rush home to pack a suitcase for the hospital. Frank was so insistent, however, that I finally promised to drop in for a minute, and I had barely entered the drawing room of their suite before Frank came to the point. "How would you like to have one of the dream jobs of all times?"

Mystified, I replied that I already had a dream job; but they said that they were creating a new position as special Washington correspondent for International News Service, and that I was their unanimous choice to fill it. Then I could understand the secrecy of Frank's call. Joseph Kingsbury Smith, a famed foreign correspondent, had recently been named president of INS and was eager to "put new life" into the Washington bureau, but Frank had not wanted to jeopardize my position by leaving his name with our operator.

The salary that they offered was considerably more than my current one. Even more important to me was the promise that I could select my own assignments and write at much greater length than we were permitted to do on the *Daily News,* which had recently ordered still further abbreviation of news stories. The offer was highly tempting, but I could scarcely bear the thought of terminating my happy association with an organization where I had so many friends. Therefore, I asked time to think it over while I was in the hospital.

For ten days following my tonsillectomy I could not talk, which must have been a welcome relief for my husband. But neither could I accept the calls from Kingsbury Smith, which gave me a reprieve. As soon as I was able to speak again, he flew to Washington with a three-year contract in hand and insisted on an answer the following morning. John O'Donnell, my bureau chief, was out of town, but I could stall no longer, so I telephoned editor in chief Richard E. Clarke in New York to tell him about the offer.

Clarke was appalled. So was publisher John F. Flynn as soon as Clarke conveyed the news to him. For the remainder of that day and evening, the two executives took turns telephoning me from

New York, trying to dissuade me. Jack Flynn wanted to meet the much higher terms of my contract, but after I pointed out that Washington bureau morale would plummet if I could pick my own assignments and write at greater length than the other staff members, Clarke reluctantly agreed with my logic. I signed the new contract the next morning but stipulated that I would not begin the "dream job" until January 1.

When the word was eventually announced, I received many poignant letters from the *Daily News* staff in New York and from numerous editors throughout the country. *Editor & Publisher* magazine ran a story saying: "Ruth Montgomery, one of America's outstanding women reporters, makes her debut January 1 as a special feature writer for International News Service in the nation's capital. This brilliant writer will report in her own bright, distinctive style the important as well as the human interest events on the Washington scene. As a Washington correspondent and syndicated columnist for the New York *Daily News* since 1944, she has interviewed countless dignitaries here and abroad, and is on first-name acquaintanceship with many of the men and women who are world figures." It also quoted numerous editors around the country, who expressed pleasure that they would now be receiving my INS copy.

My last day at the *News* was December 29, 1955, and when I returned to the office from my final assignment, the Washington bureau surprised me with the first cocktail party ever given there. John O'Donnell, news editor Ted Lewis, and my fellow correspondents presented me with two white orchids and a sterling silver cigarette case on which had been engraved "Eleven years with the right woman. Washington Bureau, New York *Daily News.*" On the other side were my initials. I could have wept with nostalgia for all those happy years together. After the ceremony, other newspaper friends arrived for cocktails, and well-wishing messages from executives in our New York office flooded our news ticker.

Newsweek magazine carried an article which read:

> Ruth Montgomery has a wide acquaintance among Washington officials, a handsome residence in the fashionable Northwest

section of the capital, a syndicated column, and a notable record of news beats scored for the New York Daily News. Last week, International News Service added more warming color to the Montgomery story. At a reported price of $25,000 a year, it hired her from The News to do a weekly Washington column and a daily 600-word feature on any topic she chooses.

For a long time Ruth Montgomery, a 26-year veteran of newspaper work, has been drawing dream assignments. She has covered the last three presidential conventions, and despite a quite feminine charm was reportedly labeled "Miss Cyanide" by Mr. Truman. The first exclusive interview ever granted by Argentine Dictator Juan Perón went to her. For INS, her acquisition represented something of a coup. Her stories of Havana in 1947 changed the course of Cuban National elections there. She once successfully posed as a member of the race-hating Black Legion in Detroit, a dangerous assignment which helped crack a murder case which revealed the fact that the city police chief was a member of this subversive group.

She hid under a waiter's tray to sneak into the honeymoon suite of Doris Duke and Jimmy Cromwell. They were so amused when five-feet-three-inch Miss Montgomery stepped from underneath the tablecloth that they gave her the first interview after their marriage—an eight-column banner story in the Detroit Times.

She has covered political conventions and important weddings such as those of Vice President Barkley and the marriage of the Marquis of Milford-Haven, the Chambers-Hiss hearings, the Axis Sally trial and the Judith Coplon case.

I covered the opening of Congress for INS on January 3, 1956, and my story included exclusive interviews with the leaders of Congress about their legislative plans. The New York *Journal-American* played my article in eight columns above the masthead on page one, with a flattering accompanying article welcoming me to the Hearst fold.

On his seventy-fourth birthday that week, I had an interview with Speaker Sam Rayburn quoting his homey philosophy of life, borrowed from his long-dead father's words: "Son, character is all I have to give you. Be a man."

"Ruth, honey," Mr. Sam's interview began, "I've tried to live by my daddy's words. Temptation just doesn't hit me. It's just so easy to be honest, and such a hard job to be dishonest. By telling no lies I don't have to remember what I told the same fellow the first time he asked me." On his favorite subject, politics, he said, "I tell you, we are going to recapture the White House this year and sweep the Democrats right back into control. The people just naturally rest better with us Democrats."

I asked Mr. Sam what he would do if he had his seventy-four years to relive, and he replied, "Why, follow the same course! My ambition was to go into politics before I could hardly talk plain. I used to read about the debates in Congress, and every biography of famous Americans I could get my hands on, and that wasn't easy down in East Texas in those days."

President Eisenhower, who had been recuperating in Key West from his heart attack and was unable to deliver his State of the Union message in person, returned to Washington and held his first press conference in five months. He seemed in excellent trim, and the long-awaited session reached its high spot when Ike said that he would not object to his name being entered in the New Hampshire Presidential primary. He also called John Foster Dulles, who had come under Democratic attack, the "best Secretary of State I have ever known." The week previously, General Matthew Ridgway had accused Ike of ignoring his advice as Army Chief of Staff and letting domestic politics influence him in cutting our military strength. Ike icily told us, in reply, that if he had listened to the narrow advice of military men, he would not yet have crossed the English Channel for D Day.

British Prime Minister Anthony Eden came to Washington early in February and confided to top members of the British embassy that he was "positively astounded at President Eisenhower's intimate grasp of all world problems, despite his heart attack."

Ike was obviously thinking of running again, and the Republicans were confident enough to be playful. Some of the GOP political posters read "Roosevelt, Truman and Eisenhower: Nero, Zero, Hero." Presidential assistant Sherman Adams was worrying some of them, however, because in recent weeks he had been advising every Republican caller to pay a visit to Governor Christian A. Herter in Massachusetts. One Midwesterner who stopped at the White House en route to New England told me that Adams asked him to "look Herter over very carefully." When he demurred, Sherm grabbed the telephone, called Herter, and personally made an appointment for him. Republicans uneasily wondered if Adams was promoting Herter as a successor for Ike or a replacement for Nixon on the Eisenhower ticket.

Later in January, I addressed the Cleveland Town Hall, where the uppermost question on everyone's mind was whether Eisenhower would seek reelection. On January 24, 1956, I published a tip-off supplied by one of his closest friends, reporting that after Ike's press conference he exclaimed, with something like awe, "You know, I'm not even tired. It didn't bother me a bit. It's amazing, because even in the old days before my heart attack a session like that used to leave me kind of limp."

Ike held another overflow news conference February 8 and indicated that he would make up his mind whether to run before the end of the month. Ruddy and relaxed, he strode into the ornate Indian Treaty Room, grinning from ear to ear, and made clear that he wanted to run again if able. But he emphasized that his decision would not be based solely on the medical report, because he had learned enough about the Presidency to understand its emotional stresses and strains better than his doctors could. This was a break for me, since the previous day my front-page story throughout the country had begun, "A top White House adviser today disclosed that the medical verdict on President Eisenhower's physical check-up next week will not settle Ike's second-term intentions. It will not be a medical decision. There are several other factors that the President feels he still must take into account before reaching his final decision. He will not, however, delay his answer unduly."

After attending his next press conference on February 29, I wrote:

President Eisenhower's "positive, affirmative" decision to seek reelection threw the largest presidential news conference in history into wild pandemonium. Chairs crashed in the aisle as correspondents from every area of the globe dashed to the doors. Only the President was calm, with a trace of the familiar boyish grin lighting his face, as he watched with amusement the mad scramble provoked by his long-awaited decision. You could almost taste the suspense as the anticipated moment arrived.

First, the President had to have a little fun with the 311 newsmen and women who crowded into the session. Forty other reporters, barred by lack of space, paced restlessly outside as the President walked composedly to the desk of the rococo treaty room in the old State Department building. If Ike was aware of the tension, he failed by so much as a flicker of his greying eyebrows to reveal it. Laying a white sheet of paper on the yellow blotter, he said that he had a few announcements to make. Then, as if teasing the press, he made a leisurely plug for contributions to the Red Cross. Next, he expressed lengthy gratification for the current visit of the Italian President. Thirdly, he urged Congressional speed on his farm bill in the Upper Colorado Basin project. The fourth announcement was it!

Seven minutes after the conference began, Ike finally disclosed that he was ready to give a "positive, that is an affirmative" answer to the American people in a TV-radio broadcast that night. He would run if they wanted him to. Laughter rocked the room when the President, stating that he would give an honest report, added that even his enemies, who may have called him stupid, had never called him dishonest. Asked if he wanted the same running mate as in 1952, he humorously retorted that Vice Presidents are nominated after the President, and he did not yet know who the Republicans' standard-bearer would be. But he immediately praised Nixon, thereby giving the impression that he favored his candidacy.

Eisenhower again drew laughter from tension-gripped correspondents when he confided that he had consulted everybody he thought was his friend, and some others he wasn't sure about, before reaching his decision. Ike said he would not presume to tell Nixon whether to run again but had asked him to chart his own course, and he stressed that he had no criticism to make of him as a man, an associate, or a running mate.

That was a cold, gray winter in Washington, and in late March Bob and I flew to Florida for a long weekend with his sister, Rhoda. While there, his fun-loving sister insisted upon taking us to a private séance with the Reverend Malcolm Panton, and although Bob and I could not believe that we had actually been in communication with our fathers and other deceased relatives, it was an exciting experience. A few weeks later, when Bob had to make a speech in St. Petersburg, we again had a sitting with the Reverend Mr. Panton, and his direct-voice demonstration was even more intriguing.

Consequently, on our return to Washington we visited a Spiritualist church with another doubting couple, and because some seemingly evidential material came through the medium, the Reverend Hugh Gordon Burroughs, I persuaded Bob to go with me to Burroughs for a private sitting. So many names of departed relatives were introduced during this session that I telephoned Kingsbury Smith to ask if he would like me to do a newspaper series on mediums, and he grabbed at the idea. After going to a number of other séances, I thereupon wrote an eight-part series which appeared in newspapers throughout America. We were overwhelmed by the reader response, as letters began arriving by the hundreds and then by the thousands. But I had become disillusioned after attending some of the sessions at Silver Bell in Ephrata, Pennsylvania, and did not pursue the interest until several years later, when Arthur Ford, the most famous living medium, came to Washington for a speech. The next day I had a private sitting with him, and the wealth of material which came through was astonishingly evidential. I made a number of long-distance telephone calls to check the "facts" stated by Fletcher, Ford's other-world control, and all of them proved true. Even more surprisingly, a "judge" who came through Fletcher told me that he had been drowned nine months before and wanted his loved ones to know what had happened to him. I had never heard of him before, but three weeks later the decomposed body of the long-missing U.S. judge was dredged up by a fisherman in Lake Michigan.

This naturally quickened my interest in psychic phenomena, and after a great deal more research I eventually wrote two best-selling books about the psychic field: *A Search for the Truth* and *Here and Hereafter*.

The children of John and Barbara Eisenhower were frequently at the White House that spring of 1956, and one day eight-year-old Dwight David Eisenhower II had a conversation with Bela Kornitzer, which I reproduced in my column. David, on introducing himself by his full name, was asked, "Who is the first Dwight D. Eisenhower?" David replied that he was.

"Now, wait a minute; who is Ike?" Bela prodded.

"Ike? He's the President," David responded. Asked why Ike was living in Washington, the son and grandson of soldiers shrugged. "Because he's stationed there."

During the early spring, romanticists were avidly reading about the approaching marriage of movie star Grace Kelly to Prince Rainier III in Monaco, but President Eisenhower apparently did not share their rapture. When a White House adviser suggested that he designate actor Robert Montgomery, his television adviser, as his official representative at the Rainier nuptials, Ike retorted, "I wouldn't insult Bob by suggesting it."

Late in April, I attended a large anniversary banquet for *Meet the Press*. Senator Alben W. Barkley, who had made his debut on that TV show at my inauguration as president of the WNPC, was the principal speaker, and during his talk he made teasing reference to "the beautiful brutality" of Ruth Montgomery as a panelist.

A day or two later, while delivering the keynote address at a mock political convention staged by Washington and Lee University, he said in reference to his new political status, "I am willing to be a junior. I am glad to sit on the back row, for I had rather be a servant in the house of the Lord than to sit in the seat of the mighty." At that moment he slumped across the podium, dead! A saddened nation heard the news of his fatal heart attack, and I wrote a column of tribute which began:

The mold was broken when Alben W. Barkley entered what he laughingly called "this veil of tears." For that reason you can't say, "The Veep is dead, long live the Veep." There was only one Veep, and even the unique title fitting the initials of Vice President passed with him.

This correspondent knew him well, and to know him was to love him. Republicans and Democrats alike will mourn his passing, but no one could be more surprised about it than 78-year-old Alben Barkley. Years ago, while on a Senate junket to Egypt, the Kentucky statesman slipped off behind the Sphinx to have his fortune read in the sand. The results pleased him more than anything except his later election as vice president.

"You will live to be a hundred and three," the fortune teller assured him, and Barkley believed it. In fact, he believed it so emphatically that he never quite forgave Harry S. Truman and the AFL-CIO bosses for turning thumbs down on his presidential aspirations at the Democratic National Convention four years ago because of age. He told me, "Why, I'm younger than anybody here. You know yourself that I'll live to a hundred and three, so I have twenty-nine years to go."

The Veep left no will, and I was not surprised. What was the rush, with a quarter-century still to go?

Immediately upon learning of his sudden death, I dispatched this telegram to his widow: "Dear Jane, Heaven will seem a little nearer and dearer to all of us because Alben is there." A number of officials who accompanied Jane on the sad train ride back to Paducah with Barkley's body told me that although thousands of telegrams had poured in from here and abroad, Jane always kept my message on top of the stack.

CHAPTER XV

That Old Ike Magic

ONCE again, Senator Estes Kefauver was wearily tramping the boondocks in search of hands to shake, but his vivacious wife, Nancy, sat out the 1956 primaries. Four years previously she had ridden planes, trains, and buses, pumping almost as many hands as Coonskin Estes, but this year she had begged him not to run. President Eisenhower seemed in the best of health, and it was obvious that he would be reelected.

Republicans were smelling victory by a walk-in, when on June 9 Ike suffered a sudden attack of ileitis and underwent an emergency operation. Once again reporters began a round-the-clock vigil, this time at Walter Reed General Hospital in Washington, but the President rallied strongly, and after a bedside conference with Ike, a White House official told me that the President still expected to make five or six major campaign addresses at Republican rallies.

Four days after Ike's operation, Commerce Secretary Sinclair Weeks flatly informed me that the President would run again, and that Vice President Nixon would also be renominated on the first ballot. The same day, a top Democratic strategist said that his party would continue to attack Eisenhower and his administration, despite his illness, "because it's perfectly obvious that Ike is going to run again, and we're not going to let him enjoy a long period of privileged sanctuary like we did after his heart attack."

The race was on in full cry, and perennial hopeful Harold Stassen was doing all in his power to keep Nixon from the Vice Presidential renomination. He repeatedly stressed the availability of Christian Herter as a replacement, but anyone who knew Stassen suspected that he had himself in mind. The Washington *Post* kept up a running attack on Nixon and carried such vicious editorial cartoons by Herblock that Mrs. Nixon barred the newspaper from their home. She did not want the two little Nixon girls to see their father unfairly depicted as a bearded monster.

Several prominent Republicans publicly criticized disarmament chief Harold Stassen for his dump-Nixon campaign. Congresswoman Edith Nourse Rogers, calling it "a cold act of disloyalty," telegraphed Stassen: "Stop this selfish aggrandizement, this disloyalty activity, this injury to the party and President Eisenhower. All you can possibly harvest is failure, contempt, and hatred."

Pat Nixon could not but have been wounded by Stassen's activities, but when she came face to face with Mrs. Stassen in a receiving line, she smilingly held out her hand and said, "So nice to see you." Mrs. Stassen said only, "Hello, I want you to meet my sister," and faded into the crowd.

Compared with Democratic bloodletting that summer, however, the Republican Party was a love-in. Kefauver's tireless campaign had netted him 360 committed delegates, but when it became obvious that he could not amass enough to win, he abruptly withdrew from the race two weeks before the convention and asked his supporters to swing to Adlai Stevenson, who desperately wanted a second try for the Presidency. But former President Truman, who wanted no part of Stevenson again, strongly endorsed New York Governor Averell Harriman, with Senator Stuart Symington as his running mate. The Senate stable, therefore, had four entries for the Vice Presidential sweepstakes: Symington, Kefauver, Hubert Humphrey, and Jack Kennedy.

This was the lineup as the curtains parted on a magnificent supper party which Perle Mesta hosted at the Blackstone Hotel in Chicago, where Democratic delegates had gathered for the nominating convention. Tired of gate-crashers, Perle had posted detectives at all entrances, but a few uninvited strolled in disguised as waiters. It was an exciting time for a party. Thicker than the cigarette smoke, more sparkling than the champagne was the suspense-laden air as hopeful candidates jostled for position at the starting gate the next day.

Former President and Mrs. Truman arrived fifteen minutes after his usual bedtime, in time to hear radio commentator H. V. Kaltenborn imitate Truman, as Truman had mimicked Kaltenborn when, in the wee hours before Truman's 1948 election became official, he had assured the nation that Thomas E. Dewey would be the next President of the United States. Truman and Bess doubled with laughter to hear Kaltenborn mimicking Truman's own mimicry.

Following this hard-to-beat act, the champagne-sipping guests broke into a chant of "Piano, piano," trying to lure a little free entertainment from Truman, but Bess Truman gave her husband a don't-you-dare look that kept him pinned to his seat. Averell Harriman had an invitation to the party but failed to show. Adlai Stevenson arrived ten minutes after Truman but ducked out before Truman was introduced. Kefauver was there in white dinner jacket, dancing with his titian-haired wife to the strains of "Tennessee Waltz."

Jack Kennedy was sitting at my table, and when Hubert Humphrey strolled over, they began laughingly praising each other as a fine Senator who should remain in the Senate. "Gad, Jack," HHH kidded, "I made five speeches praising you in Massachusetts, and then you took me seriously."

Replied thirty-nine-year-old Jack to forty-four-year-old Hubert, "Say, fellow, aren't you getting a little too old and bald for the Vice Presidency?"

Adlai Stevenson, bitterly opposed to the end by former President Truman, won the Presidential nomination the next day and then took the unprecedented action of asking the convention to make its own choice of his running mate. A Stevenson friend confided to me that the former Illinois governor preferred either Humphrey or Kennedy to Kefauver but said, "I'd be an ingrate if I didn't take Estes, after he came through at the eleventh hour when I needed him most." Stevenson had never seemed able to make up his mind about anything, even about what to say on the campaign stump until the last minute, so he threw the horse race wide open. And a horse race it was!

Intense jockeying immediately began between the three men. Humphrey, who had been openly seeking the nomination for months, was a favorite of the farm states; Kennedy had strong endorsement from New England and numerous friends in the South; but Kefauver was out in front. The exciting race on the convention floor the next day, as the lead shifted between Kennedy and Kefauver, is well known. So close was Kefauver to defeat on the second ballot that, his spectacles a little misty, he was about to leave his Convention Hall hideaway when the miracle happened, and he surged to the front.

Immediately following Estes' victory, Nancy Kefauver held a press conference in Convention Hall and told us that she would "keep right on teaching art classes" during the fall, while her husband campaigned. Neither Stevenson nor his running mate would have wifely assistance as they wooed the voters.

We correspondents moved on to San Francisco and the Republican Convention, where the story of the hour was Stassen's dump-Nixon drive. Pat Nixon invited female members of the press corps to a coffee klatch, and once again proved that she was a star-studded asset to her husband's political career. The tireless dynamo had already been to two state delegation breakfasts before welcoming us at 10 A.M., but she looked enviably fresh. Discussing her philosophy, she told us, "I'm a pretty calm person. I have a philosophy that if you are doing the very best you can, and working hard to do the things you should, everything will work out. I wouldn't be disappointed either way."

Asked how she felt about the criticism of her husband, she mused a moment and softly replied, "It hurt me in the beginning, because I have never gossiped, but now I don't read all the things they say. I feel that Dick is doing the very best that he can. I know how sincere he is and the long hours he works, and since he is doing all that he can, I refuse to worry about it."

Pat demonstrated her innate kindness when, asked if she knew Mrs. Christian Herter, she said, "I know her real well, and she is a perfectly lovely person. Dick used to be on the Herter Committee in the House, and we frequently went to their lovely house in Georgetown for small dinners. They would serve the wild game Chris had shot, and they were simply enchanting experiences. Their son went with us on our first trip around the world. We are close friends."

Nixon's fate was to be decided the next day in a San Francisco hotel suite where President Eisenhower was meeting with Sherm Adams, National Chairman Leonard Hall, Stassen, and other top advisers. At the appointed hour scores of correspondents impatiently awaited the outcome in the adjoining corridor. At last the door swung open, and as Adams strode out first, he looked unmistakably grim. Did that mean that Stassen had won or lost his dump-Nixon attempt?

We were trying to interpret the expression as he came toward us down the corridor. Then his wintry blue eyes suddenly kindling, he said, "Hi, Ruthie," as he swept me into a bear hug and planted a firm kiss on my cheek. Stassen, close on his heels, took one look at my startled reaction and broke into a broad grin. Len Hall chuckled aloud. Now how do you read the mutual secret of three men who are suddenly laughing uproariously? We had to wait another fifteen minutes before Ike called us inside to say that Stassen had thrown in the towel. Nixon would remain on the ticket.

Adams and I had become good friends during the first Eisenhower administration, and he frequently granted me exclusive interviews while denying them to others of my craft. Sherm and Rachel Adams and Bob and I were invited to all of Marjorie Merriweather Post's square dances, and although Sherm had no sense of rhythm, he had a boisterous approval of exercise. Thus, whenever the music started, he would make a dashing skid across the ballroom floor, grab my hand, and claim me as his partner. Then he would madly fling me around the squares, with little sense of musical timing, but plenty of zest for dos-à-dos.

On the night of Eisenhower's second-term nomination, the undisputed Republican queen was Mamie Doud Eisenhower, gowned in royal purple satin. It was Mamie by acclamation from the moment that the wildly cheering delegates glimpsed her royal purple pillbox bonnet bobbing above the mass of humanity. In behalf of the grateful elephant party, Leonard Hall presented Mamie with the huge organ that had been playing throughout the centennial convention, and although Mamie plays the organ, she promptly designated Fitzsimmons General Hospital in Denver as the recipient. Then Hall tendered Mamie a gold medallion naming her eight-year-old grandson David honorary chairman of the 1956 convention. Twelve years later, that same David would work far harder to help win the Presidential nomination for his new father-in-law, Richard Nixon.

Bob had joined me in San Francisco for the convention, and Mrs. Ambrose Diehl gave a "Press Go Home" party in my honor, which was thronged with Senators, editors, and other friends. Afterward, at the invitation of Austine and Bill Hearst, Bob and I drove to San Simeon, where we were houseguests for several days in the $30,000,000 castle which the late publisher William Randolph Hearst had created on a sweeping hillside overlooking the Pacific. Mary and David Sentner, head of the Hearst Washington bureau, accompanied us, and as we drove through the electrified gates and up the winding road to the crest of the Enchanted Hill, we gasped at the soaring towers of La Casa Grande, the three guesthouses which were little palaces, the great Neptune swimming pool, and the Greco-Roman templet.

Austine led us through the massive assembly hall and up a spiral staircase behind medieval choir stalls to our colossal bedrooms, each of which boasted two bathrooms and priceless works of art. Throughout our stay we roamed at will through the forty bedrooms, some two stories high with balconies, which had been purchased from cloisters and châteaus in Europe and reassembled here, stone by stone. The Henry J. Taylors arrived during our second day, but the eight of us at meals were dwarfed by the great refectory table in the dining hall, which could comfortably seat sixty.

That fall I traveled with all four candidates, beginning with Adlai Stevenson, and during a brief respite Bob and I gave a party for Bob and Millie Considine, with Mary Pickford and Buddy Rogers among the guests. Then I flew to Dayton to pick up the Nixon campaign trail, which was so rugged that I wrote a column about it beginning:

Once upon a time a presidential candidate could climb aboard a whistle-stop special, ease off his shoes, pour himself a short-snort and prepare to enjoy the comforts of home. The train might rock and roll a bit, but if the candidate was hungry he could eat. If he felt the need of a shave or a shower, his private bathroom was rolling along with him. But what goes today? The sonorous chug-chug of the train has been replaced by the siren of the motorcycle and the roar of airplane motors warming up for the inevitable take-off. Pity the poor candidate of today. In the good old times his audience conveniently awaited him at every railroad station. As the train groaned to a halt, he had merely to slip on his shoes, tie his tie, and stroll onto the rear platform with his arms raised in a victory salute. A few golden words, the same at every whistle-stop, could send the local yokels into a frenzy of cheering that was still warming the hopeful's heart as the engineer pulled the throttle for the all-aboard. A nap, a bite to eat, and the earnest crusader was refreshed and ready to repeat the same act down the line.

Nowadays the plane swoops in, taxies up the runway, and the door flies open. The candidate steps out, and may heaven help him from then on. The eager-beavers at each city frenziedly grab his coattails, and unmindful that this is his third or fourth such appearance of the day, they maul him in the crowds, shove him into a convertible, drive him up and down the streets, and finally deposit him panting at the village square or shopping center, where in the broiling sun not so much as a canopy has been provided.

As the last cheers and boos die away they push him back into the open car, turn on the siren, and gaily set out for the next stop fifteen or twenty miles away. There, without so much as a thought for his creature comforts, they joyfully nudge him on stage again; and since fifty or so radio, television and newspapermen are busily projecting his words to a waiting world, variety must be introduced into each and every address.

Should the miserable campaigner find the courage to ask for the men's room, the local arrangements man who forgot to provide for it will mutter that "it's down thataway about a hundred yards through that crowd of ten thousand people." If you think that I'm exaggerating, you should have gone campaigning with

With Vice President Alben W. Barkley.

With Bess Truman *(left)* and daughter Margaret Truman *(center)*.

Senator Styles Bridges and
Ruth at a Washington party.

With Senator Robert A. Taft.

Ruth and His Majesty Hussein I, King of Jordan, at his palace
in Amman, as she arrived to interview him.

Receiving the George R. Holmes journalism award from Barry
Faris of INS in New York.

Donning cap and gown to receive honorary Doctor of Laws degree at Baylor University.

Ruth as Mamie Eisenhower at WNPC stunt party.

Interviewing Senator Styles Bridges at opening of Congress in 1956.

Pat and Dick Nixon this week. One day we left the hotel at nine a.m., after the Vice President had already made two addresses before breakfast. An hour later, having flown across the state, he delivered the third speech at an airport and then held a news conference. A motorcade took us to the courthouse square, where we baked in the shade-less heat while covering his fourth address. We swapped our big skyliner for a battery of two engine puddle-jumpers and took off for a smaller airport, where the Vice President held another news conference. Then a motorcade carried us at sixty miles an hour to the next hall and the seventh speech.

Because this speech was to be televised, Nixon needed another shave. A cracked mirror was provided, but no towel. The water faucet spurted such a torrent that the front of Dick's only available suit was inundated. Meanwhile, Pat had meekly asked the way to a powder room, in vain. The only one in the building was hopelessly separated from her by seven thousand standees. At eleven o'clock that night, as we wearily trudged into a hotel, someone found courage to ask the Second Lady if she were tired. "Not tired, exactly," she replied gamely. "It's just that we haven't eaten since breakfast."

After a trek with the Nixons I flew to Detroit to join up with Estes Kefauver, where the chaos was well organized. Everything ran far behind schedule, and nothing went according to plan. Late in October I flew with President Eisenhower's entourage on a campaign trip to Florida, and in a driving sleet storm at one airport Ike received the news that Israel had invaded Egypt. He hastily addressed the waiting throng, after which we flew straight back to Washington.

Britain and France had also invaded Egypt, in protest against that nation's seizure of the Suez Canal, and on November 4, although Premier Imre Nagy announced that the Soviet Union had agreed to withdraw its troops from rioting Hungary, Soviet forces launched a massive surprise attack against Budapest, slaughtered tens of thousands, and put down the rebellion.

A member of Eisenhower's Cabinet told me that Ike considered the British-French invasion of Egypt "the blackest move in the past hundred years of their history." Pointing out that until British and

French forces began bombing Egypt, Russia was promising to withdraw all remaining troops from Hungary, he declared, "We believe this action gave the Kremlin the excuse it needed to rush reinforcements to Hungary and put down the revolution. The Soviets apparently decided that if the British and French could use brute force to solve a dilemma, they could also ignore world opinion." With U.S. backing, the United Nations forced British-French-Israeli withdrawal from Egypt, but the Soviets were in Hungary to stay.

President Eisenhower won reelection by a landslide, on the day of the Hungarian tragedy, but his coattails were not long enough to carry the majority of Republicans with him. Democrats would again control both houses of Congress.

CHAPTER XVI

A Doctor in the House

ONE of the highlights of my life occurred on Saturday, November 10, 1956. Immediately after President Eisenhower's reelection Bob and I flew to Waco, Texas, where I was to be awarded an honorary degree of Doctor of Laws by my alma mater, Baylor University. The mayor, several Baylor officials, and two beloved Waco friends, Asher Lowich and Helen Pool Baldwin, met our plane, and that evening Helen gave a dinner party for us. It was a family reunion as well, since my mother, sister Margaret, brother Paul, and sister-in-law Rhoda met us in Waco for the gala festivities.

Saturday morning, garbed in cap and gown, I walked beside president W. R. White in the academic processional of the Baylor faculty across the cherished campus where I had spent three happy years to Waco Hall. There I delivered a speech on freedom of the press and received my first doctorate, after this citation was read:

Ruth Shick Montgomery, as an honor student in Baylor University, gained from members of the Baylor faculty an undying love for truth, which has made her a leader in her profession. Mrs. Montgomery has been associated with some of the greatest newspapers in America. She has conferred with Presidents and Kings and other makers of history. She has traveled throughout our country and in many foreign lands, searching always for the heartbeat of humanity and recording it for the information of all who read. Her pen has written accurately, in the confidence that the truth will make men free. Therefore, Mr. President, it is with great pleasure that I present to you Mrs. Ruth Shick Montgomery, an outstanding champion of truth and freedom, that you may confer on her the honorary degree of doctor of laws.

Dr. White gave a luncheon for me afterward, and we sat in his presidential box to watch Baylor's homecoming football game with the University of Texas. That evening Asher Lowich gave a beautiful dinner party to celebrate my new honor. And what a joy it was to renew friendships with numerous college classmates and with colleagues on the Waco *News-Tribune,* where I had begun my newspaper career at the age of seventeen while working my way through Baylor University!

I was in a happy state of euphoria, not only for the honor bestowed by my alma mater, but also because of an editorial written by editor Harry Provence which had appeared in the Waco *News-Tribune.* Forgive me if I repeat it here. Under the headline WELCOME HOME, RUTH; IT'S A GREAT DAY ALL ROUND, it read in part:

> When Mrs. Montgomery speaks tomorrow about the role of a free press in our way of life, she won't be quoting from somebody's theoretical essays. She will be remembering how she and the other Washington reporters have to dig away constantly at the growing trend of official secrecy in order to tell the people what their servants are doing with the people's money and lives. She will be remembering, more specifically, what public servant it was who gave the reporters a bad time, and how the battle of wits is fought, morning and night, in the nation's capital by reporters so that the people may know.
>
> When Mrs. Montgomery speaks tomorrow about the gags and barriers in other lands that prevent citizens from knowing about their governments and their economies, it won't be a chapter out of the National Geographic magazine. She has been there, has agonized over censorships, has talked with and written about most of the leading foreign figures of our time, so that more Americans might know what was happening, and who was causing it to happen around the world.
>
> Newspapers everywhere, and the people whom they serve, can

be glad that Baylor University is paying honor to a great newspaper reporter, and by inference to the role of newspapers in helping to make this country what it is today.

Newspapers throughout the country carried stories on my doctorate award; the Waco *News-Tribune* carried the text of my speech in full, and the Waco *Times-Herald* also published a full-column editorial which enormously flattered me.

The previous year Baylor University had bestowed an honorary Doctor of Laws degree on President Eisenhower, and on learning that I was the next recipient, he wrote to Baylor's president: "Recently I learned of the award by Baylor University of an honorary doctor of laws to Miss Ruth Montgomery. This note is merely to say that I am delighted at the tribute you have thus paid to her consistently fine achievements."

Framed on my study wall is another letter which President Eisenhower wrote that day. "Dear Miss Montgomery, I have just learned of the signal compliment paid to you by Baylor University in the award of an honorary doctor of laws degree. As a recent and fellow Baylor 'alumnus,' it is a special privilege to join in warm felicitations to you on a richly deserved tribute to your outstanding achievements in the field of journalism. With personal regard, Sincerely, Dwight D. Eisenhower." My cup was running over!

Numerous members of the Texas delegation in Washington, including Senator Price Daniel, sent telegrams of congratulation, as did columnist Walter Winchell and some ambassadors and editors, but there was none from Senator Lyndon B. Johnson. LBJ's great-grandfather, George Washington Baines, had been Baylor's third president, and to a mutual friend he groused, "Why should Baylor give Ruth a doctor's degree when it has never given me one?" LBJ had been angling for such an award since he first went to the Senate, and when Bob and I later had a formal party for Dr. White in Washington, Lyndon came by to pay his respects, but he continued to be passed over. The recipients in the two years following my own award were director Cecil B. DeMille and concert pianist Van Cliburn. Not until nearly a decade later, after Lyndon Johnson had won the Presidency in his own right, did Baylor at last bestow on him the long-coveted award.

That fall I had an exclusive interview with Jack Kennedy, who had narrowly lost the Vice Presidential race, and he told me that he had given up all thought of seeking the Presidential or Vice Presidential nomination in 1960. In a frank assessment of his chances, he said that he had two strikes against him which would "rule out" the Presidency: his youth and his religion. Only thirty-nine years old at the time, he pointed out that in 1960 he would still be younger than any other elected President in history, and that as a Catholic he would have to buck the resounding defeat administered to his fellow Catholic, Alfred E. Smith, by Herbert Hoover in 1928. Asserting that the nation was ready to accept a Catholic Vice President, but not a Catholic President, he added, "Frankly, I think that being a Senator is a much more important role than being a Vice President, and that I'm too young to bury myself in the number two role."

On November 13, I wrote a headlined story which later events proved to be remarkably correct—much more correct than Kennedy's prognostications about his career. The article began:

> Secret intelligence dispatches predict that Premier Bulganin is slated for removal as top kingpin of the Soviet Union. Indications are, however, that despite disastrous loss of face in the satellite nations, Nikita Khrushchev will be able to retain control as boss of the Communist Party. Khrushchev, long considered the real power behind the Kremlin throne, is expected to survive the possible new purge of Russian leadership because agriculture, his particular baby, has enjoyed its greatest year. This naturally boosted Khrushchev's popularity with the Russian people, who were almost unaware of their government's debacle in the satellite nations, and removal of the loquacious Khrushchev would probably be too difficult to explain to the Russians unless they were also informed of the embarrassing developments abroad.
>
> Intelligence sources disclose that censorship within the Soviet Union is still so rigid that the Russian people have heard only

of a little trouble in Hungary. They know nothing of the details. Within the Kremlin hierarchy, however, the leaders reportedly blame Bulganin for the sweetness-and-light policy which backfired so disastrously in Hungary and Poland. Such a serious blooper cannot go unpunished, and the obvious fall-guy is Bulganin. The biggest mistake of Bulganin and Khrushchev was to eat crow by welcoming Yugoslav President Tito back to good party standing. This was all the encouragement that the freedom-loving Poles and Hungarians needed to begin plotting their own national communist party, free of Kremlin control.

The story continued with further details, and shortly thereafter Bulganin was ousted from power, with Khrushchev assuming control.

Lyndon Johnson, sufficiently recovered to return for the new session of Congress, was reelected majority leader and delivered such a comprehensive opening address that the press promptly dubbed it "Lyndon's State of the Union message." Styles Bridges, dean of Senate Republicans, had suffered a heart attack several years previously, but had recovered and was lavishing sympathy on both Johnson and Eisenhower. In an exclusive interview that January, LBJ told me, "Styles still clucks over me like a mother hen, and I love the guy. If he knows that I need rest but am afraid to leave the Senate floor for fear of opposition tactics, he promises me that nothing controversial will come up while I'm away. His word is as good as another man's bond."

Estes Kefauver, his hopes of the Presidency now ended, returned to his Senate seat and requested that he be given the vacancy on the Senate Foreign Relations Committee. So did John F. Kennedy, and when the Democratic Steering Committee gave the seat to Jack, Kefauver gamely congratulated him on the Senate floor, but afterward told me that he was "tired of being known as a good loser."

"There is no question but that I was entitled to that Foreign Relations seat," the soft-spoken Tennessean said. "I had the seniority over Jack, and I've wanted the post since I came to the Senate in 1949. I've attended a lot of international conferences and foreign relations briefings, and I think that my experience as well as my seniority had earned me that committee assignment." But the Kennedys were accustomed to getting what they wanted.

During that busy January, I covered President Eisenhower's State of the Union message and went to a white-tie dance given by the Ray Henles at the F Street Club, another of Marjorie Post's square dances, a black-tie dinner which Chip and Evie Robert gave in honor of newly elected Senator Herman Talmadge, a Creole luncheon which Senator Allen Ellender personally cooked in his Senate hideaway, and a square dance given by Myrtle and Homer Ferguson, who was now a judge.

A new session of Congress always prompts a rash of party-giving and 1957 was no exception. Bob and I gave a black-tie dinner party at the Sheraton Park Hotel for more than a hundred guests from the Cabinet, Capitol Hill, Embassy Row, the newspaper corps, and residential society. Former Egyptian Ambassador Aniz Azer hosted a dinner-dance at Chevy Chase Club, and Les and Liz Carpenter had a dinner party for Jenkins Lloyd Jones, their Oklahoma editor. We went to a costumed dance at Chevy Chase Club, to the Mardi Gras Ball as guests of Senator Russell Long, to a Mexican dinner given by columnist George Dixon and his wife, Ymelda, and to a white-tie dinner party at the Norwegian embassy honoring Vice President and Mrs. Nixon.

Martha Rountree and Oliver Presbrey gave a white-tie dinner party, but just before the guests arrived, Martha tripped on her Charles James velvet gown as she came down the stairs, scattering the five hundred place cards which she had held in her hand. The seating snafu merely added to the merriment.

Because January 20, 1957, fell on a Sunday, the second Eisenhower inaugural was postponed until Monday, but we went to a preinaugural party that night at the home of George and Mary Allen. On the twenty-first I covered Ike's swearing in at the Capitol and the inaugural balls that evening. The next day Vice President Nixon gave a party at the Metropolitan Club.

I wrote a series of exclusive interviews with top Eisenhower officials, including CIA Director Allen Dulles and Attorney General (now Secretary of State) William P. Rogers, and after attending the Gridiron Club party March 3, Bob and I went to Philadelphia for Perle Mesta's dinner-dance, which was held in conjunction with the opening of a new Sheraton hotel there. Since Morris Cafritz was a considerable stockholder in the chain, he and his wife, Gwen, were invited for the first time to a Mesta party, and as Gwen approached Perle in the receiving line, she observed that numerous photographers were waiting to record the event for posterity. Becoming flustered, Gwen accidentally dropped her evening bag, and as its contents rolled around the polished floor, Perle watched the scramble with a sympathetic smile. Then the rivals shook hands, and the feud melted away.

I was the only newswoman assigned to cover the Big Two Conference between President Eisenhower and Harold Macmillan, the new British Prime Minister, which opened in Bermuda on March 8. Macmillan, arriving first at the British crown colony, mustered a scant six hundred well-wishers at the airport, but practically the entire island population lined the streets of Hamilton to cheer the wartime general. Tanned and ruddy from his six-day sea voyage to Bermuda, Eisenhower stepped ashore to shake hands with Macmillan and Bermuda's governor, Sir John Woodall, who was respendent in white-and-gold uniform and red plumed helmet.

All members of the British and Bermudian welcoming party except the governor wore black cutaways, striped pants, and gray toppers, but Ike and U.S. Ambassador to Britain John Hay Whitney were in lounge suits and snap-brim hats. While Bermudians gaped at Ike's bubble-top limousine which had arrived by Navy freighter, Americans gazed in awe at the governor's landau drawn by a matched pair of black horses.

Randolph Churchill, only son of Sir Winston, was there to record proceedings for a British newspaper, but was generously hitting the bottle. One evening, joining Jock Whitney, Bob Considine, and me for a drink in the bar, Churchill said, "Your President is off his rocker, you know." We said that we knew nothing of the kind. "Crazy as can be," he continued amiably. "Why, do you know that every hour he gets down on his knees and prays for help?" We assured him that this was untrue, but Randy spread the story anyway.

One chilly March morning we watched Secretary of State Dulles plunge into the icy waters of the Atlantic for his daily swim and marveled at his fortitude. For several years he had been nursing a dread of cancer, and at the urging of his doctor the chain pipe smoker gave up his beloved vice but missed it so acutely that he wistfully told his physician, "If the medical profession should discover that there's nothing harmful in smoking, will you please cable me collect wherever I am, so that I can immediately break out my pipe again?" After giving up smoking, Dulles became a doodler, restlessly moving his pencil across a sheet of paper at Congressional hearings. At international conferences he gave his Russian counterpart the willies by constantly whittling on a pencil with a pocketknife. Then, despite his supreme sacrifice, he underwent an operation for cancer of the intestines, which apparently had nothing to do with smoking. Four months later he was diving into the chill Atlantic.

After returning from the Bermuda conference, Bob and I went to Indianapolis, where the press club's board of directors gave a luncheon in my honor. The next day I addressed the annual Matrix Table of Theta Sigma Phi, honorary journalism fraternity, and that evening the Indianapolis Press Club presented me with its Front Page Award, the first time that it had been bestowed on a woman. At the party which followed, Indiana Governor Harold W. Handley and I danced a fast Charleston number, and a picture of our twirling duet made the front page of Indianapolis newspapers.

CHAPTER XVII

Edgar Speaks His Mind

A DINNER party at the home of Barry and Peggy Goldwater on April 13, 1957, led to one of the most memorable events of my newspaper career. During that gay evening, Barry, who had just returned from the West Coast, beckoned Senator Styles Bridges and me aside to tell us that while there he had talked with Edgar Eisenhower, the President's outspoken older brother.

"Edgar is raising hell about the way Ike is running the government," he said with a broad grin. "He thinks Ike has become too left-wing, and he blames it on their liberal younger brother, Milton." He was referring to Dr. Milton Eisenhower, president of Johns Hopkins University in Baltimore.

I have made it a cardinal rule throughout my newspaper career not to take advantage of friends' confidences at parties, when their tongues are loosened by conviviality, without checking with them later. Consequently, I telephoned Barry Monday at his Senate office to ask whether he objected if I used the item about Edgar Eisenhower in my column. Chuckling reminiscently, Barry replied, "Ruth, Edgar's in town. He just called and invited me to come over this evening for a drink. Why don't you telephone him at the Statler-Hilton, use my name, and ask if you can use it?"

He gave me Edgar's suite number, and when I telephoned, Edgar personally answered the ring. I related Barry's conversation and asked if it were true that he was dissatisfied with the way his brother was running the government.

"You can say that again!" he exclaimed. "I sure am." I asked if I could print his quote, and he replied, "Why don't you come over and talk to me first? Some of the boys are coming over this evening, and I'm leaving now for the ball game, but how about one o'clock tomorrow?"

I gratefully accepted his invitation. The next morning I was still asleep when the telephone beside my bed awakened me. Edgar Eisenhower, at the other end of the line, sounded as chipper and wide-awake as a Kansas farmboy. "Say, Miss Ruth," he began. "Can't you come over and talk to me right away? I mentioned your name to some of the Senators who were here last night, and they all said you're terrific. I want to meet you, but my brother Dwight wants me to come for lunch at noon, so how about right now?"

Assuring him that I would come as quickly as possible, I scrambled into a suit and rushed to his suite at the Statler-Hilton. I was met at the door by Edgar and his blond second wife, who graciously invited me in and chatted for a few minutes. Then I opened my notebook, took out a pen, and began asking his views about the Eisenhower administration. With obvious relish, he began pouring forth his gripes. Milton and "that Sherman Adams" were obviously pulling his brother to the left. Dwight was breaking all his campaign promises by spending too much on welfare and foreign aid and failing to balance the budget. High taxation was killing private initiative and business expansion.

His torrent of words flowed so rapidly that from time to time I interrupted to say, "Mr. Eisenhower, will you please repeat that, so that I can take down your words accurately?" He affably repeated the sentences, in order for me to get his precise phraseology. Edgar was never at a loss for words, and I was so entranced by the great story that neither of us had noticed the time. At last, happening to glance at my watch, I arose in alarm, saying, "Oh, Mr. Eisenhower, you must leave immediately for the White House. It's nearly twelve o'clock."

"Sit down," he said affably, as he motioned me back into the chair. "There's no hurry. Dwight'll be there when I get there."

"But, Mr. Eisenhower," I protested, "he asked you for twelve noon, and the President's schedule is very tight. Please leave now, and I'll walk down with you to the taxi stand." He seemed in no hurry to break up our conference, but I appealed to his wife and finally started them out the door. As we reached the front of the hotel, a cab was discharging a passenger, and I urged the Eisenhowers to hop in.

"Not on your life, Miss Ruth," Edgar exclaimed. "We'll put you in this one and take the next one that comes along."

Fortunately another cab pulled up behind, so I let him hand me into the first one, and as it drove off, a clock tolled the noon hour. I rode to the INS office in a tingle of excitement. Taking time only to whisper to the news editor that I had quite a story, I rushed to my typewriter and began pounding it out, while the news editor grabbed it from me a sheet at a time. Within minutes, bulletin bells on teletype machines were jangling in client newspapers throughout the nation, and editors began tearing up the front pages of their afternoon editions to put bold, eight-column headlines above my story, which began:

Edgar Eisenhower disclosed today that he is highly disturbed about the liberal influence of Milton Eisenhower on their presidential brother, Ike. The Tacoma, Washington, lawyer told this correspondent in an exclusive interview that he also worries about the power that "Assistant President" Sherman Adams and Paul Hoffman wield at the White House.

Edgar, the most conservative of the five Eisenhower brothers, shook his head over the state of the government, and expostulated, "I can't for the life of me understand what persuaded Dwight (he never calls him Ike) to go for that big budget this year. All of his campaign speeches and promises were for decreased government spending. I'd sure like to discover what influences are at work on my brother."

Edgar reflected a moment, and then continued. "Two months ago I would have sworn that Milton was the one responsible for this turn of events. Now I'm not quite so sure." The big man from the West explained that while in Arizona for treatment of his neuritis a couple of months previously, he read a newspaper account of a speech Milton delivered, opposing federal aid to higher education.

"I immediately underscored the word HIGHER and mailed it to Milton," he recalls, "asking why he didn't apply his remarks to all education. Milton wrote back that he was speaking to a group of educators from higher schools of learning, but he carefully avoided telling me his opinion of federal aid to regular schools."

Edgar made no bones about his own stand on the subject. In Washington for lunch and dinner with Ike at the White House, he made it clear that he opposes federal aid to any school, unless a gigantic military installation temporarily swells the facilities of a local community.

Continuing, he said, "This high taxation is killing industry and killing ambition. What in the world could have made Dwight bite on this ridiculous proposition? I'm not at all sure it wasn't Milton." He praised Treasury Secretary George Humphrey as "a very sound individual," and also had good words for Defense Secretary Wilson and Commerce Secretary Weeks, but blasted Harold Stassen, Adams and Hoffman. Of the latter he said, "Hoffman's made a flop of everything he ever put his hand to. Sherm Adams and I certainly don't see alike. In fact, we rub each other the wrong way everytime, but I think he has tremendous influence on Dwight. I know Dwight listens to him all the time. He has indicated that about our brother Milton, too. They're all too liberal for me." Edgar also vented his wrath against social security, saying, "It makes me fighting mad. We're just loading this crazy burden on our great great grandchildren, and one of these days they'll revolt. They'll throw it out where it ought to be thrown. After all, what's life insurance for? I don't want to be coddled from my cradle to my grave."

As soon as my story moved on the news wires, practically every correspondent in Washington began getting call-backs from his editor, telling about my beat and asking him to try to get hold of Edgar Eisenhower for a story of his own. By this time Edgar was quietly lunching with the President, but because his name did not appear on the official list of White House callers, reporters did not know where to find him. It was nearly three hours later that he sauntered down the corridor toward his hotel suite, and by then it was jammed with a hundred shoving reporters, all of whom began asking if what Ruth Montgomery had written about his views of the administration was correct.

"Well, now, what did she say?" he asked with a broad smile. Someone read him a few quotes, and he said, "They sure are correct. Come on in, boys, and I'll pour you a drink."

The telephone in the adjoining bedroom began to ring as they walked in, and while Mrs. Eisenhower went to answer it, Edgar jovially settled down to answer newsmen's questions. In a moment he was summoned to the telephone. The caller was White House press secretary James F. Hagerty, who had just seen the story and was exploding with Irish wrath. Jim laid out the President's brother as only Jim can do it, and it was a very subdued Edgar Eisenhower who finally walked back into the jammed living room, saying, "Boys, I've been misquoted. I have nothing more to say." Two of the newsmen who were present gave me an immediate fill-in, adding that not a single reporter present believed that I had misquoted the loquacious Eisenhower.

President Eisenhower's regular weekly press conference was already scheduled for the following morning, by which time every daily newspaper in the country had picked up my story and emblazoned it on page one. With some trepidation, I took my accustomed aisle seat at the conference, and after the President had entered, the first question asked by a wire service reporter was, "Mr. President, do you have any comment on your brother Edgar Eisenhower reportedly saying that you're too liberal for him, and that he blames it on your brother Milton?"

I held my breath, but the President did not. Flashing his lopsided grin, he replied, "Edgar's been criticizing me since I was five years old." Everyone in the room broke into loud guffaws, in which Ike joined. So did I, in vast relief! Obviously he believed me, rather than his brother's denials.

At subsequent parties that week, Presidential assistant Homer Gruenther and several other White House aides drew me aside to say, "Ruth, you don't need to worry about the President's view of your Edgar Eisenhower piece. We all sat in on the huddle before the press conference, and the President said it was lucky for him that Edgar had shot off his mouth to a friendly reporter like you, instead of to some of the others." "And I know darned well that Edgar said it, too," Ike had added.

Repercussions from my Edgar story continued for some time, with many newspapers also carrying editorials about it. In the *Wall Street Journal* under date of April 18, 1957, an editorial said, "Everybody with a big brother knows exactly what President Eisenhower meant yesterday when he told his press conference that brother Edgar had been criticizing him since he was five years old." It quoted at length from my article about Edgar's complaints, and said that when reporters telephoned the White House in an effort to locate Ike's older brother, Hagerty had said, "I don't know where he is. I just hope he's left town."

Congratulatory telegrams and messages poured in to me from editors around the country, and numerous papers carried laudatory articles about my work. Even *Time* magazine, which was normally critical of Hearst writers, carried a large picture of me and an accompanying article:

> Ruth Montgomery of International News Service, an attractive news-knowing woman, has scored more than one beat with her charm and wide popularity among Washington officialdom. Her enviable talents paid off last week. At a Washington party two weeks ago, a Republican Senator told Mrs. Montgomery that he had visited recently with Edgar Eisenhower, a Tacoma lawyer and oldest of the five Eisenhower brothers. Edgar, he said, had been very outspoken about liberal influences on Dwight Eisenhower. The influences: the President's youngest brother Milton, Sherman Adams, assistant to the President, and Paul Hoffman, former ECA administrator.
>
> When Mrs. Montgomery asked if she could use the story, the Senator suggested she contact Edgar himself, who was in town for a White House dinner. At 9 a.m. last Tuesday, Mrs. Montgomery was routed out of bed by a return call from Edgar Eisenhower. The subsequent fifty-minute interview made headlines across the country. To another Washington reporter Edgar de-

nied it all. Mrs. Montgomery stood by her notes. "I even omitted a couple of points where Mr. Edgar Eisenhower was even more indiscreet. He never once called me or INS back, because he knew I could publish the whole thing."

Such assurance comes easily to Ruth Montgomery. A lively dark blonde married to Robert H. Montgomery, deputy chief of the Small Business Administration, she was good enough at her trade to cause INS to hire her away from the New York Daily News in January 1956, and to be the only woman assigned to cover the Anglo-American Conference held in Bermuda this spring.

Edgar Eisenhower, however, managed the final word. "Dwight and Milton," he said as he left for the West coast, "kiddingly gave me some advice about dealing with the press."

Apparently Edgar did not elaborate on the advice, but when I saw him a year later at a dinner party given by attorney John Mc-Clure, we had a friendly chat, and Edgar ruefully admitted that he had "gotten myself in a mess by talking too much." That time, I didn't quote him.

CHAPTER XVIII

Minor Skirmishes

PRESIDENT EISENHOWER received another comeuppance a few days after my Edgar Eisenhower story. This time it was an embattled lady who spoke her mind. The wife of Defense Secretary Charles E. Wilson, on learning that Ike had dared to call a statement of her husband's "unwise," lambasted the President as her outspoken Charlie would never have done. The statement in question was Wilson's declaration that a lot of draft dodgers entered the National Guard during the Korean War to avoid active duty. Mrs. Wilson, to whom official Washington had given ulcers, was eager to pack up her husband and go back to Michigan, where he was "more appreciated." She let it be known that she was "indignant" at the President and considered his remark about her husband's words uncalled for.

Ike was always praising John Foster Dulles, and Mrs. Wilson declared that although she also considered Dulles a "good man," she did not think he had done "one whit better" than her own man. Described by friends as "a mother hen clucking over her pet chicken," Mrs. Wilson said there was only one thing her husband had done since coming to Washington which had upset her. This was his reference to the White House, on leaving a meeting there: "This is not my dunghill." "I gave Charlie a piece of my mind for that," she muttered.

King Saud of Saudi Arabia came to America that week and, on landing in New York Harbor, distributed $20,000 worth of solid gold watches and money to the personnel of the ship which brought him. Some of the cash tips ranged as high as $400 each. His personal entourage consisted of seventy-one persons, including bodyguards with tommy guns, and he brought new kitchen wear for his voyage on the SS *Constitution* so that his royal lips would not touch food from any pot that had ever held pork.

He checked into Blair House, the President's official guesthouse across the street from the White House, which had previously lodged such colorful personalities as Haile Selassie of Ethiopia, King Paul and Queen Frederica of Greece, Queen Elizabeth II and Prince Philip of Britain, and the presidents of Liberia, Italy, Indonesia, and West Germany. Since the keeper of Mecca and Medina had left his harem behind in Saudi Arabia, Ike tossed a stag dinner for him. The king reciprocated with a dinner at the Mayflower Hotel and a reception at his embassy, which were as dry as the Arabian desert—there were no bars, since faithful Moslems do not touch liquor.

During that epic visit the king suddenly announced that he wanted to buy ladies' shoes for his harem, and Garfinckel's opened its shoe department after closing hours. Excited clerks set out samples of every shoe in the store, and the king, gowned in flowing white robes, strode majestically up and down the aisles, pointing to the slippers that met his royal fancy. Washington has since wondered whether King Saud selected his women for their looks or their tiny feet, because he ordered several hundred pairs of shoes, all in size 4½.

Among our closest friends were correspondent Marguerite Higgins and her husband, General William E. Hall, who bought a house with a garden which adjoined ours in Georgetown. When Marguerite's first child, Larry O'Higgins Hall, was born, she asked me to be his godmother, and she had to obtain a special dispensation from the Catholic Church since I am a Protestant. At Larry's christening, I held him in my arms throughout the Catholic service, with Ambassador Robert Murphy serving as godfather. When the Halls' daughter was born two years later, a different priest who had taken over the parish declined to let me serve as godmother to Linda, so Bobby and Ethel Kennedy substituted as stand-ins, and Ethel held the baby.

Two other close friends were Martha Rountree and Oliver Presbrey, and at our Women's National Press Club Stunt Party in May, 1957, we shared a table, with Senator and Mrs. John F. Kennedy, Senator and Mrs. George Smathers, Ambassador and Mrs. Hervé Alphand of France, and Ambassador and Mrs. Fernando Berckemeyer of Peru as our joint guests. The Smathers came first for cocktails at our new house in Woodley Hill, which had previously been the estate of Secretary of State Henry L. Stimson, and they liked it so much that they bought a nearby lot and borrowed our blueprints, duplicating the interior. At the WNPC dinner that evening, when waiters came around the tables to collect our tickets, Jack Kennedy had forgotten his, as he invariably did his wallet, coats, and hats.

On June 8, 1957, Bob and I were invited to a black-tie dinner party at the nearby Virginia estate of Bobby and Ethel Kennedy, in honor of Bobby's visiting sister Eunice Kennedy Shriver. We took Senator and Mrs. John McClellan in our car and talked en route about how disappointed the Kennedys must be with the weather. They had been planning to barbecue steaks on the patio, but it was still pouring rain after twelve hours, and the ground was sodden.

Among the other guests were Senators Henry Jackson, Abe Ribicoff, and Jack and Jackie Kennedy. After we had sipped cocktails for a while, we were astonished to see Bobby setting up a large outdoor grill in one of their beautiful drawing rooms. Then he began to broil the steaks without an inside flue, and we shuddered to see the greasy smoke spiraling along the white draperies and walls and drifting lazily back onto the white satin upholstery and white carpeting. Our eyes wept from the smoke, but the steaks were done to perfection.

A small dance band arrived, and after dinner we began tripping the Charleston, which was undergoing a popular revival. Teddy Kennedy, enjoying a weekend respite from law classes at the University of Virginia, groused about the play given in newspapers that week to a ticket which he had received for speeding and reckless driving, complaining, "Jack and Bobby used to get tickets for speeding all the time, but nobody knew about it. Now, just because Jack's a Senator, I get mine blasted all over the newspapers."

His mind soon lightened, and he began whirling Ethel in a lively modern dance. Each time that they backed away from each other, Ethel would pick up a different vase of flowers, which she emptied over Teddy's head as they swung together again. Teddy seemed indifferent to his sopping-wet tuxedo, but the rest of us were eyeing the puddles of water on the highly polished floors and the rugs. At last I called out, "Ethel, have you forgotten that this is your house that you're ruining?" Without missing a beat of the rhythm, she retorted merrily, "The house is two hundred years old anyway, so this won't make it any older."

A male guest who had disappeared for a while returned, leading the Kennedys' pet burro in from the barn. The burro's feet were covered with thick mud, which it began tracking over the white rugs, but Ethel and Bobby seemed to consider this hilarious. Eventually the animal was returned to the barn, and as we were leaving, we searched everywhere for my French petit-point bag, which had been lying on the hall table.

"Don't worry, we'll find it," Ethel graciously reassured, "and I'll bring it to you tomorrow." Two days later she telephoned, and with a giggle exclaimed, "Say, Ruth, you must have had a better time last night than we thought you did. We found your evening bag in the barn."

She dropped it off on her way to the Capitol and for once seemed rather concerned. The bag which was supposed to last a lifetime had been trampled into the dung, its gold frame mangled, the petit point ruined, and the compact and lipstick hopelessly smashed within. All we could surmise was that either the burro or a prankster guest had carried it to the barn.

My brother and his wife arrived from Indianapolis a few days later, and since they were active in Republican politics we had a "Grand Old Party" for them, with Senators Barry Goldwater, William F. Knowland, William Jenner, their wives, and the widow of Senator

Joe McCarthy as guests, along with the Presbreys and Halls. It was a hilarious evening of dancing, after which we all gathered around the piano to harmonize on old Methodist hymns. A week later we gave a large cocktail party for my visiting sister, Margaret Overbeck, with a dozen ambassadors in attendance.

In late June, I went to Philadelphia with Martha Rountree and Larry Spivak for a televised *Meet the Press* show before a large audience. Jack Kennedy, his eye already on the White House, had agreed to be interviewed, although the Sunday show interrupted his Cape Cod weekend. Bob and I had meanwhile bought a fourth interest in Martha's WKTF radio station in Warrenton, Virginia, and we made numerous trips there with the Presbreys to hire announcers and get it on the air. It was a harrowing, time-consuming experience, and a year later we thankfully sold the station to sports announcer Harry Wismer, who owned the New York Jets.

Vice President Nixon did not always see eye to eye with his boss at the White House during the Eisenhower administration. Ike had labeled the full appropriation of $144,000,000 for the U.S. Information Agency "an absolute must," but as the Senate prepared to vote on a proposed cut of $34,000,000 from the propaganda agency's budget, presiding officer Nixon reached for his briefcase and departed. Asked by friends for an explanation, he replied, "I'm just getting out of here, that's all. The vote on this may be close, and I don't want to break the tie, because I personally favor the cut." Sixty-one Senators, feeling as Nixon did, sustained the reduction.

Nixon was not the only future President who had strong feelings on the measure. Majority Leader Johnson, leading the fight for a cut in the appropriations measure, became irked when Senator Kennedy wanted to know why, if the agency was so bad, Johnson had agreed to its big appropriation the year before. Beginning another question, Kennedy prefaced, "This is something I don't know a great deal about, but—" Before he could proceed, Johnson snapped, "I certainly want to agree with the Senator on that." Johnson later deleted his crack from the *Congressional Record*.

Our relations with France were severely strained because of U.S. action in the United Nations against the Israeli-French-British invasion of Egypt, and when France found herself involved in deep trouble in Algeria, the administration was gingerly walking on eggs to avoid further antagonizing the French. In early July, however, Jack Kennedy delivered a Senate speech, widely billed in advance as a major policy address, in which he lambasted France for its colonialism in Algeria. The next day a high-ranking White House assistant called to give me a tip on a story, and I wrote:

> The White House is seething over what it regards as a brashly political move by Democratic Senator John F. Kennedy to embarrass the administration's slowly mending relations with France. An unimpeachable source discloses that President Eisenhower and his top foreign policy advisers have concluded that Kennedy's "meddlesome" speech on the delicate French-Algerian crisis was designed to present himself as "an impartial statesman on world affairs." They see it as part and parcel of a carefully designed move by Kennedy to gain stature as 1960 presidential timber. The source revealed that Ike and his staff held a full-fledged policy meeting to pool their thinking on the whys underlying Kennedy's "damaging fishing in troubled waters" at this time. He says the White House conclusion is that Kennedy, the most junior member of the Senate Foreign Relations Committee, was eager to gain stature as a world-thinking statesman. The White House source said that Kennedy's action not only embarrassed us in our relations with the French, which had been strained since our UN action against them in the invasion of Egypt, but that he could also dangerously encourage the Algerians to further excesses in their revolt against French rule.

Before writing the article, I had vainly tried to reach Jack Kennedy in order to present his "answer" at the same time, but his secretary would only tell me that he was out of town until the following Tuesday. As soon as my syndicated article appeared, however, I had no trouble hearing from Jack. Reaching me by telephone, he exploded, "Ruth, I thought we were friends! Why would you write that story without first checking with me?" I recounted my vain attempt to learn his whereabouts from his secretary, and he sputtered, "Well, you surely know that I spend my weekends in Hyannisport."

I replied that I had no idea he was spending four-day weekends away from Senate business, and he replied in more subdued tones, "Well, for heaven's sake, next time get in touch with me before you write a damaging story like that about me."

"Well, for heaven's sake," I kiddingly replied, "from now on tell your staff not to be so secretive when I try to reach you." As usual, we parted as friends.

President Eisenhower was meanwhile holding weekly press conferences in the completely airless, unair-conditioned Indian Treaty Room of the old State Department Building next door to the White House, and the addition of television lights brought the temperature well above 100 degrees. We would emerge from the crowded room with our clothing literally dripping perspiration, and as the humid summer dragged on, reporters beseeched Jim Hagerty to have air conditioning installed. After checking, he reported back that since the room had no usable windows, engineers said that it was impossible to air-condition it.

On a stifling August day, Ike strode in from the icily cool White House, looking as unrumpled as usual. He recognized me for a question, and knowing that he particularly relished questions on foreign affairs, I asked, "Mr. President, why is it that a great nation like ours which can send submarines under the North Pole, and rockets to orbit the moon, cannot figure out a way to air-condition this room?" He had been listening intently to my question, his head cocked to one side, and at the surprise ending he joined in the roar of laughter. Then he turned, said something to Jim Hagerty, and replied, "We'll check on that." When we arrived for the next week's press conference, the room was delightfully air-conditioned, and has been ever since.

Bob and I flew to Europe later that month for a tour of London, Paris, Rome, Nice, Monaco, Barcelona, Majorca, Lisbon, and Estoril. And in October Queen Elizabeth II and Prince Philip came to America for a state visit. I was assigned by INS to cover their trip to Jamestown, Williamsburg, Washington, and New York, and on a bitterly cold day I accompanied them to the University of Maryland's stadium, where the sports-loving queen was to see her first American football game. Bundled in a new gunmetal mink coat designed by Leo Ritter, which had been presented to her by Canadian mink growers, she sat beside Maryland Governor Theodore McKeldon.

The high spot of the game was an 81-yard run that clinched a 21–7 victory for underdog Maryland over North Carolina, and it was witnessed by everyone in the stadium except Her Majesty. She desperately tried to see it, but the towering governor began jumping up and down in front of her, completely blocking her view. All that the petite queen saw of the touchdown was the rear view of McKeldon's flying coattails. Bob and I were formally presented to Elizabeth and Philip that evening at a British embassy party, and the next day in New York I rode behind her in a ticker-tape parade down Broadway.

King Mohammed V of Morocco arrived for a state visit in late November, 1957, and President Eisenhower went to the airport to greet him. It was a raw, windswept day, and Ike stood bareheaded throughout the lengthy welcoming ceremonies. The two heads of state then rode in the President's open limousine on the chilly ride from the airport to the White House.

Shortly before the state dinner for King Mohammed that evening at the White House, Ike suffered what was initially described as a chill, and he asked Vice President Nixon to substitute as host. He also insisted that Mamie go downstairs to the party, and the First Lady put guests at ease by declaring, "Ike was simply furious because the doctors wouldn't let him come."

The next morning it was announced that the President had suffered a cerebral occlusion, his third serious illness during the Presidency. News of Ike's stroke had Washington's "golf widows" up in arms. They kept reminding their husbands that the President had played thirty-six holes of golf only a few hours before his 1955 heart attack and six consecutive days of golf only four days before his latest illness. They could not understand why doctors permitted a sixty-seven-year-old man, on whose health the free world teetered, to take such sporadic, strenuous exercise, and they were concerned that he had stood bareheaded on such a raw day for the lengthy airport ceremony.

A White House source confided that a few days after his stroke, Ike told close friends, "The minute I can't do this job anymore, I'm going to resign in favor of Vice President Nixon. I'm pleased and gratified with the way he has conducted himself throughout my three illnesses." Ike's illness once more projected Presidential assistant Sherman Adams into a position of almost unprecedented power for a nonelected official. When Eisenhower assumed office in 1953, he had set up a military type of staff system under which problems of a similar nature either were handed to one person for decision or were to be analyzed by him and passed upward for resolution. Adams was the chief of staff. Ike made an unusually rapid recovery, however, and on December 9 Adams announced, "The President is back in the saddle. His grip on the reins is tight and sure."

Early in President Eisenhower's second administration he had broken precedent by naming Wiley Buchanan, our retiring ambassador to Luxembourg, chief of protocol. Unlike his predecessors in the protocol post, Wiley was a political appointee who had helped win Texas for Ike in 1952, but he and his pretty wife, Ruth, had an unusual flair for entertaining and putting VIP guests at ease. When twenty-three-year-old Prince Harold of Norway came to Washington, the Buchanans gave a swinging party for the jazz buff at their beautiful Washington estate, and among the guests were John and Barbara Eisenhower, Pat and Dick Nixon, and Bob and I. They imported Dick Ridgely and his two-piece jazz band from Southampton, and while drummer Ridgely and pianist Buddy Smith played several instruments simultaneously, we watched with such fascination that Norway's heir apparent, who had summoned his car for midnight, stayed on for two more hours.

The Buchanans gave another brilliant party for Vice President and

Mrs. Nixon in January, 1958, and while we danced, I asked Dick if I could have an interview with him. He set the date for the following morning and gave me so much good material that I divided it into two full-length articles. During the interview he expressed the fear that history would look back on that period and record that we were properly alert to military danger, but not adequately aware of the far greater peril of Soviet nonmilitary penetration. We were then in the throes of a recession, and when I remarked, "I'll bet that if you were President you would take more drastic action to halt it," he replied firmly, "You can bet your life I would."

One of the most revealing aspects of that personal interview was Nixon's comments on his wife. Although her name had not yet been mentioned, the Vice President abruptly declared, "Ruth, the effect that Pat has had overseas is nothing short of incredible. She has made as much impact as any man who has ever represented America abroad. Hardly a day goes by but that I receive a letter from overseas which sings Pat's praises. The writers tell what a wonderful impression she made in their country and how much the women who are struggling for emancipation admire her."

Reminiscing about their official trip through Africa, during which Pat tramped dusty streets of native villages to visit hospitals and schools, he continued: "Pat has that rare ability to look fresh at all times, even on eighteen-hour-a-day schedules in tropical heat. I have never once heard her complain of being tired. She is never snooty, and believe me the greatest sin that Americans can commit abroad is to appear snobbish. Pat is a wonder!"

My brother Paul and his wife came to Washington for a large dinner party which Bob and I gave at the Sheraton Park Hotel, with Postmaster General Arthur E. Summerfield, Attorney General William P. Rogers, Speaker Sam Rayburn, former Speaker Joseph W. Martin, French Ambassador Herve Alphand, Commerce Secretary Sinclair Weeks, Senator Herman Talmadge, Senator Styles Bridges, Senator John McClellan, Robert Kennedy, and their wives among the guests. Paul had a joyful reunion with Assistant Secretary of State (later to be Ambassador to Mexico) Thomas Mann, who had been Paul's closest friend during their years at Baylor University. Nancy Mann, Tommy's wife, had also been a close college friend of mine.

On February 21, 1958, I went to New York to receive the George R. Holmes Memorial Trophy, which INS bestowed each year on its "most outstanding writer." The award included a gold medallion and money, but the part that I liked best was the plaque which read: "In recognition of her consistently outstanding reporting from Washington, and particularly her remarkable interview with Edgar Eisenhower, judged to be the finest and most distinctive work by an International News Service reporter during the year." At the presentation an official declared, "Ruth has provided INS with something it has never had before: a daily exclusive."

The next month I was made an honorary national member of Alpha Chi Omega sorority, and later I went to Ashland, Ohio, where I delivered the commencement address at Ashland College in cap and gown and received for the second time an honorary Doctor of Laws degree.

CHAPTER XIX

Tragedies Here and There

THE shrinking Hearst empire was about to shrink some more. I had been tipped off in advance that International News Service was about to merge with United Press, and Kingsbury Smith flew down from New York to sign me up for an extended contract. I learned that Hearst was planning to retain only five of its INS writers, including Louella Parsons, Bob Considine, and myself. After signing the new contract, I flew to Columbus, Ohio, to address the annual Matrix Table of Theta Sigma Phi, and on my return Kingsbury Smith telephoned that the merger was now official. "Merger" was a polite word, since United Press would be unaffected, but all except a handful of INS writers who were being absorbed into UPI were being dismissed with severance pay.

Kingsbury Smith invited INS Washington bureau chief William Hutchinson to New York to break the news of the merger, and on his way back to Washington Bill died of a heart attack. It is a heart-rending experience to witness the demise of a newspaper or news service, the angry shock of men suddenly thrown out of work, the destruction of their dreams and their security. Their severance pay was generous, but it was an emotion-charged bureau which attended the funeral of Bill Hutchinson at Arlington Cemetery on May 28, 1958. No one in that grieving assemblage so much as spoke to Kingsbury Smith, who had come from New York for the services. No one except me. I was the only member of the Washington bureau to be retained, and I sensed the understandable hostility of my colleagues.

The Eisenhower administration was becoming increasingly embarrassed by the Bernard Goldfine hearings, which were playing to packed houses on Capitol Hill, and on July 14 a White House assistant leaked to me a story that President Eisenhower would now welcome the resignation of his controversial chief aide. Ike had previously said of Adams, "I need him," and he was still convinced of his personal loyalty, but he was said to be disappointed in Adams because of industrialist Goldfine's evasive testimony before a House committee. The source said that the President would prefer to have Adams choose his own exit date, with some face-saving device, than to discharge him, and I wrote that Adams' resignation was expected no later than Labor Day weekend.

The enigma which most puzzled Ike was how taciturn, straitlaced Adams could have enjoyed the personal friendship of brash, name-dropping Goldfine and how artistic, reserved Rachel Adams could have been on friendly terms with his diamond-bedecked spouse. I was equally puzzled, because I was genuinely fond of Rachel and Sherm but repelled by the pushiness of the Goldfines, whom I saw for the first time during the hearings.

My prediction about Adams was off by three weeks. On September 22, the onetime knight in shining armor, who had managed Ike's 1952 "crusade," bowed out of the political arena with tarnish showing. He admitted having received gifts and favors from Goldfine but insisted that his intercession for him with governmental agencies was solely in the line of duty. His resignation, complete with klieg lights and cameras, was dramatically staged. The White House had requested free television time on all networks in order for Sherm to defend himself as he resigned, and Ike accepted the resignation "with sadness, warm regard and highest esteem."

His grand exit was reminiscent of that of another Eisenhower "crusader," Air Force Secretary Harold Talbott, three years earlier. In August, 1955, Sherman Adams strode into President Eisenhower's office and told him that Talbott must go, because he had been mixing public and private business. Ike, always reluctant to lose a bridge-playing friend, agreed to Talbott's discharge, but gave his blessing for the Air Force to arrange the greatest parade and flyover ever accorded a retiring sub-Cabinet officer. Only the complication of a hurricane, which curtailed the flyover, prevented Talbott from receiving the most flamboyant farewell party in Pentagon history.

Edgar Eisenhower told me that he saw "a vast improvement in the administration" after Sherman Adams departed, and most of the legislators were also delighted because of the changed climate. Adams' successor was Major General Wilton B. Persons, a longtime friend of Eisenhower's who had spent most of the past decade charming legislators on behalf of the executive branch. His soft drawl, bountiful tact, and warm personality were in sharp contrast with the taciturn, often rude New Englander, and he was much more accessible to Congressmen.

It was a busy social season in Washington. Bob and I went to a dinner party which George Abell gave for Aristotle Onassis and his beautiful Greek wife; since she was wealthy in her own right, we wondered what she could see in the swarthy, squat Ari. As all the world now knows, he had a public love affair with Marie Callas, his marriage ended in divorce, and he has since married Jacqueline Kennedy, who was not at the party that evening.

We went to parties at the Egyptian embassy, the Korean embassy, the Peruvian and Iranian embassies, and to others given by Senator John Sherman Cooper, the Robert Guggenheims, Liz and Les Carpenter, Mrs. Alben W. Barkley, Mrs. Thurmond Chatham, Morris and Gwen Cafritz, Congressman Albert Thomas, Louise Gore, Postmaster General Arthur Summerfield, and the Bobby Kennedys. Madame Chiang Kai-shek paid a visit to Washington, and I had an exclusive interview with her at the Chinese embassy. I also did a series of interviews with all of the Eisenhower Cabinet.

The West German government invited me for a tour of Germany, and Bob and Mother went along. After my interviews with a number of high German officials we took a boat trip up the Rhine and revisited Heidelberg, Munich, Garmisch-Partenkirchen, and Oberammergau, plus Austria and Switzerland. En route home on our supposedly nonstop flight, we were over the North Atlantic at 4:30 A.M.

when the pilot announced that he had just feathered one engine. As soon as he could fly low enough to dump our excess fuel, he would try for an emergency landing at Gander, Newfoundland. We made it, with fire trucks standing by, and after twelve weary hours in the airport we caught another flight home.

Later that fall the Mexican government invited Bob and me to attend the inauguration of its new President, Adolfo López Mateos, and since Bob could not spare the time, my sister Margaret went with me, along with George and Ymelda Dixon, Les and Liz Carpenter, and the Considines.

After my return home, I wrote a series of articles in which I flatly labeled Fidel Castro a Communist. I had had numerous contacts with Cubans since my sensational first visit there in 1947, and another of my sources was Father Joseph Thorning, a Catholic priest who had wide acquaintanceship throughout Latin America. I had an exclusive interview with CIA Director Allen Dulles, during which my old friend declared, "Ruth, I can tell you flatly that Fidel Castro is not a Communist. A liberal, yes, but not a Red. We here at CIA do not see a Communist under every bed, like Father Thorning does."

I refused to believe Allen Dulles on that one, however, and continued throughout the spring and summer of 1959 to warn my newspaper readers of Castro's Communist espousal. There is an interesting footnote to this story. A few years later, during a top-level CIA strategy meeting on the deepening crisis in Cuba, which by then was completely Red, a high official wearily remarked, "If only we had known before that Castro was a Communist!"

"Ruth Montgomery knew it," a top-ranking colonel declared, and reaching into his briefcase, he slapped a complete file of my articles on the conference table.

In late March, 1959, King Hussein of Jordan came to Washington for a state visit, and I was able to secure the only exclusive interview which he gave while in America. The next time that I interviewed him, we sat together at his palace at Amman, and still later I talked with him at a state dinner which the Johnsons gave for the Arab ruler at the White House.

Syndicated columnist George Dixon wrote an article about me, which said:

Ruth Montgomery and I were among the press passengers on the first commercial airlines flight from New York to Buenos Aires a dozen years ago. We made a stop-over at Belem, Brazil, where we were bundled into an ancient ruin of a car for a tour of this old rubber capital near the mouth of the Amazon. The driver turned out to be a madman with a great sense of humor.

He screamed around tight corners on half a wheel, rocketed through narrow streets teeming with natives, and used only his horn as he shot across blind intersections. The more terrified we became, the funnier he found it.

He had all of us clutching at anything we could clutch, including our hair. All of us—except Ruth Montgomery. Our heroine leaned back, a resigned smile on her face, and murmured, "This is going to make my mother feel pretty silly. She's been predicting for years that I'd be killed in an airplane."

When we finally landed in Argentina, pretty much all in one piece, the first thing we craved was to interview Juan Peron, the new dictator. We were assured this was impossible, that Peron never granted interviews. The rest of us accepted this. But there is a streak of the skeptic in Ruth Montgomery. She refused to believe it. She not only obtained an interview with Peron, but an exclusive one. Moreover, it proved to be one of the few that the now fallen dictator ever granted.

This blonde was born Ruth Shick in Sumner, Ill., which had a population of 1,000 then and now. I asked Ruthie to enumerate all the places she had lived and worked. "I don't mind giving you the run-down," she said with that Mona Lisa smile, "but I warn you—it's going to read like a time-table." She changed high schools three times in her senior year alone—Vincennes and Terre Haute, Ind., and Waco, Tex.

She got a reporter's job on the Waco News Tribune and worked her way through Baylor University. Because her family moved again, Ruth left Baylor without graduating, but two years ago she was made a doctor of laws. After Waco, Ruthie Shick lived in Louisville, Ky., where she got a job as woman's editor on the Herald Post, but it soon went out of business. She moved with her family to Lafayette, Ind., and enrolled in Purdue University.

Ruth Shick was dating a young fellow in Lafayette when his best friend came to visit from Detroit, Robert H. Montgomery. Nothing of interest came of the meeting until months later, when Ruth got a job on the Detroit Times. Seven weeks later she eloped with Bob Montgomery. She eloped, because the city editor had announced he wanted no married women on the staff. The city editor found out about the elopement two weeks later, but his only punitive action was to make Ruth listen to a lot of advice on marriage. Bob is now deputy administrator of the Small Business Administration.

I have skipped all manner of fascinating side stories about Ruth. For instance, she was the first woman ever to receive the "Big Story" award for a Black Legion case she covered, and have it dramatized on radio.

Ruthie is now chief Washington correspondent for the Hearst Headline Service. She has won such admiration, and achieved such standing, that the great of the nation seek her out to give her news. It is nothing for her to lift the phone and hear a familiar voice ask, "Ruthie?" before identifying himself as the postmaster general, or a high ranking senator.

She and her husband attend most of the more important sociopolitical functions, but they also entertain extensively in return. You meet some odd combinations of people at their parties because they suffer from a phobia comparatively rare in Washington. They invite only people they like. As a consequence you will see sworn foes having a wonderful time together at a Montgomery party. Why, they had the French and Egyptian ambassadors right after France invaded Egypt!

Ruth Montgomery is a past president of the Women's National Press Club—and she's the most wonderful newspaperwoman ever to hit Washington.

John Foster Dulles died in May, 1959, and I covered his funeral at the National Cathedral, with a grieving President Eisenhower in attendance. Shortly thereafter I flew to Baton Rouge, Louisiana, to investigate the antics of Governor Earl Long. The series of articles which I wrote while there made front pages throughout the nation, and I was a runner-up for the Pulitzer Prize that year.

The weird world of Governor Long was a whimsical conglomeration of catfish, cornpone, crackpot and cracker-barrel politics. To decent, hardworking taxpayers of Louisiana it was a sore that festered on their pride and their conscience. To "Uncle Earl," it was "my state, by damn, and to hell with the consequences." Huey Long, the Louisiana Kingfish who established the family dynasty and met death by assassination in 1935, rose to power on a share-the-wealth platform that had for its slogan "Every man a king." His younger brother Earl, who viciously attacked Huey during his lifetime but eagerly seized his vacated throne, was a different kettle of fish. Always jealous of the brilliant, colorful, power-hungry Huey, Earl wanted no man to be a king except himself. A vindictive man of unpredictable whims, he prided himself on raising his satraps to positions of power, watching them swell, and then thrusting in the stiletto that collapsed the balloon and the man.

His weight dropped nearly fifty pounds while he loudly fought off federal income tax investigators, hurled invective at loyal cohorts, and defied the state constitution to seek an unprecedented fourth term. But the man whom outstanding doctors and psychiatrists had diagnosed as a dangerous paranoid-schizophrenic still held the full range of his powerful office. One of his friends who helped kidnap him for the night ride to a psychiatric hospital said of the governor, "He would kill a glass of bourbon before breakfast, and then keep going all night on gin, wine and vodka. He wouldn't sleep over an hour a night because he kept changing from benzedrine to tranquilizers, back and forth. The night we took him away, we put sleeping pills in his liquor and then gave him three hypodermics, any one of which was enough to knock out a normal man for twenty-four hours, but ol' Earl didn't even go to sleep."

Convinced that her husband was not only crazy, but dying, Mrs. Long summoned his nephew Senator Russell Long and two other family members, and while they tried to quiet the raging man, Long escaped their clutches and smashed a mirror, broke a window with a chair, wrecked a four-poster bed, and began tossing furniture to the ground below. His cursing, shouting, struggling stay in the state mental hospital ended only after he fired the head of the hospital board and appointed a crony, who immediately declared him sane.

The series completed, I returned to Washington, where Bob and I attended the wedding of Attorney General William P. Rogers' daughter, as well as parties given by Perle Mesta and the Nixons. By this time I had received a long-hoped-for visa to accompany the Nixons on their official tour of Soviet Russia.

CHAPTER XX

Our Merry Comrades

WHAT an excited group we were, as we soared off from Idlewild Airport on July 22, 1959, en route nonstop to Moscow on Pan American's new 707 jet! As we crossed the airspace above the iron curtain, five Soviet navigators who had been riding with us entered the pilot's compartment, and although we were forced to circle for some time before landing, we nonetheless broke the world's speed record from New York to Moscow. Frol R. Kozlov, a member of the Presidium, met Vice President Nixon for ceremonies at the airport, after which we rode buses through a city of garish new yellow apartment buildings to the Ukraina Hotel, where we were lodged.

After writing our arrival stories, some of us went dinner-dancing at the Praga to sample Soviet night life. Although it was the most expensive restaurant in Moscow, nearly every male was tieless and coatless, and many of the Russian women wore cotton ankle socks with their high-heeled shoes. The dancing was sedate and rather listless until editor George Healy of the New Orleans *Times-Picayune* and I, fortified by a vodka, decided to introduce the Charleston to Moscow. Our energetic demonstration promptly emptied the ballroom floor, as Moscovites watched in undisguised amazement and then applauded enthusiastically. As soon as the music resumed, they flooded back to try an imitation of our steps, and the café turned into swirling pandemonium. One Russian, after practicing a few minutes, abandoned his girlfriend and came over to beg me to dance with him.

I reluctantly consented, and the workout he gave me left blistered feet for my subsequent tramping tours with Pat Nixon.

Leaving the restaurant about midnight, George Healy and I tried fruitlessly to find an empty cab, but at last a taxi with one Russian passenger stopped to give us a lift to the hotel. The Russian spoke no English, but he graciously refused to let us pay for the ride "because you are Americans."

The next morning we went to Spaso House, the lovely U.S. embassy, for a visit with Ambassador and Mrs. Lewellyn Thompson, after which Nixon engaged in his famous "kitchen debate" on Communism versus Democracy at the American Exposition. The debate did not dampen the high spirits of Nikita Khrushchev for long, and that afternoon he exuberantly pumped my hand before touring the remainder of the American exhibit with Pat and Dick Nixon.

In the evening I went with Rear Admiral Hyman Rickover to the American embassy for dinner and the next day accompanied Pat Nixon on a tour of hospitals and the GUM department store. Jinx Falkenburg and I also visited the Kremlin and its three beautiful cathedrals, which are now museums, and rode down the amazingly rapid escalators to Moscow's extraordinarily deep subways. Khrushchev later told me that the subways were designed at great depth in order to serve as bomb shelters in the event of aerial attack.

The next day we again went to the Kremlin, this time to see the tombs of Lenin and Stalin and the jewels and court dress of the late czars and czarinas. Then we took off by Russian jet to Leningrad, and while airborne, Jinx, George Healy, Mike Flynn, and I began a bridge game which was to continue on every plane flight until we eventually landed at Washington ten days later.

On our arrival at the Leningrad airport, Pat Nixon was surrounded by a group of official Russian women who proposed taking her to some kindergartens and Soviet youth camps. We hastily whispered to Pat that she should ask to see the Hermitage Museum, but she had never heard of it and seemed completely uninterested when we mentioned its priceless works of art. When I also mentioned that it had previously been the winter palace of the czars, her eyes sparkled with anticipation, and she firmly told the women that we must go first to the Hermitage. Our Russian escorts seemed non-plussed at the change in plans but eventually consented, and we reporters gasped with delight as we strolled through the rooms containing some of the world's greatest Rembrandts and other master-pieces.

It soon became apparent, however, that art was not Pat's dish of tea. She barely glanced at the paintings, but as she walked rapidly through the palace, she occasionally stopped to exclaim, "Oh, girls, look at this pretty doorway." At last, however, there was something to capture her interest. In glass cases were miniature rooms of furniture, fashioned in gold by seventeenth-century French artisans, which had once belonged to the czars, and as Pat stooped to examine each delicate piece, she repeatedly exclaimed, "Wouldn't my two girls love these!"

Pat Nixon never ceased to amaze me as she tripped tirelessly along on the highest, thinnest spike heels I have ever seen. By contrast, Mrs. Kozlov's plump feet gave her so much trouble that halfway through the Hermitage tour she exchanged her white high-heeled pumps for green house slippers, but she adamantly insisted that Pat must visit the Young Pioneers headquarters. Pat politely agreed, and the highlight was a Soviet-slanted planetarium show for children, depicting Russia's third satellite circling the solar system and preparing to land on Mars. Sitting next to me in the darkened room, Pat repeatedly nudged my ribs to show that she wasn't buying that brain-washing.

Afterward, despite a drenching hailstorm which pelted the streets with huge ice pellets, our hostesses insisted that we continue the tour to the Palace of Pioneers, and Mrs. Kozlov seemed to be having the time of her life in her damp, limp lavender dress.

Bob Considine and I made a tour of Leningrad, the lovely old St. Petersburg founded by Peter the Great, where we viewed Lenin's revolutionary headquarters and saw the ships from which the first guns of the Russian Revolution were fired and the once-lovely cathedrals which were now closed by atheist Russians. We also engaged in a running debate with our Intourist guide, who patronizingly assured us that even idiots knew there was no God.

One engagement which the Nixons had eagerly anticipated in Leningrad was a night at the ballet, but while still airborne, our Soviet chaperons announced that the ballet had been canceled. Disappointed, the Nixons hastily scheduled a dinner with U.S. officials, and during the afternoon Pat asked to see the building where the ballet would have been performed. Properly impressed with the beautiful theater, she charmingly thanked the manager and murmured her regret that the evening's performance would not be held.

"But the ballet is performing tonight," he exclaimed in astonishment, "and we would love to have you as our guests." There went the dinner party! Plans were hastily switched for the second time within hours, and that evening the Nixons went to the same theater on which Pat had earlier wasted a precious half hour. This incident was typical of the Alice-in-Wonderland tour arranged by the comrades. Pat always knew where she was, but she never knew where she was going until minutes beforehand.

Nixon had been promised that he could visit Novosibirsk, the Soviet "Chicago" midway in Siberia which was off limits to all Westerners, but Russian officialdom seemed to be placing every kind of obstacle in his path. At last Dick won the battle of nerves, and we took off in larger Russian jets for our exciting date halfway around the world from Washington. Russian officials had warned us that because of limited hotel accommodations, we reporters would have to double up, but we were unprepared for what followed. While still airborne, Soviet press officers began handing out our room assignments, which were promptly greeted with male guffaws and feminine shrieks. With total disregard for separation of the sexes, Jinx Falkenburg was assigned a room with three male reporters, and although married couples were permitted to share the same chamber, two other men were assigned to their room.

My three roommates fortunately were women, but as soon as we checked into the hotel, the other wives and female scribes began dragging their cots through my door, and that night eight of us slept in a room designed for two. Slept? No! That is the night when I discovered that snoring is not confined to the male sex, and I tossed all night on my hard cot.

By the time we reached Novosibirsk, we had written so many stories about Pat's visits to nursery schools and Young Pioneer camps that we told her if she wanted to get in the newspapers back home, she would have to insist on something different. Thus, when we landed at the airport and the official greeters began ticking off her schedule—the same type she had endured in Moscow and Leningrad —Pat found the courage to ask, "What else is there to see?" The Russians were chagrined, but grudgingly conceded that a style show was then in progress, with ninety buyers gathered from the Urals to Vladivostok. I quickly signaled Pat to accept, and off we went to a large building where lumpy models were demonstrating the latest fashions, Soviet style. The materials were sleazy, the styles antiquated, and the zippers bare of covering, but we received a surprisingly friendly welcome from the large audience.

Because I had to write and cable a story about the style show, I was late in arriving at the beautiful civic center in downtown Novosibirsk, and the Nixons had already gone inside to see a performance of Dick Nixon's favorite ballet, *Swan Lake*. The company which was presenting it that evening had just returned from a triumphant tour of Red China, and although our Siberian hosts had announced that the performance was canceled, the Nixons expressed such disappointment that it was suddenly "on" again.

Arriving by cab midway in the first act, I was impressed by the thousands of Siberians who, having watched Vice President and Mrs. Nixon enter the opera building, still stood outside in silent observance. At the end of the third act, walking outside with George Healy for a breath of fresh air, we discovered that the thousands of Siberians were still standing there. Slipping back inside, we told Nixon of the phenomenon. He followed us out, climbed atop an automobile, and addressed the vast throng about the friendship of America for the Soviet people, as opposed to their government's policies. An interpreter translated his remarks, and the friendly crowd clapped warmly.

Nixon then returned to his seat for the final act of *Swan Lake*, but George and I were so intrigued by the friendliness of Siberians, that we decided to remain among them. As we slowly moved through the throng, shaking outstretched hands, young Russians rushed over to pin Soviet buttons on our lapels. Many requested our autographs, and when we eventually reached the empty press bus, a young Russian asked in English if we would answer some questions while he translated for the rest.

Gladly agreeing, we stood on the steps of the bus, smiling down into the thousands of intent, upturned faces, eager to "sell" American democracy to our hosts. But pride goeth before a fall! The first question asked of us was: "Why do young people have to pay to go to college in America?" Hmmmm! How to explain our pride in free enterprise, which often was keeping needy, worthy young men and women from obtaining the higher education that would make them more useful members of society? In Russia, we knew, it was free. We did our best to explain our system, and to point out the availability of scholarships for honor students and athletes, but in 1959 such scholarships were far less plentiful than they are today, and it was disquieting to admit (only to ourselves) that the world's richest nation often wasted the talents of bright youngsters.

The next question was even more difficult. "Why," they wanted to know, "do people have to pay to go to the hospital in America when they're sick?" I, who had always scorned the welfare state, suddenly found my mind swarming with recollections of innumerable Americans whose slim savings had been wiped out by astronomical hospital bills.

"You take this one. It's your turn," I whispered to George, but since he seemed as nonplussed as I was, we plunged in together to tell about our charity wards for the very poor and the hospital insurance carried by many others. But we were dissatisfied with our answers, and we noted with cowardly relief that *Swan Lake* had ended. The rest of our press group was surging toward the bus.

Returning to our so-called hotel, which boasted only two bathrooms for the entire building, we found the dining room locked for the night. Since I had written a column instead of having dinner, I went to bed hungry, and the next morning we were given no opportunity for breakfast before leaving early for a visit to a new hydraulic plant on the river. After our stiff uphill climb to the bridge, a Soviet official extolled its magnificence to Dick Nixon, while Ambassador George A. Allen whispered to me, "Look down at the fish killing themselves against the dam. The stupid engineers failed to install lifts so that the fish could swim upstream to spawn."

We were next taken on a boat trip, where I had my first food in thirty-six hours, and then flew to Sverdlovsk. Checking into the Bolshoi Urals Hotel, I was happy to have a private room again, but less enchanted to learn that the lavatory was at the other end of the long corridor and the only shower five floors below. And the elevator would carry passengers up, but not down! We had dinner in the hotel and then sat in a plaza across the street, where a man who spoke some English asked us questions for the benefit of a group which hastily gathered around us. It seemed significant that the farther we traveled from Moscow, with its forbidding shadow of the Kremlin towers, the friendlier and happier the citizens appeared to be.

Our hosts in Sverdlovsk seemed unusually attentive, and the next day some of our press group decided to live dangerously by accepting their invitation to a picnic "at a sandy beach." Hastily grabbing our bathing suits, we set off by bus with a daredevil driver who charged down the bumpy road at eighty miles an hour, darting between monstrous trucks and fleeing pedestrians. After half an hour of terror, we spotted a beautiful sandy beach beside a shimmering lake, but our fiendish driver was apparently well briefed on the dangers of permitting subversive Americans to associate with relaxing Russians.

Our bus veered off cross-country around the lake, grazing trees and leveling rocky mounds while we desperately clung to our bumpy seats. Finally we halted at the rockiest, ugliest spot we had seen, and our Intourist guides told us to take our choice. We could change clothes in the bus or behind one of the skinny pine trees ahead. Jinx and I chose the bus, while Crosby Noyes, George Healy, and publisher John Johnson of *Ebony* magazine took to the woods. Then we gingerly waded into the ice-cold water, shrieking in anguish at the rapier-sharp rocks which pierced our tender feet. By the time we and our goose pimples emerged from the freezing water our Russian hosts, who had been busily guzzling vodka, gleefully motioned us to join the picnic. We painfully dropped down on the rocky ground, which was generously covered with prickly pine needles, and our hosts poured each of us a stiff drink of vodka in paper cups; but before we could down the first fiery sip, the bottom of the cups began to dissolve. Laughing like hyenas, the Russians stuck a second cup under them, then another and another, but it would have required a Houdini to add cups fast enough to entrap the vodka, which kept trickling out the bottoms.

All the while a Russian photographer, who was feeling no pain, howled with laughter, while popping corks off warm vodka bottles and spraying us with the contents. The Mack Sennett comedies of yore had nothing on our playful Russian comrades. En route back to town, we insisted on stopping at the building where a Red firing squad had disposed of Czar Nicholas and his family, and our gleeful hosts thought that was funny, too.

We tramped through a few more kindergartens and youth camps with Pat, but communications were breaking down. Once we arrived ahead of Dick Nixon at a steel mill, where officials mistook trimly dressed newsman Austin Kiplinger for the Vice President and began ushering him through the plant. We did not realize that they had made a mistake until we ran into Nixon, who, looking rather perplexed, was wandering around with only his Secret Service escort.

When we returned to Moscow, our once-scorned Ukraina Hotel seemed like a palace. That night, fortified by only two and a half hours' sleep in the last twenty-four, Nixon made a television address that was unprecedented in Soviet Russia. I was one of the three pool reporters who were permitted to accompany him to the television station, and during his one-hour broadcast we watched several dozen Russians who, ignoring the ample supply of chairs in the lobby, stood massed around the TV screen, motionless and impassive, listening intently to his words about the free world. No eye strayed from the screen, as within the shadow of the Kremlin he dared to hit out at lying propaganda behind the iron curtain. A dropped pin would have sounded like a jet rocket in that quiet room.

The next morning we took a taxi to the Baptist church, the only Protestant one permitted in the Russian capital, and although we arrived early for the service, it was already jammed with worshipers, some of whom had been there two hours in order to assure a seat. Hundreds of others, unable to get in, were clustered outside, but a young Russian seminarian found two seats for us in the balcony.

After the service we went to a Russian Orthodox church where mass was in progress, but no more than a dozen worshipers sat in the cathedral, which could easily have accommodated eight hundred. Either Russians were afraid to be seen there, or reports were true that they still held the Orthodox Church accountable for the dissolute conditions which brought on the Russian Revolution.

Back at the hotel we finished our packing and then went to the American embassy for a press conference with the Vice President. In the afternoon we flew to Warsaw, Poland, and although the Communist regime had carefully concealed our arrival time and the route that we would follow into town, word had spread clandestinely. A quarter of a million smiling Poles lined the streets from the airport to the hotel, cheering and clapping in unison, while many women and children spread flowers along the Nixons' path.

The Warsaw Press Club had a reception for us that evening, and almost to a man they made evident their distaste for Russian Communism. They implored our group to remove the Russian buttons which adorned our hats and lapels, and we hastily acquiesced. Someone mentioned the monstrous Ministers' Palace, a huge edifice which Soviets had erected in the center of Warsaw as a gift to the Polish people, and a Polish newsman told us the current joke: "The only good view in Warsaw is from the palace, because you can't see the palace from there."

Jinx Falkenburg and I accompanied Pat to a spectacular new children's hospital, where we were surprised to notice Catholic medals and saints' pictures beside many of the little beds. Then we lunched at the American embassy with Mrs. Nixon and several ranking Polish women. I laughingly handed Mrs. Oscar Lange, wife of the Vice Chairman of Poland, an "I like Pat" button left over from the '56 campaign, with an explanation of its meaning, and she proudly wore it on her gray flannel suit the remainder of the day.

We went with Vice President Nixon to the once-loathsome Jewish ghetto which had largely been replaced by a new housing development, although part of the ghetto had been left as a monument to Poles murdered by Nazis during World War II, and that evening we attended a formal reception for the Nixons at the Council of Ministers' Palace.

After another day in Warsaw, we rode to the airport past cheering throngs who had again discovered our departure time, and freedom-loving Poles heaped the open Nixon car with hundreds of bouquets, despite efforts of the Polish police to keep them back. Our hearts ached for the Poles, some of whom were crying as they waved good-bye. Within a few hours we would return to the free world, but they were to be left behind.

Vice President Nixon rode with us on our TWA 707 jet as far as Iceland in order to hold a background press conference on board. He had just learned from Washington that Soviet Premier Khrushchev had accepted President Eisenhower's invitation to visit America the following month, and Nixon seemed rather perturbed that Ike had not shown him the courtesy of delaying the historic announcement until his return to America. The conference continued while our plane refueled at the Keflavik, Iceland, airport; then Nixon returned to his own plane, while Jinx, George, Mike, and I resumed our interrupted bridge game which had flourished halfway around the globe and back.

On our return to Washington, Bob and I went to a party at Senator Goldwater's and then flew to New York, where Earl Mazo, Frank Holeman, and I were grilled by David Susskind for three hours about our trip to Russia on his *Open End* television show. Later Jinx, Frances Lewine, and I addressed the Women's National Press Club about our Soviet safari. I had interviews with Pat and Dick Nixon for an article about them in *Cosmopolitan* magazine and attended the first meeting of Nixon's "Kitchen Cabinet," where each of us who had accompanied him to Russia was presented with a framed membership scroll. Superimposed on a red etching of the Kremlin towers was the familiar picture of Nixon poking his index finger at a scowling Khrushchev during the "kitchen debate," and the password on our membership scrolls was *mir y druzhba*. These were the words, meaning "peace and friendship," with which Russians had greeted us everywhere that we went.

Like news reporters the world over, we found our greatest enjoyment in swapping stories about the humorous sidelights of our trips, and I also recounted some of them when I addressed the Indianapolis Press Club later that month. For instance:

We had no sooner arrived in Moscow than a male reporter received a cable from his editor ordering an "immediate and comprehensive round-up of Communist subversion throughout the world." A half hour later the same editor sent him another cable requesting a quick article about humor in the Soviet Union. The luckless correspondent promptly cabled back, "The biggest joke in Soviet Russia is your first cable."

George Healy, as an editor, had been invited to travel with the Nixon entourage, which had plush accommodations, but he chose to join the press group instead. He had written frequent editorials in the New Orleans *Times-Picayune* about the mental instability of Governor Earl Long, and on the morning when more than twenty newsmen lined up to await their turn to shave in the one bathroom at our hotel in Novosibirsk, Scotty Reston smilingly asked George, "Who's crazy now?"

Marguerite Higgins of the New York *Herald Tribune* was eight months pregnant during the Russian trip and consequently had difficulty in trying to outsprint the bevy of New York *Times* reporters; but in Sverdlovsk she made a dash for the nearest telephone and miraculously made quick connections with the *Tribune* office in Paris. Aware that she was ahead of her *Times* rivals, she pantingly told the editor that she had an important story to dictate, but he replied, "Sorry. Everyone's out to lunch now. Call back in an hour."

In Siberia, when a Russian apparently made a slighting remark to our press group on a bus, one of his female compatriots slugged him in the jaw. Both were ejected by the impassive driver.

After our return to Moscow from the rigors of the Soviet hinterland, some of us ran into Dr. Milton Eisenhower at GUM department store. The President's brother, who had shared the Nixon accommodations in dachas and palaces, said wearily, "This is the roughest, most tiring trip I've ever been on in my life." We nearly clobbered him!

President Eisenhower's invitation to Khrushchev to visit America kicked up such a political storm that House Majority Leader John McCormack threatened to resign his leadership post and lead a fight against a Congressional invitation for the Red boss to address a joint session. Senate Majority Leader Lyndon Johnson quietly spread the word that Congress should get out of town before Khrushchev's arrival, to obviate the necessity of inviting him, and this was done. Security officers were so fearful of an attempt on Khrushchev's life that they decided not to assign him the master suite on the second-floor front of Blair House, the suite President Truman had occupied when Puerto Ricans tried to assassinate him.

The U.S. government had to buy several additional beds for Blair House because Khrushchev insisted on crowding twenty-two members of his party into quarters which normally accommodate no more than fifteen people. The Kremlin declined to answer the State Department's repeated inquiries about what the Khrushchevs wanted to see in America or even whether they preferred twin or double beds.

Khrushchev and his wife, Nina, arrived in Washington on September 15, and I was at the airport to cover their reception by President Eisenhower and Vice President Nixon. Mrs. Khrushchev, her already-plump feet and ankles badly swollen from the long jet flight, limped down the red carpet leading to the land of the free, but her grandmotherly face was wreathed in smiles. Mrs. Henry Cabot Lodge, who was to be her official escort, suggested that she might like to see such typical American wonders as a supermarket, a public school, or a department store, but Nina replied, "We are too tired. We want to rest."

Nina's two stepdaughters, Julia Nikitichna and Rada Adzhubei, accompanied the Khrushchevs to America, but when it was learned that a daughter named Yelena had been left behind, not even members of the accompanying Russian press knew whether Yelena was Nina's daughter or Nikita's offspring by his first wife—such was the security behind the iron curtain. A State Department specialist in

Soviet affairs told me he thought it unlikely that other Kremlin officials would have permitted Khrushchev to bring his entire family, that Yelena was a sort of hostage to assure their willing return to Russia.

We women of the Washington press corps have a soft spot in our hearts for roly-poly Nikita Khrushchev. Male reporters had always refused to let us cover speeches by prominent dignitaries at the National Press Club, but Khrushchev declined to address that forum unless qualified newswomen could also attend. The "democratic" U.S. newsmen had to buckle under!

CHAPTER XXI

Visions of Sugar Plums

PRACTICALLY every Representative who looked in the mirror was seeing himself as a possible Senator, and nearly every member of the Senate was viewing himself as Presidential timber during the summer and fall of 1959. President Eisenhower could not run again, because of the two-term limitation, and politicians were hopefully playing musical chairs with their own futures.

Vice President Nixon, who was a cinch to try for the Presidency, sent out press invitations to a party in late August, but by the time our acceptances had been mailed he was confined to a hospital bed, in traction for a bad back, and we assumed that the party would be canceled. But the overworked Nixon staff stopped more pressing duties to telephone each of us that we were still expected, and Pat Nixon stood alone in the receiving line to greet more than a hundred correspondents. Thanks to her remarkable memory and our shared experiences on foreign travels, she knew nearly all the guests by name.

I interviewed her at the Nixon's eleven-room Tudor house and wrote a series of articles in which I said that if Pat had her preference, Dick would not be in politics. She had no desire to live in the White House. Asked to analyze her feelings about her husband's expected candidacy for the Presidency in 1960, she said, "I just never think ahead. I'm so busy now that I almost live from day to day. If I looked ahead at my schedule, I would feel unable to meet it. I try to do the job that I'm doing well, and let the future take care of itself."

Knowing how exhausting her schedule had been in Russia and Siberia, I asked how she trained for such marathons, and she said, "I've always been very strong. I didn't even have the usual childhood diseases, and I have such enthusiasm. I feel that if you're enthusiastic you don't tire. I can shake thousands of hands with pleasure, because I like people so much. These trips are hard, but when you feel you're accomplishing something and that people are glad you came, then it makes it all worthwhile."

Queried about Earl Mazo's appraisal of Dick Nixon as an extremely complex man, she mused, "Dick is the least complicated individual I know. He has not changed from the first day I knew him, except naturally to grow with experience. He enjoys his home tremendously, and I let him enjoy it. When he comes in at night, I never tell him the day's woes or complain about a broken faucet."

I asked if he ever shouted in anger, and she smiled mischievously. "He hasn't anything to shout or holler about. I never ply him with questions. If he wants to talk politics or discuss a meeting he has attended, we do it. Otherwise we don't. Dick has never scolded the children in his life. He's gay and fun. That's what so few people seem to know about him. In small groups he is the life of the party, telling funny stories and mimicking until he has us doubled up with laughter. He is very affectionate, and so are our daughters. We like the simple life, and home means everything to us."

Her eyes sweeping their tastefully furnished house, she summarized, "We're happy here, even though we need more hours in every day. Dick is an extremely easy man to live with. He's always trying to make it fun for the girls and myself."

Lady Bird Johnson had meanwhile been taking a public speaking course, and since LBJ was casting hopeful eyes toward the 1960 nominating convention, she invited a group of newswomen to her house one evening when she was sure that Lyndon would be away. Refreshments were served, and then the questions began to fly. Did Mrs. Johnson want her husband to run for the Presidency? Did she think that he could win the nomination? Would she like to be the chatelaine of the White House? Lady Bird was fielding questions with reasonable aplomb when the door swung open, and in came Lyndon. Grinning at his disconcerted wife, he lounged around the room, giving us each a hug or a kiss, while confessing that as soon as the lights had dimmed for entertainment at the National Press Club stag party, he had slipped away from the head table "to see how Bird was a-doin' with you girls."

Since all the chairs were occupied, the extroverted politician sprawled on the floor and promptly took over the press conference. No matter what we asked Lady Bird, he answered it. LBJ's monologues are always fascinating, but when he told us that he was "just talkin' off the record," we laughingly ordered him to leave the room, because his wife's remarks were on the record. He amiably ambled upstairs but in a few minutes returned to share the spotlight.

Johnson was generous with his compliments for possible rivals in the opposition party. He said that Nixon was an "extremely fair" presiding officer of the Senate, and that Republican Everett Dirksen was "a joy to work with." He did not mention his possible Demo cratic rivals, but Jack Kennedy subsequently said of Lyndon, "I know all the other candidates pretty well, and I frankly think I'm as able to handle the Presidency as any of them, or abler. All except Lyndon, and he hasn't got a chance for the nomination."

Senate Whip Mike Mansfield sought to boost Johnson's chances for the Democratic nomination by declaring that LBJ had "a great deal of strength" in the Rocky Mountain states as well as the South. Lyndon announced that he considered himself a Westerner rather than a Southerner, to avoid the Presidential onus of being a son of Dixie, and Speaker Sam Rayburn threw LBJ's big Stetson in the ring.

Jack Kennedy was delivering a series of speeches in California, Oregon, New York, and Stevenson's home state of Illinois. Stu Symington, while claiming that he was not a candidate, was maintaining a backbreaking schedule of partisan speeches throughout the country, and Hubert Humphrey was barnstorming through a dozen states.

With tension mounting to fever pitch as election year approached,

Jeane Dixon looked into her crystal ball for the benefit of my annual New Year's column about her predictions and in retrospect made a dismal showing. She said that pro-Western Iran would fall to the Communists through internal subversion and that Fidel Castro would fall from power in Cuba during the coming year. She also declared that John F. Kennedy would fail to win the Presidency and that Russia would be the first nation to land a man on the moon, probably during 1960. It was a clouded crystal ball!

With the dawn of the new year, I covered Jack Kennedy's klieg-lighted press conference in which he openly declared his Presidential candidacy. The race was on, and when I telephoned Jack a few days later to ask if I could write a column about his little daughter, Caroline, he thought it was a great idea. Jacqueline was away on one of her frequent trips, so he asked me to call Maud Shaw, Caroline's English nanny, but he had to ask his secretary for his own telephone number. Afterward he wrote me a warm letter of appreciation for the column that I wrote about the twenty-six-month-old child whose first three words were "Daddy," "airplane," and "car." He was always traveling!

With all five front-runners for the Presidential nominations sitting in the Senate, the world's most exclusive club began to fester with bad blood and bitter rivalry. Stu Symington was feeling no love for Jack Kennedy since the youthful Solon insinuated that any Presidential hopeful was a coward if he refused to try out his vote-getting appeal in state primaries. The long-standing friendship between Jack and Hubert Humphrey was also wearing thin after Kennedy decided to oppose the Minnesota Senator in his "own backyard," the Wisconsin primary.

Nixon, presiding over the Senate, was forced to look at Humphrey, who at a weekend rally had called him a "juvenile delinquent." He had to face Symington, who had termed him "Sir Richard the Nimble," and also Kennedy, who had sarcastically referred to Nixon as "the only surviving heir to the throne." And there sat Lyndon Johnson, who had made slurring remarks about Nixon's settlement of the eight-month steel strike. But Nixon was leading all others in the public opinion polls, and they eyed him with frosty glances on the rare occasions when they bothered to attend a Senate session.

Kennedy, Humphrey, and Symington were absent so often, while beating the grass roots for delegates, that during a marathon debate on civil rights legislation during March, 1960, Mansfield dubbed the proceedings "Hamlet and the Three Ghosts." Mansfield cast Johnson in the hero's role of Hamlet, declaring, "Lyndon is more liberal than most of his liberal critics. While they are off proclaiming their dedication to civil rights, he's the man who is trying to do something about it. He's the hardest worker we have, and even though he knows he is being hurt in the South, he is sticking to his duty."

Referring to Kennedy, Humphrey, and Symington, Mansfield continued, "The three ghosts occasionally slip in the side door, deliver a soliloquy on the dire state of our defenses, and then slither offstage and into the outer darkness. When next heard from, they're monologuing their way through the embattled ramparts of Wisconsin, New Hampshire, West Virginia, or California."

In the fourth week of debate, with the Senate sitting around the clock to break the Dixie filibuster, Johnson had a letter-perfect attendance at the eerie midnight quorum calls. Humphrey and Symington had been on hand only twice, and Kennedy not at all. New York Governor Nelson Rockefeller was pouring family gold into his drive for the GOP Presidential nomination, but Nixon managed to maintain his sense of humor. Seeing Nixon at a debutante dance at the lavish estate of Wiley and Ruth Buchanan, I remarked, "Isn't it nice to have such rich friends!" Grinning broadly at his close friend, Nixon replied, "Yes, Wiley is my Rockefeller."

Not since the gold rush days had California seen anything like the avalanche of free-spending Kennedys who began pouring into California before the convention. The close-knit clan had chipped in to buy Jack a private plane, complete with pilot, for the primary campaign, and Bobby Kennedy had resigned as chief counsel for the Senate Labor Racketeering Committee to direct the onslaught. Teddy Kennedy, fresh out of law school, virtually deserted his new bride to woo delegates in the Rocky Mountain states. Brothers-in-law Sargent Shriver and Stephen Smith took leave from their jobs to join the campaign, and sisters Eunice, Pat, and Jean flew to the hustings to hold coffee klatches in behalf of their brother. Papa Joseph P. Kennedy spread wide his ample purse and manned telephones to powerful friends throughout the country, while Mama Rose Kennedy toured Wisconsin and West Virginia to help achieve her son's victory.

Long before the 1960 convention opened, the Kennedy clan had staked out its claim in the Golden State. Palatial homes were leased to house the descendants of Boston Mayor John "Honey Fitz" Fitzpatrick, and Papa Joe Kennedy rented Marion Davies' Beverly Hills estate for his campaign headquarters.

On June 25, 1960, shortly before the Kennedy entourage descended on Los Angeles, Bobby and Ethel Kennedy invited Bob and me to a dinner party in honor of Clark Mollenhoff, a newspaperman who was taking a sabbatical year's leave to visit England and Africa. Clark had suffered a broken neck in an automobile accident the year before, and this was the first day that he had been permitted to remove the heavy neck cast.

The Kennedys were in bathing suits, but the rest of our group was in summer party attire. A plank had been placed across the swimming pool, and when the Mollenhoffs arrived, Bobby motioned for Clark to walk across it in order to greet the other guests on the far side. Clark, a heavyset man who towers several inches above six feet started across the plank, when, to our horror, Bobby took a running leap from behind and gave him a hard shove which was designed to knock the guest of honor into the swimming pool.

Clark, who was wearing his best suit and wristwatch, desperately tried to maintain his balance on the plank, while plunging ahead toward the other side. Bobby had thrown him off-balance, however, and he had such momentum that when he reached the concrete patio he turned a complete somersault on the pavement, landing on the back of his neck, with his long legs dangling in a bush. For a moment, everyone was too stunned to move. Then some of the men rushed to help Clark, and as he slowly unwound, he reached into his pocket and brought out a celluloid collar which he gingerly fastened around his mending neck, before trying to straighten his head. We women, watching mutely from the sidelines, were paralyzed with fright as we thought of Clark's broken neck and the heedless act of our host.

Bobby Kennedy, appearing somewhat subdued, came over and slouched at my feet, and as he leaned back against my chair I found voice to say, "Oh, Bobby, how could you!"

"It was his own fault," Bobby muttered. "If he'd gone in the water like I intended, he wouldn't have been hurt."

"Oh, shame!" I cried. "Doesn't it occur to you that some people can't afford to have their clothes ruined?"

Bobby began to shake as if he were having a chill, and after sitting in silence for a few minutes, I finally said, "Come on, Bobby. You must go up to the house and put on some dry clothes. You're taking cold." He rose as docilely as a small child and walked around the swimming pool with me, but as we reached the other side, he suddenly said, "Ruth, wait. I want you to meet Jack's best friend in all the world." He introduced me to LeMoyne Billings, who said with a grin, "Ruth, you're next in the swimming pool"; then, as he saw my husband approaching, he added, "And Bob is next."

I had had my fill of their childish antics and disregard for others. Eyes blazing, I turned on the two men and said testily, "I want to serve notice right now that if anyone else is shoved in the swimming pool here today, Jack Kennedy will not be the next President if I have to defeat him in person."

Bobby meekly went in the house to dress, and when he returned, we found our place cards at the round tables set up near the pool. My place was next to Bobby's, with Mrs. Mollenhoff on his other side, and the dinner conversation was somewhat reserved. We had reached the dessert course when one of the Kennedy intimates suddenly climbed the big tree over our heads, despite the fact that she was wearing high-heeled shoes and a chiffon dress. All that we needed was one more casualty that evening, so some of the men persuaded her to descend.

Afterward I walked to the house with Mrs. Mollenhoff, who said, "I want to apologize for that piercing shriek I uttered when Bobby pushed Clark, but I could just see another year of hospitalization with a broken neck, if he survived at all."

"Did you really think that you screamed?" I asked with concern. "You did not utter a sound." She had stood silently, as if paralyzed, throughout that horrible scene, and when I telephoned the next day to see how Clark was feeling, he replied, "My wife is in worse shape than I am, from the shock." Is it any wonder that Clark Mollenhoff has since worked for President Nixon as a White House adviser?

CHAPTER XXII

Distaff Politicking

I FLEW to Los Angeles on July 7, 1960, to cover the competitive Democratic Convention, and had an interview with seventy-one-year-old Rose Kennedy, who said that she knew exactly what she would do when her son became President. "I'll just pray more than ever. I know that Jack will win the Presidency, and it will be the culmination of my dreams. The most that he can do for mankind and for himself is to become President of the United States, and I want that for Jack."

The Kennedy clan tossed a lavish party to which all Democratic delegates were invited, and the hotel lobby resembled a mob scene as several thousand bewildered, bedraggled, bedazzled Democrats fought their way to the crowded reception. Clutching invitations in hot hands, they finally elbowed their way into the grand ballroom, only to discover that nobody was on hand to welcome them except Kennedy hirelings. While delegates milled aimlessly around, staring distastefully at the pink punch, a paid hostess frantically dispatched a page boy to a nearby restaurant with a message for the Kennedys to break up their luncheon dawdling and come on.

Pat Kennedy Lawford eventually strolled in, accompanied by Jean Kennedy Smith and the wives of Bobby and Teddy Kennedy. By this time the delegates who held Jack's fate in their hands were furious, but the girls kept them waiting another ten minutes while they posed for cameramen. "When is this going to get started?" sister Jean finally asked me. When I told her that it had been under way for some time and that these restless people were important delegates, she lined up the family in a receiving line and began pumping hands. Jean, who was eight months pregnant, looked wearily around from time to time, asking, "Where in the world is Eunice? I want to sit down, but I don't like to leave until she gets here to take my place."

Three-quarters of an hour later, when neither Eunice Shriver nor Rose Kennedy had shown, Jean Smith gave up and left. In another five minutes so did Pat Lawford. Eventually Teddy Kennedy put in an appearance, and five minutes later candidate Jack Kennedy arrived. The four-piece orchestra struck up a victory tune, and a two-way crush began, half the delegates trying to shake his hand, while the other half fought disgustedly for the exits.

Meanwhile, Lyndon Johnson was entertaining delegates at another party down the hall. LBJ had flown into Los Angeles waving his Texas Stetson and brandishing his wife and daughters. Lynda Bird, sixteen, clung to her father's arm, beamed at him adoringly, and hung on his every word as if each syllable were too precious to miss. Twelve-year-old Lucy Baines (later to be called Luci), made a little speech in which she said that she was frankly there to shop for boyfriends. Johnson then took over the loudspeaker and offered himself as the one man who could "save us in these perilous times." With a meaningful nod down the hall toward Kennedy headquarters, he declared, "We've seen enough of this razzle-dazzle, Madison Avenue type of campaigning, with the toothpaste smiles and the attempt to outglamor glamor. I have the utmost respect for you Democratic delegates, and I think your decision will be based on who ought to win, instead of who might win. This is not an issue of age. It's an issue of maturity. It's not a question of who can kiss the most babies in the most places, but a question of selecting a trustee for your children."

The next day Lyndon and Jack finally met for an off-again, on-again debate before the Texas delegation and a smattering of delegates from Massachusetts. Lyndon Johnson, speaking first, made a strong pitch for support and pointed out that as majority leader he was always in the Senate for every vote, while Jack was usually off somewhere else. When Kennedy rose to reply, he won a good-natured wave of applause by quipping, "I've always believed that Lyndon was a great Senator, and that's where I want him to stay."

On July 11, I wrote a column which began:

A few thousand people will be dropping in on Perle Mesta tomorrow for breakfast. The famed party-dropper doesn't know exactly how many, and she doesn't really care so long as every delegate who samples her ample larder pumps the hand of her presidential candidate, Lyndon Baines Johnson. Those who dismiss Madame Mesta as a mere hostess are making a Texas-sized mistake. She's a shrewd operator, and she's figured out the neatest trick of the week to avoid asking other presidential hopefuls to share Lyndon's spotlight at her shindig. "I'm only inviting delegates," she murmurs disarmingly. "I'm told that Jack Kennedy isn't a delegate, but Lyndon just happens to head the Texas delegation."

That convention is now history. During the final balloting Peter Lawford and Frank Sinatra crowded into our Hearst section below the podium; then Jack Kennedy strode triumphantly onstage with his sister Pat Lawford to receive the jubilant cheers of the delegates.

The next day, to the consternation of every columnist who had taken LBJ at his word and written that he would not consider the number two Throttlebottom spot, Johnson accepted the Vice Presidential nomination. Lady Bird Johnson, later telling about it in my book, *Mrs. LBJ*, recalled:

After Lyndon lost the presidential race, I had the best night's sleep I'd had in some time. Early the next morning the phone rang. It was for Lyndon. I had a mind to tell the caller that he was sleeping, but when the voice identified itself as Mr. Kennedy, I awakened Lyndon. That's when they first began to talk about his accepting the vice presidency, and the first time that I had even considered such a possibility.

Johnson had only a few hours in which to decide. The Vice President was to be chosen by the convention that day, and the delegates were obviously going to elect whomever the new Presidential nominee wanted. Johnson consulted with Speaker Rayburn and John Connally, both of whom opposed his acceptance; but the Kennedys applied pressure on Mr. Sam, and at last he growled his consent for "my boy Lyndon" to join the ticket. Jacqueline Kennedy, pregnant again, did not attend the convention, and because of her history of miscarriages, the distaff campaigning chore would fall to Lady Bird Johnson and Jack's female relatives.

After the Democratic Convention we moved on to Chicago, with only a week's respite, to cover the Republican conclave. Compared with the Kennedy steamroller, the GOP convention seemed a rather cut-and-dried affair. Everyone knew that Nixon would be nominated, despite Rockefeller's abortive attempts to split the delegates. On July 27, I visited with the Nixon women in their Chicago hotel suite, while they waited out the long day until Dick was to be nominated. Julie and Tricia were barefoot, clad in shorts. Hannah Nixon, Dick's mother, was comfortably settled before the TV set. So was Pat, who wore two white orchids sent by admirers, but giggled to me, "I'm allergic to orchids."

I asked each of the four women closest to Nixon to recall their greatest moment with him. Pat spoke first, saying, "Oh, it was definitely that night here in Chicago eight years ago when I learned that Dick had been selected by General Eisenhower as his running mate. It was so completely unexpected, you know! I was sitting in the Stockyard Inn with a friend, munching on a sandwich, and a grade-B movie was grinding away on TV, when suddenly a flash bulletin interrupted the movie. I honestly couldn't believe my ears. The announcer said that Eisenhower had just chosen Nixon. What a moment! How could I ever forget it?"

Twelve-year-old Julie, the extrovert of the family, recalled her most unforgettable triumph, the September before in the recreation room of the Nixon house, when Dick and Pat returned from their tour of Russia. Julie as a surprise had written and staged for them a musical entitled *Cinderella,* and so professional was the production that the Nixons, who themselves had met at a little theater production a generation before, agreed that Julie could have a theatrical career if she wanted it. Pat broke in to say, "I don't think I ever saw Dick so proud!"

Then Tricia dug her bare toes luxuriously into the pile carpeting and said that her abiding passion was baseball, so how could she fail to choose that sensational day two years previously, when a long-distance operator announced that the Vice President was calling Miss Tricia Nixon? If she would be willing to fly alone to Pittsburgh, Dick told his excited daughter, he would meet her and escort her to the All-Star Game. Could she be ready? Could she! Her feet flew and her heart raced as Pat helped pack her overnight bag, and soon she was flying toward Pittsburgh for a private date with her father.

Mrs. Hannah Nixon, drawing on seventy-eight years of wisdom, spoke last, saying, "Dick has made his mother proud many, many times. We were proud about his surprise election to Congress, but I guess the proudest was when my husband and I sat in the auditorium of Fullerton high school three decades ago, when Dick won the regional oratorical contest. He had worked so hard for it!"

After the convention Bob and I spent our vacation in Palm Beach, and on returning to Washington, I wrote a column in which Jeane Dixon flatly predicted that Richard M. Nixon would be elected President in November. Not until a few days before the balloting that fall did she see "snakes crawling from the Democratic to the Republican side" in her crystal ball and interpret it to mean that unless the GOP guarded every polling box, the Democrats would "steal the election."

Shortly before the two conventions, Johnson and Rayburn had decreed that Congress should return for a rump session immediately afterward. The powerful Texans had hoped that Lyndon would win the Presidential nomination and that this would provide a perfect forum from which to demonstrate his skill to the voters. Jack Kennedy had won, however, and if there was any place that the restive young man did not want to be that summer, it was in the Senate.

Nixon was also grounded in Washington during this period, presiding over the Senate, but his wife, Pat, was proving a potent weapon. In mid-August she made a political sortie to Connecticut, her father's birthplace, and despite torrential rains, made a big hit with the citizens. Nixon had chosen UN Ambassador Henry Cabot Lodge, Jr., as his running mate, and during the hiatus I interviewed the wives of all four men who headed the two tickets.

The first was Pat Nixon, who had nothing but praise for the three other women who would share the national spotlight in the months ahead. Of Jacqueline Kennedy she said, "I've only met her a few times because she seldom attends our Senate Wives' Club, but I think she's very glamorous." Of Lady Bird she said, "She's very well liked by all the Senate ladies. I think she's a very charming, sweet person." Of the wife of her husband's running mate, she said, "I know Emily Lodge quite well, and I admire so much the way she conducted herself during the Khrushchev visit here. She was such a good sport about everything, and she has beautifully handled her hostess role at the United Nations. Emily is a real charmer, and a wonderful asset to the ticket."

When I asked how she would like to be First Lady, her laugh rang out merrily as she said, "You won't believe me, Ruth, but I actually haven't given it any thought. It would be presumptuous of me anyway, and I'm not the type to take anything for granted." Asked about the possible effect on her children of the goldfish-bowl life in the White House, she replied, "I just haven't looked that far ahead, but we have always been able to adjust to every situation as it comes. In every campaign I have refused to look ahead, because I know that all situations can be met. I don't think we've changed personally in any way since we came to Washington, except that our lives are more crowded with official duties. Our home life is the same." Then, with quiet intensity, she added, "Dick and I have no personal interest in this. I don't quite know how to say it, but ever since he has been in politics he has felt a real dedication, a pride at the opportunity to serve. Dick realizes that one man can't do too much, but he knows that a lot of men working together can do wonders, and he wants to be a part of the whole scene, the progress."

To interview Jackie Kennedy I flew to Boston and then drove with a photographer to Hyannisport, where she was spending the summer. In those days the Kennedy Compound was unfenced and unguarded, and when no one answered my ring, I walked through the open house to the rear, where I glimpsed Jackie and Caroline approaching from the beach. Jackie was expecting me, and she waved gaily; then she invited me to have lunch with them, but since a photographer was with me and he was not included, we returned to the compound after lunch at a restaurant.

Jackie was dressed and ready by then, but she insisted that no full-length pictures be taken of her, because of her pregnancy. I heartily agreed, but the photographer considered her the most stubborn woman he had ever met. Jackie and I had a long chat after the picture taking, and it was apparent that she was leading a life of quiet desperation while her husband was off campaigning. "I married into a whirlwind," she said expressively. "Jack has been running for Vice President or President ever since our marriage seven years ago, and I have learned to adjust. This suspense is the worst, though. It's terribly frustrating to sit back, when I want so much to be helping. There are so many things I could do for him on those eighteen-hour days: pack his bags, lay out his clothes, order food when he forgets to eat."

I asked if she worried about the possibility of Caroline living in the White House limelight, and she replied, "Oh, yes. Anyone with young children would worry about that. The greatest responsibility is your children. If my children turned out badly, I'd feel that nothing I had done was worthwhile." She said that the most important role for a First Lady was "to take care of your husband so that he can be the best possible President. The President needs every ounce of his energy and judgment. His wife must devote herself to him, releasing him from needless burdens and making home a sanctuary." Asked if she thought that Jack would win, she mused a moment before replying, "I don't know. Everyone thinks it will be a very even race, and that we won't know until almost the end, if then." Her words were oddly prophetic.

After a warm, sprightly interview with my old friend Emily Lodge, I talked to Lady Bird Johnson at their white-painted Colonial brick house where they had lived since 1952, and she said, "We've parlayed this very simple little John Citizen home as far as it will go. We're bursting at the seams, and if Lyndon became Vice President, I'd need more than the one long evening dress a year that I buy now. We have to have more closet space."

Lynda, sixteen, and Lucy, thirteen, occasionally wandered in and out to consult their mother about clothes, dates, and schedules. I asked what effect Lyndon's possible election might have on the girls, and she grimaced. "I've really tried to impress on them that their father's job is important, but I tell them this doesn't rub off on them, and that self-importance is nuts. Self-responsibility is the thing to aspire to." With an indulgent smile she added, "We have the usual teen-age problems. They're on the phone all the time, and they won't pick up their clothes."

At that moment Lucy burst into the room, wailing, "Mother, you've ruined my whole life! You had the telephone tied up all morning, when he might have been trying to ask me to meet him for lunch." The "he" was a brand-new flame, a Senate page boy, and she decided to go down to her father's office on the chance that he might be loafing around and ask her for a date. I gave her a lift in my car, and she said excitedly, "Somehow I can't get over having boys pay attention to me. You see, I was always a wallflower until now. At the parties none of the boys would ask me to dance, even though I'm a very good dancer. I was simply flabbergasted when a boy actually asked me to go out for a Coke with him. I just couldn't believe it was true." Explaining why she was so upset about her mother's telephone calls that morning, she said that her new beau had promised to call her the night before, but hadn't, so she finally called him. "Mrs. Montgomery," she sighed, "I know I did wrong, but I've been a wallflower for so long, it's terribly hard for me to play hard to get."

CHAPTER XXIII

The Kennedy Upset

THE special session of Congress finally adjourned, without noticeable accomplishment, and just as Presidential candidate Dick Nixon prepared to kick off his campaign through fifty states he developed an infected knee, which hospitalized him for nearly two of the precious ten weeks allotted for that swing. Still walking stiff-legged after the traction, he invited us to a party at the Nixon home on September 14, 1960, and the next day set out for the grass roots.

The day was a killer! Hurricane-driven rains angrily lashed the sodden Baltimore airport and kept to pygmy size the crowd that was to have seen him off. But as we flew westward, the skies cleared, and he was greeted by a tumultuous crowd in Indianapolis. At our next stop, Dallas, 100,000 Texans lined the streets to give him a king-sized welcome, and the Dallas police chief said it was "the biggest turnout this town has seen since we gave a hero's welcome to Admiral Nimitz after World War II."

On and on we flew, eventually winding up at a night rally in San Francisco, which by our getting-up time in Washington was held at 12:30 A.M. Tuesday was more of the same. The weather was balmy and the crops were bountiful as we hopped across Iowa. Nixon's audiences were warm and folksy and seemed more interested in what he had to say about peace and foreign affairs than domestic policies, a sure sign that they were not suffering in the pocketbook department. Schools had been dismissed for the occasion, and as we landed in each city, we sensed a carnival air as our caravan moved along flag-bedecked streets.

Nixon was suffering from hay fever because of the pollen in the air, and he talked through a stopped-up nose at the plowing contest in Guthrie Center, but the thousands of farmers and their well-dressed spouses seemed to like what they heard as he unrolled the first half of his proposed farm program. The second half was delivered at the National Plowing Contest in Sioux Falls, South Dakota. Our planes finally touched down in Omaha at 1:30 A.M. to cap a twenty-one-hour day. We had expected to creep silently off to bed, but several thousand wildly cheering, bright-eyed Nebraskans who had been standing since 10:30 P.M. warmly welcomed Pat and Dick. After only a few hours' sleep, the Nixons turned up at a "rooster rally" at 7:30 A.M. to drink coffee with 7,000 Republicans. Then we plane-hopped through the great Northwest, and the sensational turn-out in Portland, Oregon, seemed to infuse Nixon with new strength. "There's nothing like a good crowd," he quipped, "to cure a sore knee."

En route to Boise, Idaho, the next day, the "Pat and Dick Nixon Special" plane lost an engine, and Nixon remarked, "If this plane can fly with three motors, I can certainly campaign with one knee." We eventually fell into bed at 3 A.M. in St. Louis, and it was later still when we reached Omaha the next night. After six of these grueling days, the Nixons and the press finally reached Washington at 4 A.M. on a Sunday morning.

The first of the televised Nixon-Kennedy debates was held on September 26, and I was less shocked than most viewers by Dick's wan appearance, since I knew that he had not fully recovered from the effects of the wonder drugs and had been in constant pain. Jack Kennedy was in great form, however, and so captured the imagination of the nation that thereafter his sparsely attended rallies began to swell. Teen-agers and women squealed and jumped with joy at the sight of him, and there is little question but that the televised debates reversed the tide of history.

Presidential campaigns are an endurance contest which glorifies brawn over brain. Lugging my typewriter and suitcase into hotel lobbies in the wee hours of the morning, with only three or four hours' sleep at night, and typing my dispatches on my lap in swaying buses took its toll. Midway in the campaign I landed in the hospital, where I lay in double traction because of excruciating muscular spasms in my back, and one of my news colleagues telegraphed: "You'll envy us, knowing that we're getting the most out of every twenty-six-hour day."

The peripatetic Kennedy clan was constantly on the go that fall. So many Kennedy women were holding coffee klatches that in Chicago an eighty-five-year-old woman confused Bobby's wife with Mama Rose Kennedy and cooed, "My dear, I haven't seen you since you gave that embassy lawn party in London before the war."

I wrote of that day's schedule: "The reason why Pat Kennedy Lawford, who lives in California, flew to a Washington tea was because Ethel Kennedy, who was supposed to be the guest of honor, was campaigning in Chicago, since Eunice Kennedy Shriver, who lives in Chicago and was scheduled to be there, was campaigning in Ohio instead. Get it?"

Jacqueline Kennedy and Jean Kennedy Smith were excused from the campaign to increase the tribal numbers, but Jean produced a bouncing baby boy in September and was soon back on the hustings. Jackie, who was reared a Republican, managed to pour tea at a few Democratic shindigs, while Pat Nixon, who was reared a Democrat, was the best distaff campaigner in the Republican stable. Jackie's mother, the very Republican Mrs. Hugh D. Auchincloss, lent her Potomac River estate to the Democratic Women's Committee for a fund-raising coffee klatch, while Perle Mesta, who had been all out for Lyndon Johnson, switched parties again and campaigned for Dick Nixon. It was a crazy, mixed-up campaign, and when the votes were finally tallied Kennedy had won by only two-tenths of one percent, the smallest margin in our history.

After the election I had an exclusive interview with Bobby Kennedy and asked what position he wanted in the new administration of his brother. To my amazement, he said that he was thinking of Secretary of State, Secretary of Defense, or Attorney General. He had the grace, however, to say that he was worried about the charge of nepotism, and since I considered him too immature for State or Defense, I urged him to become Attorney General instead, saying, "You would indeed be criticized for thinking of the first two, but since you were Jack's campaign manager, and Eisenhower appointed his campaign manager, Herb Brownell, Attorney General, you could probably get away with that."

I wrote a column about our interview, indicating that Bobby would probably be his brother's Attorney General, and shortly thereafter the appointment was made. As was expected, some criticism resounded from his lack of experience, but Jack took care of that in a speech before the Alfalfa Club. "I see no harm in letting Bobby get a little legal experience," he quipped, "before he starts to practice law."

Capital society matrons, hopeful of a White House invitation during the new administration, began taking a hard look at their wardrobes. Jackie was a pacesetter in fashions and favored daring innovations. During an interview she told me, "I know what I look best in. The only way to be correctly dressed is to be ruthless. Keep your wardrobe small but right, wear it out in a single season, and discard it. Leftover dresses never look well the next year. My wardrobe is really very small. Each spring and fall I buy a suit, coat, two wool dresses, two afternoon dresses, and an evening gown. Each must be absolutely perfect for what it is. I wear my clothes very hard and try to avoid having any leftovers." Admitting that her wardrobe included several Paris gowns, she added, "Until now it was nobody's business whether I wore French gowns, but now that I will have an official position, I will wear only American clothes." This was a promise that she kept about as well as most male politicians keep their campaign pledges.

Shortly after the election President-elect John F. Kennedy flew to his father's oceanside estate in Palm Beach, accompanied by staff advisers, ten Secret Service men, and a retinue of newsmen. While Jack leisurely sunned himself on the beach and worked on Presidential appointments, the future First Lady remained in Washington to be near her doctor. Jack flew to Washington for Thanksgiving dinner and that evening took off again for Palm Beach; but by the time he reached Florida Jackie was in labor, and he jumped into the faster press plane for the return trip north. The stork won the race, and before Jack arrived, Jacqueline gave birth to a boy, who was christened John F. Kennedy, Jr.

Mrs. Kennedy's doctor shortly thereafter announced that because of her Caesarian section, she could do very little entertaining during her first six months in the White House. She was known to dislike large parties with politicians present; so rumors spread that she had asked her physician to make the announcement, saying, "Give me as much time as you can, like six months." The parties Jackie relished were candlelit dinners for eight or ten sophisticated friends, and she confided that the only White House parties she looked forward to were state dinners for visiting heads of state.

Jack's own party preference ran to the kind of bashes which Ethel and Bobby Kennedy customarily gave. After that exuberant one during which the burro muddily trampled the white rugs and Ethel poured water over Teddy's head and tux, Jack had confided to another Senator, "You should have been at Bobby's party last night. Everyone had a terrific time. I wish I could get my wife to give parties like that."

Lyndon B. Johnson was meanwhile preparing to take over the Vice Presidency, and on a trip to London he ordered five side-vent suits made to order on Savile Row, despite the "buy American" campaign at home. He was also expanding his office space. During the previous eight years he had appropriated fifty-six rooms in the Capitol for his own purposes, while allowing Vice President Nixon only ten widely scattered ones. Now, while still holding onto a sizable chunk of his Capitol space, he also acquired a large suite in the old State Department Building next door to the White House. Jack Kennedy allocated him no office space in the White House itself.

While Kennedy was settling on his Cabinet appointees, he also named Frank Sinatra to head the inaugural gala, and Sinatra chose such close friends as Sammy Davis, Jr., Joey Bishop, Peter Lawford, and Tony Curtis as featured entertainers. The only private party which Jack Kennedy had attended during the nominating convention was one given by brother-in-law Peter Lawford, at which Sinatra and his "rat pack" turned out en masse, and on election night Sinatra had the gall to keep trying by telephone to get Nixon to concede the election before the results were in. Some Republicans had tried to persuade Nixon to demand a recount, but he refused.

A few nights before Christmas of 1960 Bob and I went to a party at the Nixons'. The Christmas lights etched brilliant patterns on the snow beside the stoop. The door swung open, wafting pine-scented air and the lyrical strains of *Swan Lake*. Just inside, smiles wreathing their relaxed faces, stood Pat and Dick Nixon to greet their invited guests. The tension had dropped from their shoulders, and the taut lines drawn by the strenuous campaign had softened into laugh wrinkles.

As they stood with hands outstretched to greet their favorite members of the Cabinet, press corps, and campaign staff, they looked a perfect picture of contented bliss. The English-style manor house where they had spent their happiest and most productive years glowed with soft light, massive red poinsettia plants, balsam runners, and holly sprigs. Dick Nixon seemed ten years younger than the haggard man who confronted challenger Jack Kennedy in the first of the TV "great debates."

A government official, pressing Pat's hand, told her that in his opinion the election had been "stolen" by the Democrats. Her laugh tinkled hollowly as she replied, "Isn't it a dreadful thing if in this great country we lack the right to have our ballots counted correctly! That will be a goal for Bobby Kennedy to set himself as Attorney General, won't it?"

Another friend sputtered, "If the votes had been counted honestly in Texas and Cook County, Illinois, you can be sure the results would have been different."

Pat's ramrod shoulders sagged for the merest moment as she replied, "Just those two states were all we needed. Think of it!"

Jacqueline Kennedy was meanwhile convalescing at her father-in-law's estate in Palm Beach, but before leaving Washington, she had arranged to lease a Virginia country estate, Glen Ora, for use as a weekend house. Both the Kennedy and Nixon houses were quietly for sale, although Pat would stay on in Washington until June, for the remainder of Julie and Tricia's school year, after Dick went to Los Angeles to practice law.

During the hiatus before the new administration came to power, I talked with Lyndon and Lady Bird Johnson at a party, and they told me of a recent happening, about which I wrote:

> The phone rang raucously on the busiest desk at Capitol Hill. The big, rangy Texan ignored it as long as possible, and then reached for its clamorous throat. The call must be important, or it could never have cleared his large and efficient staff. "Daddy," sighed a soft voice at the other end of the wire, "You'll just have to come and help me. I've found the most heavenly suit, but it might be just a little too sophisticated for me."
>
> Vice President-elect Lyndon B. Johnson grinned and began to relax. His desk pad was crowded with appointments and re-minders, but here was a challenge that obviously called for the kind of expert judgment that only a man like himself could provide. Buzzing for his confidential secretary, he explained the crisis and headed for a Washington department store. Thirteen-year-old Lucy and 16-year-old Lynda were eagerly awaiting their father's arrival in the ready-to-wear department.
>
> This was the first time they had summoned their father alone, without mother along, to pass judgment on their feminine pur-chases. They knew by experience, however, that when Lady Bird Johnson met her husband at apparel shops, he invariably had her buy more than she had in mind. Lyndon, flattered to be consulted on such a weighty matter by the junior misses in his family, came through with flying colors. The four-piece blue wool suit, com-plete with matching sport coat, was exactly right for his younger teen-ager, he judiciously decided.

Second-Lady-to-be Lady Bird, more adept than Lyndon at seeing through feminine wiles, was appropriately suspicious of the lure that Lucy offered her father to get him to the store. "I just can't get over Lucy worrying about anything in the world being too sophisticated for her," she mused ruefully. "She's been bulldozing me for too long about pushing ahead too fast, and trying to get into clothes more grown up than she is."

LBJ also bought Lynda a similar beige suit and both girls spectacular bathrobes. In Texas for Christmas, the three women ordered inaugural gowns from Nieman Marcus, and Lady Bird confided to me, "I'm trying to draw together all the threads of my life and making sure that all my kin folks and Alabama cousins are invited to the inauguration. I keep having dreams that I might forget my shoes or some of my oldest and dearest friends."

A new era was about to begin.

CHAPTER XXIV

The New Frontier

INAUGURATION day dawned white, bright, and bitingly cold, and we shivered in the press bleachers at the Capitol for Jack Kennedy's swearing in, despite fur coat and heavy galoshes. The previous day, Washington had been inundated by the heaviest snow in recorded history, and I wrote a column which began:

> What do you do in a snowstorm the day before your brother is to be inaugurated President of the United States? Answer: If you're a member of the high-spirited Kennedy clan you play touch football out at Bobby's in the snow, naturally. That is how the next Attorney General, his younger brother Teddy, and their wives and assorted pals spent midday before going to three receptions, a symphony concert, the Inaugural Gala and a post-midnight supper hosted by papa Joe Kennedy.

The gathering of the clan from the northern regions of Boston to the sunny shores of Southern California was an event in itself. They arrived by jet and turbo-prop, pouring trunkloads of jewels, furs, and couturier creations into a half-dozen Georgetown mansions which they had leased for inaugural week, at an average cost of $200 a day each. They impressed even blasé Georgetown with a fabulously decorated party staged in a heated tent behind sister Jean Smith's eighteenth-century abode, which set the night-owl pace for a rollicking week and kept the Kennedys with their dancing shoes on.

Bobby and Ethel Kennedy, aware of my ailing back, had repeatedly

234

urged me to go to New York City for consultations with Dr. Janet Travell, the specialist who had been treating Jack Kennedy's back for several years, but I was suffering too much to make the trip. Thus, when Dr. Travell came to Washington as a guest of the Kennedys for inauguration, they sent her to my house, and her injections of procaine brought the first relief that I had known in months. Before her departure by White House limousine for the Kennedys' residence in nearby Georgetown it had begun to snow, and by the time I had finished writing a column at the Hearst bureau the snow had become a battering blizzard. Bob picked me up in the car, and the drive home, which ordinarily required ten minutes, consumed four hours, through mountainous snow drifts. By morning, 550 snow plows and dump trucks were mustered just to clear Pennsylvania Avenue for the grand march to the White House from the Capitol.

Inauguration night the new President went to a dinner party at the home of George Y. Wheeler and then to five inaugural balls. Jacqueline accompanied him to the first two balls but waited outside the Statler-Hilton Hotel in the Presidential limousine while he ducked upstairs to a party being given by Sinatra. It was a long wait, and when he returned to the car, she asked to be driven to the White House, after which he touched bases at the last three balls alone.

During Kennedy's first week as President he called a televised press conference at the unheard-of hour of 6 P.M., dropped by a newsman's private party at 1:30 A.M. and stayed until 3 A.M., stopped unannounced at a former neighbor's house and yoo-hooed up the stairs to them, and took slacks-clad Jackie on a tour of the White House executive wing and press room. He was obviously relishing his new position, and its duties had not yet begun to weigh on him. Unlike Eisenhower, who was always at his desk by 7:45 A.M., Jack usually strolled in around 9.

During the campaign he had accused the Eisenhower administration of permitting a "missiles gap" with Russia, but Defense Secretary Robert McNamara, after assuming office, admitted that he could not find one. Kennedy had also criticized President Eisenhower for "too much personal diplomacy," but during his own first hundred days he held more meetings with foreign heads of state than any

Chief Executive in our history. Candidate Kennedy had further said that the place for a Secretary of State was at home running his department, not running around the world, but in those same hundred days the new Secretary of State, Dean Rusk, made far-flung trips to the SEATO Conference in Bangkok, the CENTO Conference in Angora, and the NATO Conference in Oslo. During the campaign, Kennedy slurred Eisenhower by saying, "I would think that whoever was President would see the press at least once a week." This campaign promise also fell by the wayside, and during his first ten months as President he held only seventeen news conferences.

But his Irish wit was bubbling out all over. Addressing the Gridiron Club, he reminded the members of the famous joke about Catholic Presidential candidate Al Smith, who after losing the election supposedly sent the Pope a one-word cable: "Unpack." Then he topped it by saying, "Well, after my stand against federal aid to parochial schools last week I received a one-word cable from the Pope, 'Pack.'"

In another speech he spoofed his father by claiming to have received this telegram from him during the campaign: "Dear Jack, don't buy a single vote more than is necessary. I'll be damned if I'm going to pay for a landslide." When Republicans struck at his youthful inexperience, he said of his campaign rival, "Mr. Nixon may be very experienced in kitchen debates. So are a great many other married men I know." When a small boy asked President Kennedy how he became a war hero, Jack ad-libbed, "It was absolutely involuntary. They sank my boat." And at his forty-fourth birthday party a few months after becoming President, Kennedy joked that when he took office, the thing that surprised him most was "to find things were just as bad as we were saying they were."

One of Kennedy's first official acts as President was to appoint Dr. Janet Travell White House physician, the only woman ever to have been so honored. JFK badly needed her ministrations for his ailing back, and so did I. But now that she was on the government payroll, she told me that she could no longer treat private patients. I was desolate, because the good effects of her first treatment had been voided by that freezing, four-hour struggle to reach home through snowdrifts on inaugural eve.

The day that I covered Kennedy's first State of the Union message at the Capitol, I ran into Bobby and Ethel Kennedy on the marble staircase, and when they solicitously inquired about my back, I told them of Dr. Travell's decision. Ethel exclaimed, "We'll fix that, won't we, Bobby?" And they did! A few days later, Dr. Travell telephoned to say that she was coming over, and the second treatment proved highly successful. I gratefully telephoned my thanks to Ethel, and the next evening when President Kennedy came to a party honoring former President Truman, he strode over to me and exclaimed, "Isn't she terrific! I hear that your back is much better."

A nation which rocked with laughter at the uninhibited antics of the Theodore Roosevelt ménage, in the early years of the century, now had a new cast of elfin characters to applaud. Bobby's exuberant youngsters romped in and out of the White House, but center stage belonged to three-year-old Caroline Kennedy. During the first months of the new administration, she was being given a somewhat free run of the Executive Mansion, and when a newsman once asked what her daddy was doing, she replied, "He's just sitting up there with his shoes off."

In early February, 1961, Speaker Rayburn, Vice President Johnson, and Senators Mike Mansfield, Hubert Humphrey, and George Smathers assembled in the White House dining room for a legislative leadership breakfast, and when the President strode in, he was not alone. Peddling along beside him on her tricycle was Caroline, who roguishly made eyes at the Congressmen as she wheeled around the room several times. Then, at a word from her father, she amiably peddled down the hallway and into the waiting elevator, which whisked her back upstairs.

Enchanting little Caroline had developed into quite a scene-stealer even before inauguration. Once Jack took her to mass, where she spent the time crawling under pews, whispering to her vexed father, and making eyes at amused worshipers. Afterward the President-elect walked out of the Catholic church carrying her rag doll under one arm, while his blond daughter skipped merrily ahead of him toward waiting cameramen. Another time she interrupted her father's televised press conference at Palm Beach by blithely clumping into the center of the group in her mother's high-heeled pumps. JFK started to do what comes naturally, grasping her firmly by the arm. Then, remembering that TV and newsreel cameras were recording the event for posterity, he grinned broadly and led Caroline sociably back to the house.

Caroline was never spanked, perhaps because the one paddling administered to her mother was such a monumental flop. Mrs. Auchincloss told me that Jacqueline, at the age of six, liked nothing better than to dial her grown-up relatives and chatter on the telephone. Once her mother asked Jackie to call her grandfather, but the little girl rudely refused. Rebuked, she alibied that she did not know how. Mrs. Auchincloss patiently repeated the telephone number, which Jackie knew by heart, but to no avail. Nettled beyond endurance by her daughter's well-developed stubborn streak, she finally spanked her; but the phone call remained unmade, and physical punishment ended in the Bouvier household that day. "I couldn't help but think that Jackie got the better of me," Mrs. Auchincloss explained ruefully.

Living at the White House, Caroline saw much more of her father than she ever had before, and she invariably accompanied him on his walks to and from the executive West Wing. Mrs. Kennedy, a devotee of ballet, enrolled Caroline in a ballet school, but the moppet heartily disliked it and refused to cooperate with the teacher and other children.

Despite the buy-American campaign, Congressman William Ayres of Ohio read that the Kennedy White House had ordered six hundred meters of carpeting from France, so he bought a made-in-America tricycle for Caroline and took it to the White House the day that he was invited there for a stag meeting. President Kennedy accepted it but refused to let Caroline pose on it. Ayres prankishly straddled it for the benefit of photographers, and the pictures appeared in newspapers the next day. A White House gagster thereupon signed Caroline's name to a telegram to Ayres which read: "I'm so busy with my dancing lessons that my mommy hasn't time

to teach me to read, but I can look at pictures, so get off my bike."
White House assistant Lawrence O'Brien denied that the White
House intended to buy rugs from France, and the next day an article
out of Paris said that the carpeting order had been canceled.

The new First Lady made unfavorable headlines when press dispatches from London revealed that she had asked her sister, Lee
Radziwill, to try to hire for the White House the incomparable
French chef of the French embassy. To the *haut monde,* few sins
are as unpardonable as trying to steal another's cook, and this attempt
could have provoked an international incident. Jacqueline for once
was stopped in her tracks, but she soon managed to lure another
French chef from the Carlyle Hotel in New York City. The Kennedys had been occupying the White House less than a month when
they required all servants and secretaries to sign affidavits promising
not to write about their experiences as Kennedy employees, even if
they left the White House, but judging by the swarm of books in
recent years, they could have saved the paper on which the affidavits
were written.

President Kennedy had been enjoying a remarkable honeymoon
with the Republican opposition and the press. Then, on April 17,
came the abortive invasion of Cuba by U.S.-backed Cuban refugees,
and thereafter JFK became a more sobered young man. Much of the
play had gone out of the Presidency. Two years previously, after a
three-hour session with Fidel Castro in his Vice Presidential office,
Dick Nixon had warned the Eisenhower administration that Castro
was "a captive of Communism." Nixon spoke no public criticism of
Kennedy's handling of the Bay of Pigs fiasco, but he privately told
me that the worst mistake for a poker player is to throw in his hole
card before it is necessary. While the rebels were pouring onto Cuban
beaches in the hope of inspiring others to defect and liberate their
homeland, President Kennedy and Secretary Rusk were telling the
world that the United States would not raise a finger to intervene.
This was the hole card that turned up too soon. Many Cubans were
afraid to defect, and the invasion was crushed.

Nixon pointed out that by contrast, President Eisenhower and

Secretary Dulles carefully concealed the hole card during the tense days and weeks of the Quemoy-Matsu crisis. They left doubt in the Communist mind as to what extent they would be willing to commit U.S. strength in the Formosa strait, and the Reds finally backed down.

On May 5, 1961, Navy Commander Alan B. Shepard, Jr., successfully returned from outer space, and on that joyous note President and Mrs. Kennedy flew to Canada for a good-neighbor visit. While there, JFK participated in the ceremonial planting of a tree, which wrenched his already ailing back, and he suffered untold agonies with it all that summer. Simultaneously, Vice President and Mrs. Johnson were touring the Orient, with JFK's sister and brother-in-law Jean and Steve Smith in tow, and while in Pakistan LBJ invited a camel driver to come to America. No one was more astonished than the Vice President when Bashir Ahmed took him seriously and requested money for the trip. Johnson's harried staff appealed to the People to People program, which furnished a round-trip ticket, and soon Bashir Ahmed was stealing headlines from coast to coast. Kennedy, marveling at Johnson's flair for dramatics, muttered, "If I had done that, there would have been camel dung all over the White House lawn."

At the end of May President and Mrs. Kennedy went to Europe, where JFK failed to impress Soviet Premier Nikita Khrushchev at the international conference table in Vienna. But his beautiful wife of French descent made such a sensational hit with Parisian masses that the President quipped, "I am the man who accompanied Jacqueline Kennedy to Paris."

The exquisitely gowned First Lady traveled with forty pieces of luggage, and while in Paris, she purchased a French gown to wear at the glittering dinner-ballet at Versailles Palace. Her personal maid took care of the wardrobe, and Jackie devoted long hours each day to French, Austrian, and English hairdressers, who tried to outdo one another with elaborate coiffures for the photogenic First Lady.

No sooner had President and Mrs. Kennedy returned from their official visit than Jacqueline began making plans for a tour of the Greek islands with her sister, Lee Radziwill, while Jack worked at

the White House on crutches. After Jackie's return she spent most
of the remainder of the summer in Cape Cod and Newport, and
because the President needed a hostess for a state luncheon in honor
of the visiting President of Ecuador and his wife, Rose Kennedy flew
to Washington to preside opposite her son. Sleeping at the White
House was no novelty for Mama Rose, as she and her husband had
been houseguests there during the Franklin D. Roosevelt era. She
recalled to me that on one occasion, when she descended the White
House stairs in a pencil-slim evening gown, FDR's son-in-law, John
Boettiger, took one look at the mother of nine children and whistled.
"Now I believe in the stork!"

Jackie was spending as little time as possible at the White House.
Beautiful, elusive, and independent, she was also doing everything
that her White House press secretary, Pamela Turnure, said that she
would not. Jackie presumably cleared the announcement that she
would not be able to ride with the hunt or do any official entertaining
that first spring because of the Caesarian delivery of John, Jr., the
preceding fall; but she joined the Orange County hunt and immediately began riding for hours over fences, through woods and fields,
in pursuit of the fox.

Pamela repeatedly emphasized that Mrs. Kennedy would use Glen
Ora only for family outings, so that the children could enjoy weekends with their parents, and the family did spend a few days there
in the spring of 1961, although baby John remained at the White
House. Jackie's next visit there lasted eleven days, while JFK worked
in Washington. Then, instead of returning to the White House,
Jackie hopped a plane for Palm Beach while the White House was
denying that she had any plans to go to Florida.

On moving to the White House, Jackie had said that the First
Lady she most admired was Bess Truman, who had stayed close to
the family fireside; but after her conquest of Paris and her water-
skiing vacation in the Greek islands, she began to emulate the fast-
traveling Eleanor Roosevelt more than homey Bess Truman. From
June until November she scarcely set foot in the Executive Mansion,
and reporters began to add up the days of her absences, as they had
once done with Eleanor.

The White House first announced, and then canceled, a trip for her that November to India and Pakistan, but she spent nine days in Glen Ora and then flew to Palm Beach again. She returned to the White House briefly to see her visiting sister, Lee, but the two sisters promptly left for four days at Glen Ora, after which they went directly to New York for fittings on clothes and theatergoing.

When Jackie wished to turn her attention to entertaining, she could do so with remarkable flair. Unafraid to be an innovator, she abolished the stiff receiving lines at White House soirees, and although some guests bitterly complained that they therefore had no opportunity to greet the President, others were grateful to be spared the dull, hour-long wait in line for a brief handshake.

Whereas the Truman guest lists favored old Senatorial and political pals and the Eisenhower lists read like a Who's Who of Big Business, the Kennedy roster was generously sprinkled with artists, musicians, singers, actors, Harvard professors, and enormously wealthy collectors of rare antiques. Jackie's triumphal tour of Europe inspired other innovations. For the state visit of the President of Pakistan, three yachts equipped with bars and dance orchestras transported guests to Mount Vernon, where they dined on the lawn while the National Symphony Orchestra played background music. On another evening, opera was provided for the President of Peru, and at a state dinner for the President of the Sudan, a program of Shakespearean drama was the *pièce de résistance*.

But the proud marines were doing a slow burn. For the first time in memory, the Kennedys bypassed the famed Marine Dance Band, which had been playing at White House parties since time immemorial, in favor of Lester Lanin's society band from New York. The first occasion was a dance honoring Lee Radziwill, and if Lanin ever writes his memoirs, he can claim credit for introducing the twist to the decorous East Room of the White House. A Marine Band member told me wistfully, "We can play the twist, too, but we would have considered it rather undignified for the White House."

Speaker Sam Rayburn had been seriously ailing since August, and during the Congressional adjournment that fall the Grim Reaper took both "Mr. Democrat" of the House and Styles Bridges, "Mr. Republican" of the Senate. When the new Congress convened in January, 1962, the House elected Majority Leader John W. McCormack Speaker, and the eyes of the nation focused on Massachusetts politics. Everyone knew that McCormack's favorite nephew, Eddie McCormack, and the President's youngest brother, Teddy Kennedy, were planning to run for the Senate seat which JFK had vacated. It was currently being warmed by amiable Benjamin A. Smith II, JFK's former Harvard roommate who had agreed not to run again in return for the favor of the appointment. Thus, most Massachusetts Congressmen began practicing the art of brinkmanship to avoid offending either the powerful new Speaker or the President by taking sides in the Democratic primary. Rose Kennedy was preparing to campaign vigorously for her "baby," and she telephoned me twice from Palm Beach to ask for ideas about what she should say in her speeches.

In January, 1962, I was inaugurated "Fall Gal" of the Circus Saints and Sinners Club, and a thousand roisterous Senators, ambassadors, members, and friends assembled for the dinner and the roasting. In years past, the all-male group had unmercifully roasted such "Fall Guys" as Vice Presidents Barkley and Nixon, Speaker Rayburn, and dozens of other top politicians, but only three women had previously enjoyed the dubious honor of being named "Fall Gal"—Perle Mesta, Gwendolyn Cafritz, and Arlene Francis. It was a hilarious evening! A saucy girl in a skimpy Charleston costume paraded a sign reading, "Ruthie, the worst of Hearst." Famed television raconteur Walter Kiernan came down from New York to recount my biography, and any resemblance between his sidesplitting account and the real life and times of Ruth Montgomery was coincidental.

"There's nothing President Kennedy wouldn't do for Ruth," Kiernan summarized, "and nothing Ruth wouldn't do for him. That's why they're always doing nothing for each other." A girl dressed as Caroline Kennedy asked, "Is a Fall Gal the same as a fallen woman?" Roars of laughter drowned out the reply.

Shortly after resumption of the White House social season in 1962, social secretary Letitia Baldrige and press secretary Pamela Turnure summoned society writers to the White House for a course in how to seem invisible. Tall, sophisticated Tish began with a personal gripe. She had been dying to meet astronaut John Glenn when he came to a White House party but couldn't get within a martini's reach of him because newswomen surrounded him all evening. Tish and Pamela told society writers that they must not monopolize guests, eavesdrop on conversations, or talk to the President. When one news-woman huffily asked what she was supposed to do if President Kennedy came up to talk to her, Tish quipped, "Why don't you get behind a pillar and stay there? Let's face it. The President used to be a newspaperman, so he probably feels more at ease with members of the press than a scientist like Linus Pauling. Nonetheless, these people came to meet the President of the United States, and they want to talk without eavesdropping."

The First Lady also let it be known that she considered a couple of the society reporters repulsive, and that she wanted all female scribes to understand that they were there not as guests, but as work-ing people, even though they had to dress in long evening gowns. This seemed fair enough to me—but of course I was not writing society!

In December, 1962, there was another clash of tempers. Engraved invitations cordially invited newswomen to a White House reception from 12:30 to 2 P.M., and since this was the lunch hour, women re-porters arrived dressed to the teeth for what they assumed to be a luncheon with the First Lady. In the downstairs reception room we were greeted by Tish and Pamela and then taken on a tour of the White House public rooms which we had seen hundreds of times before, while guides delivered the same loquacious lecture that they give to out-of-town tourists. At last we were handed small glasses of wine, and when a newswoman asked when the First Lady would appear, Tish said that she was too busy getting ready to leave the next day for Palm Beach to come downstairs. No food was in evi-dence, and the newswomen irately departed to buy their own lunch at the Press Club.

Madame Perle Mesta was definitely "out" during the Kennedy era because she had supported Nixon's candidacy, but the gregarious Kennedy clan became party givers extraordinary. The Bobby Kennedys gave large dinner parties around their swimming pool and continued to shove fully dressed guests into the water. Jean and Steve Smith thought nothing of inviting sixty to a hundred friends for an evening of dancing by simply calling a caterer to provide the food, orchestra, folding chairs, and liquor. Eunice and Sargent Shriver (he was by now director of the Peace Corps) also entertained frequently at their nearby Maryland estate, but often with more serious overtones than the rest of the clan, since Eunice was doing a great deal of work with handicapped children. Sarge Shriver, a handsome, dynamic man, seemed restive at being overshadowed by the peripatetic family into which he had married, and during one of my frequent interviews with him, he remarked bitingly, "Mine is a much older family than the Kennedys; we could have bought and sold them several times over."

Jacqueline was not one of Eunice's favorite in-laws. On the weekend that Jack and Jackie paid a state visit to Mexico, Bob and I were invited to the Shrivers' for a quiet Sunday luncheon. Eunice and I were sunning ourselves beside the swimming pool, when the radio brought news of the President's warm reception below the Rio Grande, and Eunice exclaimed, "Isn't it wonderful that Brother is getting the attention this time, instead of Jackie. Honestly, when I think how she has never lifted a finger to help Jack politically and then reaped all that attention in Europe!"

Early in 1962 the Kennedy troupe, like the flying Wallendas of Big Top fame, put the show on the road. All except President Kennedy, who stuck to the main ring at the White House. Attorney General and Mrs. Kennedy were playing to packed houses in the Orient, and rave notices began to filter back to the U.S. Ethel introduced a comical act which included a slapstick spill from a sailboat into the Pacific and a novelty act of trying to eat noodles with chopsticks. She also attempted a little speech in Japanese but comically abandoned it, sighing, "Oh, dear!"

Brother Teddy Kennedy, youngest and handsomest of the performing artists, took off for a solo act in Poland, and Jackie Kennedy and her sister Lee finally went to India and Pakistan, where Ambassador Kenneth Galbraith provided the laughs. The longtime family friend barely made it to the Delhi airport in time for the welcoming ceremony, because his young son had been playing in the government limousine and had locked all its doors, with the only set of keys inside. A few days later, when President Kennedy told Jackie by telephone that Caroline had not received any letters from her, Jackie discovered that the mail which she had given Galbraith was still in the absentminded ex-professor's briefcase. Visiting a silk-weaving center, Jackie bought $630 worth of handloomed fabrics but ran short of money and had to borrow from Secret Service agents, because Galbraith had neglected to bring any. In Jaipur she was showered with good-luck rice and lotus blossoms and then was expected to throw a coin from her own country into a silver pot to reciprocate the good wishes. Neither Jackie nor Galbraith had so much as a dime, so she borrowed from touring newsmen.

Before Jacqueline's return home, the Secret Service asked for eighty additional employees and more than a million dollars in extra appropriations, and no one could doubt the reason. Although the White House stressed that Jackie was paying her own expenses, taxpayers had to foot the bill for the dozen or so Secret Service agents who always traveled with her on her adventuresome extravaganzas, paying their airline tickets, hotels, food, ground transportation, and laundry, besides their salaries. Because the Kennedy clan was ceaselessly commuting between the various vacation headquarters in Palm Beach, Middleburg, Hyannisport, and Newport, Secret Service agents were among the government's most overworked employees. In addition, after JFK's multimillionaire father suffered a stroke, Secret Service agents stood guard at both the Palm Beach hospital and his estate.

Jacqueline came home laden with costly gifts from heads of states, including a five-strand pearl necklace studded with diamonds, rubies, and emeralds and a bay gelding named Sardar.

President Kennedy was meanwhile having troubles on his own doorstep, with Canada and Mexico. After Cuba fell to the Communist orbit and we cut off all trade with the island, Canada breezily

stepped up her own Cuban trade a hundred-fold. While the administration was refusing to trade with Red China, Canada shipped it
100,000,000 bushels of wheat and 26,000,000 bushels of barley for cold
cash. When a Foreign Minister's council of the Organization of
American States held a meeting about Communist Cuba, Mexico
joined five other Latin-American nations in refusing to support our
resolution to exclude Cuba from the OAS.

But JFK's Irish wit was still quick and honed. At a press conference on April 2, 1962, I asked him, "If you had it to do over again,
would you work for the Presidency? And can you recommend the
job to others?" JFK flashed a broad grin, and his blue eyes twinkled
as he replied, "The answer to the first is yes, and to the second is no."

CHAPTER XXV

Visions of Camelot

JACQUELINE KENNEDY, in the short space of a year, had become the most written-about, talked-about, photographed woman in America. A picture snapped at the precise moment that she spilled across a split-rail jump fence with the Orange County Hunt showed her floating flawlessly toward earth, sans horse, and when she irately protested to her husband about newspapers printing it, he grinningly informed her that a First Lady landing on her derriere was legitimate news.

President Eisenhower had once flushed with anger when a newsman suggested that he might be planning to use government helicopters to transport him from the White House to nearby Burning Tree Golf Club, but Jackie breezily ordered a government helicopter if she wanted to go fox hunting in Middleburg, Virginia.

When elegantly gowned in shimmering sheaths, her hair piled high in regal Empire fashion, Jackie's photographs made her look as fragile as a Dresden doll. Actually she is large-boned and about as frail as a steel girder. Until she became First Lady, her hair was notoriously ill kempt, and she bit her fingernails to the quick. She wore slacks to the stores in Georgetown but for some reason angrily denied that she had worn them.

It was an open secret that her marriage had not always had smooth sailing. Both Jack and Jackie, accustomed to luxury, were high-spirited, pampered, and determined to have their own way. A cleaning woman who used to serve the households of both Senator Kennedy and Senator Bridges regularly reported to the latter on the marital battles at the Kennedy ménage. Once, she said, Jack and Jackie angrily hurled cups and plates at each other during breakfast, but they managed to weather the storms.

Thirty-year-old Teddy Kennedy, who had never held a salaried job, announced his candidacy for the Senate in the spring of 1962. As expected, Teddy defeated Speaker McCormack's nephew Eddie for the Democratic nomination, and then faced George Lodge, son of Henry Cabot Lodge, Jr., in the general election. Even the news that Teddy had once been kicked out of Harvard for cheating failed to slow his steamroller, and when he inevitably won, Rose Kennedy told me in an interview, "At last we have evened the score with the Lodges!"

As a matter of fact, the score had long since been tallied in favor of the descendants of her father, John Fitzgerald, who had once been defeated for the Senate by the first Henry Cabot Lodge. JFK had captured the Senate seat of Henry Cabot Lodge, Jr., in 1952, and when he went on to win the Presidency, Lodge, Jr., had been Nixon's running mate.

When Teddy Kennedy swore the Senatorial oath in January, 1963, every member of the Kennedy clan except his ailing father gathered in Washington for the event. Addressing the Women's National Press Club Congressional dinner a few days later, he demonstrated that he had his share of the Kennedy's Irish wit by beginning, "Well, now that we are all here..." It brought down the house, as did his subsequent remark that when he dropped by the White House to give the President his ideas for the upcoming State of the Union message, his brother remarked, "Are you still using that greasy-kid stuff on your hair?"

I had long yearned to visit the Holy Land, and late in January I flew there to write a six-part series for the Lenten season. It was a soul-stirring experience, and on my return I brought the Second

Lady a Roman oil lamp dating from the time of Jesus that had been excavated in Jerusalem. Elizabeth Carpenter had asked me to try to find an artifact for Lady Bird Johnson's collection, and when I mentioned her interest in archaeology to the curator of the Jerusalem museum, he gave me the lamp for her.

Restless, gregarious Lyndon Baines Johnson was looming bigger than life on the Washington scene in those days, despite his desperate attempt to stay out of the Kennedy limelight. Shortly after his election to the number two spot, he and Lady Bird had purchased Perle Mesta's luxurious Washington estate, Les Ormes, and prudently renamed it The Elms. In May, 1963, I went there for an exclusive interview with LBJ, and although he was expecting me, he was lounging beside the swimming pool clad only in swim trunks. Since I was fully dressed and the sun was shining mercilessly, it was one of the hottest interviews that I have ever had. It also had one of the funniest aftermaths.

For two hours LBJ freely discussed a wide range of problems, and as we watched the billowing tail of a streaking jet in the blue sky overhead, he philosophized, "How can we be second in space and first on earth? These people who discount the importance of the race to the moon never cease to astound me. Suppose the Russians conquered space first? Suppose they began determining the weather and turning America into an arid plain? Suppose they controlled the world militarily from outer space?" His hypothetical questions about space reminded me of what the political pros had been asking about Lyndon three years earlier, "How can he be second to any man, after being first in the Senate for so many years?"

As Vice President he headed the President's National Aeronautics and Space Council and was number two man on the National Security Council, which was the single most powerful unit of our government, but he knew that Bobby Kennedy did not like him, and he was wary about too much personal publicity. During our interview Lucy came out to the pool to tell him good-bye, before leaving for a weekend at the Annapolis Naval Academy. He ambled over to kiss her, then pulled a large roll of bills from his swim trunk pocket and, peeling off a $50 bill, said, "That lipstick's too dark. Buy yourself a new one."

My lengthy interview with the Vice President received front-page spread throughout the country the next day, and shortly afterward the telephone rang. It was LBJ saying, "Ruth, I'm calling you from my automobile. I just left the White House, where the President had a copy of our interview on his desk, and he said to me, 'I'll bet you've been entertaining Ruth down at the ranch, to get such a good story. She never writes that good a one about me.' I bet him ten dollars that you've never been to the ranch. Have you?"

When I replied that I had not, he chortled, "Well, will you do me a favor? Will you write out a little thing saying you've never been there, and I'll send my driver by your house to pick it up. I sure do want to win that bet with the President, and thanks for the swell write-up." I dutifully wrote out "a little thing," the driver came, and Jack paid Lyndon $10.

I continued to be rather mystified, however, by one aspect of the interview. The only part that LBJ had asked me not to print was the fact that he gave Lucy a $50 bill; yet I was aware of his sometimes lavish generosity. Liz Carpenter, his executive assistant, had told a group of us that when she threatened to resign in order to earn more money in the newspaper business, Lyndon had driven a brand-new car to her house and handed over the keys, saying that it was hers as long as she stayed with him. Liz said that he had given similar new cars to his favorite secretary, Mary Margaret Valenti, and another member of his staff. When Liz and Les Carpenter joined Bob and me on a Sheraton Hotel junket to Venezuela, LBJ impetuously handed Liz a roll of bills, with which she bought herself a gold necklace and some articles of apparel. What was so secret about giving his daughter a large bill?

Not until later, when the Bobby Baker scandal broke on Capitol Hill and some witnesses alluded to the large amounts of cash which LBJ, as well as Baker, carried, did I understand his unusual reticence. By that time LBJ was President, however, and although the Senate committee took hundreds of pages of testimony about Bobby Baker's penchant for accepting Congressional campaign donations in cash while serving as Majority Leader Johnson's right-hand man, it avoided allusions to LBJ's free-spending ways.

In April, 1963, the Palm Beach White House announced that the First Lady was canceling all engagements because of the anticipated birth of a baby in August. By that time, plans for the annual Congressional brunch and the Senate Ladies' luncheon in honor of the President's wife were too far advanced for cancellation, and the parties were held without her. No tempers flared until it was afterward revealed that on the same day that Jackie skipped the Congressional brunch and a White House reception for the military, she was feeling well enough to go shopping in New York City and attend the opera that evening.

The miffed Congressional wives were quick to recall that although Jacqueline had presided at the elegant state dinner for 170 guests honoring the Grand Duchess of Luxembourg, she failed to greet Congressional leaders and their wives who had assembled on the family floor of the White House preceding the reception below. They muttered that since she was only a few doors down the hall, she could at least have paid that much tribute to the men who were struggling with her husband's legislative program on Capitol Hill.

The impending arrival of three new Kennedy babies that summer had slowed Mrs. John F. Kennedy and Mrs. Edward Kennedy to a walk, but the only apparent effect that it had on Mrs. Robert Kennedy was to take her out of the touch-football starting lineup. Ethel was expecting her eighth child in July but was continuing to play tennis every day, and when I asked whether she was still beating Bobby now that she was six months pregnant, she laughingly replied, "He's fantastic. He never gives up. He usually beats me." Then she laughed so uproariously that I asked her who was really winning, and she said, "Listen, I have to live with Bobby. Don't ask me."

Ethel's doctor, like Jackie's, advised his patient to stop going to parties until after her confinement. Ethel pretended to obey but scheduled a staggering list of functions at which she would have to play the much more difficult role of hostess. She gave a picnic at Hickory Hill for 250 Foreign Service children, a lawn party for the

Christ Child Society which included a boat trip down the Potomac, and another party for nearly 300 moppets and parents. Meanwhile, the Kennedys were having a heating unit installed in their swimming pool, and Ethel was busily conferring with architects who were preparing to add four more bedrooms and a huge new drawing room to their house.

Jacqueline, Ethel, and Joan Kennedy spent that summer of 1963 on Cape Cod. Joan by then had miscarried, but the other two were eagerly awaiting the additions to their families. Ethel's eighth child arrived without incident in July, and on August 7 the First Lady gave birth prematurely to a 4-pound 10½-ounce son at Otis Air Force Base Hospital on Cape Cod. President Kennedy, rushing to her bedside, learned that little Patrick Bouvier Kennedy was suffering from a serious respiratory ailment, and although he sped with his little son to another hospital in Boston, doctors could not save his life. The President openly wept, and the nation mourned.

In the fall of 1962, Mrs. Kennedy had inaugurated a kindergarten for Caroline and some of her friends on the top floor of the White House. Now that Caroline was nearly six years old, the Kennedy school was divided into two parts so that Caroline and nine others could attend first-grade classes in a converted third-floor bedroom, while the younger ones continued kindergarten in the solarium. School opened in late September. When Emperor Haile Selassie of Ethiopia was entertained with a state dinner at the White House on October 1, Mrs. Kennedy did not attend. Her press secretary explained that the recuperating First Lady did not feel like sitting through a formal dinner, but the next day she left for Greece by commercial jet, on a ten-hour flight. A few days later, I wrote this column:

> If a picture is worth ten thousand words, it would be interesting to know whether an equal number of votes could be affected by the pathetic picture of little John F. Kennedy, Jr. sobbing bitterly at the airport, as his father waved goodbye. The President was flying to Arkansas to dedicate a dam and mend a few political fences in the Deep South. Little John-John was doubly grief-

stricken, however, because his mother had also departed two days earlier for a yachting vacation in Greece.

Caroline has her schoolmates, who come each day to classes on the White House third floor, but John-John, too young for kindergarten, seemed to think that he had only the panda doll that he clutched to his heaving heart.

The First Lady, checking in at the White House for only a few days after a summer in Hyannisport, where she lost a baby son, and a visit with her mother in Newport, is now holidaying with her brother-in-law and sister, Prince and Princess Stanislaws Radziwill, at a rented villa near Athens. A White House spokesman said that a change of scenery would be good for her.

The high spot of her vacation is the sea-going trip aboard the gleaming white yacht of Greek shipping magnate Aristotle Onassis. The yacht 'Christina' is named for Onassis' ex-wife, whom he discarded in favor of Opera Diva Marie Callas. From all reports, the storied love affair between Callas and Onassis has now cooled by several degrees, but Christina (Tina) Onassis subsequently hit the jackpot by marrying the Marquis of Blandford, son of the Duke of Marlborough, who was considered the top-catch of the international jet set.

The Onassis yacht on which America's First Lady will put to sea is probably the largest privately owned ship afloat. Well over three hundred feet long, it carries its own canary yellow seaplane which merrily flies off to collect fresh caviar and other delicacies for the gay parties on board. A matching yellow speed boat is also on deck. The octagon-shaped dining salon of the vessel boasts priceless art by such French impressionists as Renoir and Manet. The furniture is Louis XVI, and each of the many guest suites features bathroom fixtures and other appointments in rose quartz, jade, amethyst quartz, or gold. There is even a fireplace mantle of lapis lazuli, a rich blue semiprecious jewel. Guests are assigned personal maids and stewards, and need merely press a buzzer to secure pedicures, manicures, massages and hair-setting services.

Sir Winston Churchill, since retiring from his top post as prime minister, has made several trips on the Onassis yacht, but has been subjected to British editorial criticism for accepting the hospitality of the Greek shipping magnate who is also chief owner of the famed Monte Carlo gambling casino. Rumors are current that Onassis is beginning to pull out of Monte Carlo, where his relations with the Prince of Monaco and Princess Grace have been none too warm of late. Some of his freighters and tankers are reportedly now flying the Panamanian flag, and some U.S. officials are concerned that he may be planning to move his gambling operations to the Caribbean area off our Florida coastline.

These same officials are privately questioning the wisdom of our First Lady putting herself under obligation to the fabulously wealthy but somewhat mysterious Onassis.

CHAPTER XXVI

Three Shots Heard Round the World

POLITICS was bustin' out all over in the summer and fall of 1963. John F. Kennedy had regained much of his international stature through his adroit handling of the Cuban missiles crisis the previous October, and although Congress was still turning its back on much of his New Frontier legislation, everyone knew that he would again be the Democratic standard-bearer the following year. Richard M. Nixon, who had built a "dream house" for his family in California and then suffered bitter defeat in his campaign for the governorship of the Golden State, had by now moved to New York, where he joined a prestigious law firm, but was keeping his national fences mended.

The right wing of the Republican Party, patently unhappy at the thought of Nixon as the GOP standard-bearer in 1964, was rallying around attractive, conservative Barry Goldwater, and when the Arizona Senator addressed a $1,000-a-plate campaign dinner in Washington, Nixon, Nelson Rockefeller, former President Eisenhower, and Governor William Scranton of Pennsylvania sent their regrets. Only Michigan Governor George Romney shared the speakers' platform with him.

Goldwater-for-President headquarters opened unofficially in Washington the day that President Kennedy returned from a political swing through five Western states, and when I interviewed Barry, he said, "I've made up my mind on one thing. If I do decide to seek the Republican nomination, I will not run simultaneously for reelection to the Senate. I could, but I won't." This was a crack at LBJ, who had run so scared for Vice President in 1960 that he cautiously ran for reelection to the Senate from Texas as well.

Barry and JFK, poles apart in their political thinking, frankly liked each other, even as they kidded and teased. A picture of President Kennedy, snapped two years earlier by Barry Goldwater and hung on his Senate office wall, was autographed "For Barry Goldwater, whom I urge to follow the career for which he has shown much talent—photography. From his friend, Jack Kennedy." They had even shared the same doctor for their ailing backs, Dr. Janet Travell, and Barry grinningly remarked that Janet was one holdover that he would retain if he moved to the White House.

President Kennedy was beset by problems on both the domestic and the international fronts. On August 28, 1963, civil rights advocates led several hundred thousand blacks in a March on Washington, which with its massive numbers turned out to be both impressive and peaceful. In South Vietnam several Buddhist monks were committing self-immolation as a protest against that government's alleged persecution of Buddhists, and tart-tongued Madame Ngo Dinh Nhu horrified the world by referring to the fiery suicides as "a monk barbecue show."

The beautiful Madame Nhu was a Catholic, as were her influential husband and his bachelor brother, President Ngo Dinh Diem, but she had earned the nickname "dragon lady" by spearheading anti-Buddhist demonstrations. The Kennedy administration was not amused by her antics, since we were helping finance South Vietnam's war efforts against the Communist Vietcong, and neither were her parents. Her Confucian father, Dr. Tran Van Chuong, was South Vietnam's ambassador to the United States and her mother, a devout Buddhist, was that country's permanent observer at the United Nations.

In late August both resigned their posts in protest against the policies of their daughter's family, and when Madame Nhu announced that she was flying to Washington on October 7, both her parents and the Kennedy administration pulled in the welcome mats. I had an exclusive interview with her father, who told me, "No, no.

We will not receive her, because of what she and her husband's family have done to our country. They have lost all touch with reality."

A State Department official said that neither President Kennedy nor Secretary Dean Rusk would see her, even if she requested a meeting. She had scornfully labeled U.S. military officers, who were trying to save her country from Communist seizure, "little soldiers of fortune," and when she addressed the Women's National Press Club October 16, she said that the Kennedy administration was "not red but pink." Looking deceptively demure in an unadorned sapphire-blue brocade gown, Madame Nhu blasted the administration for cutting off economic aid to South Vietnam. Asked for her opinion of Henry Cabot Lodge, Jr., whom Kennedy had recently sent as our ambassador to South Vietnam, she snapped, "I have not met him yet, but he is becoming more mysterious than an Asian."

During that tempestuous visit, Madame Nhu and her exquisite seventeen-year-old daughter, Le Thuy, came to tea with Marguerite Higgins and me, and during our two-hour chat her quicksilver moods ran the gamut from fiery anger to little-girl hurt. Her anger was reserved for the Kennedy administration, which had publicly snubbed the First Lady of an allied nation who was also a member of its Parliament. Her hurt stemmed from the equal snubbing administered by her father and mother.

Marguerite and I gently tried to point out to her the mistakes that she had been making. We suggested milder synonyms for such inflammatory words as "liar" and "coward," which she so freely hurled at U.S. officials, and we urged her to express more appreciation for the million and a half dollars a day that Americans were pouring into Vietnam's war effort, but she could not really grasp the point. Her daughter said, "I agree with you," but Madame Nhu proudly retorted, "They would think I am begging. Why should I beg?"

"I telephoned my husband last night," she continued, "and told him—let's break off diplomatic relations with America and just take their military aid."

Trying to smother our laughter at the naïveté of her remark, I asked for her husband's reaction to the suggestion, and she pouted, "He didn't answer me."

And what of her charges that our Central Intelligence Agency had tried to promote a *coup d'état* against President Diem? An arrogant smile flitted across her scarlet lips and her eyes burned fire as she replied, "It is true, but they were wasting their time. After all, my husband has the youth with him, and I have the women. How could a *coup* accomplish anything?"

Madame Nhu continued her cross-country speaking tour, and nine days after our chat over the teacups, the event that she had termed "impossible" occurred. A *coup d'état* masterminded by three Vietnamese generals began shortly after noon on November 1. During the night President Diem and Police Chief Ngo Dinh Nhu, the "dragon lady's" husband, escaped from the palace. Early the next morning they took communion at a Catholic church in the suburbs, and there they met death. The new provisional government termed it "accidental suicide" in a struggle over a gun, but others said that they were shot to death. The White House and State Department denied reports that Americans were behind the plot, but neither Madame Nhu nor a lot of other people believed the denials. Six days later we recognized the new regime, and the war continued.

President Kennedy was considering selling some of our surplus wheat to Soviet Russia, which had had another bad crop year, but because the Kremlin was obviously stirring the bitter caldrons in Cuba and Vietnam, many members of both political parties were opposed to helping Russia "pull their fat out of the fire."

In whimsical vein I wrote a parody on the Biblical famine, which was widely reproduced in newspapers throughout the country:

> And there was a famine in the land. And Patriarch Nikita Khrushchev, who was not a God-fearing man, looked around for a way to save himself and his Communist clan. Now when Nikita saw that there was wheat in America, he said unto Gromyko, "Some Capitalist dreamer has been storing up surpluses against the lean years, which are now upon us. Get you down thither, and buy for us from thence, that we may live and not die."
>
> And Gromyko said unto the Patriarch, "But what if our

brothers the Americans remember that you said you would bury them?"

Khrushchev spake harshly, saying he had already sold some of his favorite comrades into Siberian bondage for less back-talk than that, and for Gromyko to hurry and get himself thither without further gabbing. The Patriarch then loaded Gromyko's sacks with gold, so that he could bring back that which the Communist system had failed to produce. And Gromyko took some of his comrades and went to the land of plenty, and the governor over all the land was John, the many-coated son of Joseph P.

Now this was the same young man to whom Gromyko had sold a bill of goods exactly one year previously, by claiming that Patriarch Nikita was putting only defensive weapons and agrarian reformers in Cuba. But lo, even as Gromyko spake thus, aerial spies dispatched by John, the son of Joseph P., were spotting missile installations in the island to the southward.

Now Gromyko pondered on these things as he went hat in hand to Governor John, but he did not bow down before him with his face to the earth. After all, his bags were loaded with gold which the Communist Patriarch had given him to buy capitalist friendship and grain. But John, remembering the former treachery, said unto Gromyko, "Whence come ye? Ye are spies, to see the nakedness of the land ye are come."

Gromyko, maintaining an unbowed head and straight face, replied, "Nay, my Lord, but to buy food are thy servants come. We are true men; thy servants are no spies."

Now John, the son of Joseph P., was a very understanding sort who realized that Patriarch Nikita did not really want to bury us, but merely to wipe us off the face of the earth. This wise young Governor also knew that his own people were becoming restive because they had too much to eat, and were tired of storing so much plenty against a rainy day.

John therefore assembled his advisors, and although some spake in favor of punishing the Communist comrades for their previous treachery, most of them were dazzled by the exotic foreign gold. The wise young Governor at first thought of detaining one of the comrades as a hostage, but realizing that one more defector would make little difference in a thousand years, he commanded his officials to fill the Communist sacks with grain, and to restore every man's money into his sack.

And they loaded their asses with the grain, and departed thence. And one of them, opening his sack to feed his ass, espied his money and said unto his brethren, "My money is restored, and lo, it is even in my sack."

And their hearts nearly failed them, but when they returned to Patriarch Nikita and told him what had happened he comforted them, saying, "Have no fear, my comrades. This is the way the capitalist Americans do business. They subsidize their farmers to grow far more grain than they can use; then they taketh up taxes to pay for storing it; and when the time is ripe and we hunger, they sell it to us at half the market price, which they call the world price."

Gromyko beamed and said, "Good father, then you mean they meant to put our money as well as the grain in our sacks?"

"Aye, even so," Nikita replied. "At this price there is no further point in our trying to grow grain at home. We will hereafter use our farmers to produce missiles, and we will feed ourselves with subsidized American produce. Prepare to return ye, then, to the land of plenty to buy also cotton, milk, butter and feed grains."

And it came to pass that a lively trade developed, and many many moons elapsed before the American taxpayers finally realized they were supporting the Communist economy.

Lady Bird Johnson was meanwhile off and running to help reelect the Kennedy-Johnson ticket the following year, although it was an open secret that Bobby Kennedy wanted LBJ dumped in 1964. Even before New York Governor Nelson Rockefeller tossed his hat in the Republican ring, Mrs. Johnson hit the whistle-stops of three New England states. She returned home only long enough to repack her suitcases and give a dinner party for Lucy, before flying to California for two days of Democratic women's rallies. Returning for three days, she attended State Department briefings on the European Common Market and departed with LBJ for a week in the Benelux countries. Her first act on returning home was to entertain twenty-five wives of Cabinet officers and other high officials, to map female strategy for JFK's reelection campaign.

Because of Jacqueline Kennedy's obvious distaste for politics, Lady Bird had been dubbed the administration's number one pinch hitter. Not only was she campaigning in Jackie's stead, but she had frequently substituted for her at White House functions and ladies' luncheons which were traditionally attended by the First Lady. Interviewing Lady Bird in mid-November, I asked how she managed to keep up her own household duties, and she mused, "Every time I get back to the ranch I sort of sigh at the way the closets are, but when there's a two weeks' lull in the summer I try to get caught up on things and see that the peach preserves get put up." During the previous two years she and LBJ had traveled 120,000 miles to thirty foreign countries on official duties, and she had crisscrossed America innumerable times in quest of votes for the Democratic ticket.

Lady Bird was full of plans for playing host to President and Mrs. Kennedy during the Texas swing that the two top-ranking families would make together to mend political fences. She was happy that this would be the fourth time that a head of state had partaken of Johnson hospitality—the Kennedys were to spend the night of November 22 at the ranch—and she had even managed for her favorite walking horse, who was undergoing training in Tennessee, to be returned so that Jacqueline could ride her.

The First Lady had just returned from her vacation aboard the Onassis yacht in Greece and to everyone's surprise had agreed to accompany her husband on the political swing through Texas. The trip was being billed as "nonpolitical," so that taxpayers rather than the Democratic National Committee would pick up the expense tab, although it included a $100-a-plate Democratic dinner in Austin, a Houston dinner to spark the reelection campaign of Democratic Congressman Albert Thomas, and several receptions, airport rallies, street parades, and luncheons.

On November 20, 1963, President and Mrs. Kennedy held the annual judicial reception in honor of members of the Supreme Court and officials of the Justice Department at the White House. Six hundred of the nation's leading federal jurists and attorneys went to the cocktail party, which was Mrs. Kennedy's first official appearance since the death of her premature baby and her vacation in Greece. She was radiantly beautiful in a raspberry velvet suit, as she descended the staircase with her husband to the stirring strains of "Hail to the Chief." President Kennedy plunged zestfully into the assembled crowd, shaking hands and circulating through the state rooms, with Jackie following close behind. Because it was Attorney General Robert F. Kennedy's birthday, he and Ethel left shortly for a celebration at home, and JFK and Jacqueline remained only twenty-two minutes, before slipping upstairs to prepare for their Texas trip the following morning.

Two days later I was writing a column at my desk in Washington when the telephone rang. It was Milton Kaplan, Washington bureau chief for Hearst newspapers, calling to say that President Kennedy had been shot in Dallas. No one yet knew whether it was serious, but would I come at once to the office? Grabbing a transistor radio, I hailed a taxi and sped to the Pennsylvania Building. I rode in a state of shock.

Even before we knew the final verdict, I was pounding away at my typewriter. As the only member of the Washington bureau who personally knew the Johnsons, I had been directed to begin writing immediately a comprehensive series of articles about the man who would shortly be the next President of the United States. While I numbly filled the pages with a complete chronicle of the life and times of Lyndon Baines Johnson, he was swearing the Presidential oath inside the Presidential jet on a runway at Love Field in Dallas.

While heads of state flew to Washington from all parts of the world, the body of President Kennedy lay in state at the White House, and with other members of the White House press corps I was invited to pay last respects to my longtime friend beside his flag-draped casket in the East Room, where I had covered President Roosevelt's funeral eighteen years before.

The Kennedy era with its brilliant eclat, verve, and high style had come to a tragic close. Only historians of the future, viewing it with the detachment of time, will be able to appraise its accomplishments.

We are too close to it, too emotionally involved. Glamorous, youthful, witty Jack Kennedy had passed from our mortal stage, soon to become a legendary folk hero in much the same mold as King Arthur and his Knights of Camelot, to which the Kennedy White House had often been compared.

It is, of course, impossible to know whether America and the world would have been better off had Jack Kennedy lived, but since death must come to all men, it is probable that some of our past Presidents would have been willing to exchange a lackluster old age for the hero's mold into which John Fitzgerald Kennedy was cast by his senseless murder. Ecclesiastes tells us, "To every thing there is a season, and a time to every purpose under the heaven: A time to be born, and a time to die ..."

Would Abraham Lincoln be so highly revered after a hundred years if he had been forced to deal with the heartbreaking problems of reconstruction in the South? Would not Woodrow Wilson have been a greater hero if he had died during his period of greatest triumph after forging the League of Nations, instead of losing that battle with Congress and suffering a debilitating stroke which affected his capacity to function? What if Herbert Hoover had met the Grim Reaper while America was enjoying unprecedented prosperity, instead of becoming the despised symbol of the Great Depression?

And what of Jacqueline Kennedy? She had captured the fancy of America with her sophistication and high style, her highly successful transformation of the White House, and her beauty. But judging by my mail from readers, her popularity was beginning to ebb, and many letters sharply criticized her long absences from the White House and her wifely duties. Had she still been skiing off the Onassis yacht in Greek waters when a murderer struck down her lonely husband, she might have been one of the most vilified women in American history. Instead, she had returned in time to accompany her husband for the first time in years on a political trip. Thus she was at his side when the tragedy befell, and by her magnificent calm she gave courage to a stricken nation. Jacqueline Kennedy was already heading the list of the Ten Best-Dressed Women. Now she also led the polls as the World's Most Admired Woman.

Jack Kennedy himself had recognized the difficulties of becoming an ex-President, when at his forty-fourth birthday celebration he lightheartedly quipped that after eight years in the White House he would be "too young to write my memoirs and too old to start a new career." Now he would never have to undergo the frustrations of being a has-been or the debilitating ailments of old age. His youthful vibrance was forever stamped on our hearts.

CHAPTER XXVII

The Great Society

IMMEDIATELY after the Kennedy assassination, a publisher telephoned to ask if I would write a book about the new First Lady. Thus, while busily turning out daily columns concerning the shift of power, I also began work on a book entitled *Mrs. LBJ,* which was completed in six weeks. The Johnsons had no sooner moved into the White House, with Caroline Kennedy's classroom still continuing on the third floor, than I went there to interview Lady Bird Johnson, and as she was recounting the chilling events which transpired that dreadful day in Dallas, she became so choked with emotion that she briefly left the room to regain control.

She told me how Secret Service Agent Rufus Youngblood, as the first shot rang out, vaulted over the front seat of their car to cover the Vice President with his body, while shouting to Lady Bird and Senator Ralph Yarborough to "get down." Since the huge bodies of Youngblood and Johnson were occupying the available space in the bottom of the car, all that she and the Senator could do was stoop their heads.

She recounted that emotional wait at Parkland Memorial Hospital while doctors fought vainly to save the life of the stricken President and the shock that she underwent when someone came into their heavily guarded waiting room and addressed LBJ as "Mr. President." Then, trying to recapture her feelings as she stood beside her rangy husband in the Presidential plane while he swore the time-hallowed oath, she said, "I felt that I was stalking across the stage in a Greek tragedy, just putting one foot before the other. There was a sense of unreality and nightmare and great tragedy. Yet there was also a sense of wanting to take in, and remember everything that was going on. It was a state of intense aliveness, yet of intense cessation of the normal processes. I only remember an infinite compassion for Lyndon, that's all. Then I sat down, and each person was wrapped in his own thoughts. I think someone served us hot bouillon, or perhaps it was coffee, and the plane was off the ground within seven minutes after the swearing-in." A new chapter in the life of Claudia "Lady Bird" Taylor Johnson had begun.

To round out the book *Mrs. LBJ*, I also had an exclusive interview with President Johnson in his White House Oval Office. The winter twilight had faded into dusk as I approached the White House at the appointed hour. The bumper-to-bumper rush-hour traffic had completed its homeward crawl, but the big man in "the world's loneliest job" was still struggling with affairs of state, as he had been since he swung his long legs out of bed at 6:30 that morning. Not until 3 P.M. had he found time for a midday snack.

Violence was flaring in Panama, and he had decided to dispatch a blue-ribbon group of Latin American experts to the trouble spot. Consequently, I waited nearly an hour before the scheduled appointment, during which time Attorney General Robert Kennedy, who had tried to reach me at home to give me a column tip, telephoned the White House. I talked to him from the Cabinet room, and fervently hoped that President Johnson would not hear about it.

It was nearly 7 P.M. when President Johnson strode out of his office, laid a friendly arm across my shoulders, and escorted me inside. Disregarding his own stresses, he profusely apologized for the delay and offered me coffee or an orange soda. A white-coated attendant served the beverages, and while LBJ's personal photographer snapped numerous pictures of us, the interview proceeded.

The President, seated in a specially made rocker which was nearly a duplicate of the one Dr. Janet Travell had also prescribed for President Kennedy, said of his wife, "No one has ever had to carry a load for her in her life. She has just never stepped in the mud and had to be lifted out. She is one of the best planners, best organizers, and best directors ever born. She's one of the few people who never feels sorry for herself. No matter how complicated things get, she never feels that she's being imposed upon. She never loses her dignity. She's a lady. You can't get an argument out of her, because she's above it all."

The tall Texan took a sip of orange soda, and continued, "As a companion she has no equal. She's soft and kind and understanding. She's always willing to meet you more than halfway. She's wonderful with our children. I've never heard her correct either of them." One of LBJ's many telephones rang, and after talking briefly with a Cabinet officer, he neatly picked up the thread of conversation, saying, "Lady Bird is the soul of efficiency. When she comes in to see me, she has maybe five things jotted down, which she presents in logical and orderly fashion. She is very executive in her approach to problems. She always puts others' interests above her own. For instance, our first house guests at the White House are not rich people, and they're not Bird's relatives. They're my eighty-one-year-old uncle, Huffman Baines, and his wife, and my mother's only sister, Josefa Saunders.

"As a companion Lady Bird is the best, and as a housekeeper she's perfection. She runs a house just like she would a well-managed hotel. Your clothes are always in place. As a mother ... well, in my opinion no mother in the world could do a better job than she does of managing her children. She's the most generous person in the world, yet she never makes anyone feel indebted to her. She's totally adaptable. She is equally as comfortable with President Charles de Gaulle of France as with a visitor from Texas. She's a woman of great depth and excellent judgment."

The interview lasted well past the dinner hour, but the President never once glanced at the clock. He seemed totally relaxed, even while he occasionally took telephone calls. When I arose to leave, he walked along, steering me to his Texas-sized desk where he showed me a number of new photographs of himself. Studying one, in which his rangy figure was silhouetted at twilight against the white colonnade of the walkway to the Executive Mansion, he said with a deprecatory smile, "The loneliest man in the world."

He didn't believe it, and neither did I, for this many-faceted man had never permitted himself to be alone. He seemed to have a compulsion for surrounding himself with people, and even on the first night of his Presidency, on returning from Dallas, he had insisted that an aide talk to him in his bedroom until he fell asleep.

The day after my interview a White House car delivered an enormous brown envelope to me. It contained a number of beautifully mounted photographs taken of the two of us during our animated conversation, and each was autographed by the President with such flattering lines as "Much love to Ruth, from Lyndon" and "With deep affection." My favorite one was signed "To Bob Montgomery's terrific wife, Ruth, with high regards, Lyndon B. Johnson."

Lyndon Baines Johnson is many men, and his indulgent wife has learned to live with all of them. A highly complex individual, he soars to the heights one moment and plunges to the depths of gloom the next. He is a hard taskmaster, and his highly volatile nature seeks the nearest scapegoat when things go awry, yet he never forgets a kindness, and he is a warmhearted husband, father, and friend. He is thin-skinned to a fault, and he can be arrogant and overbearing, but he proved that he is a master of self-discipline during those trying years of his Vice Presidency. Impulsive and quick-tempered? Yes. But also compassionate and forgiving.

Lyndon Johnson seized the reins of power as if he had been born to the Presidency. Congressmen who had been dragging their feet over the "must" legislation of the New Frontier now set to work in earnest, and the "can-do" new President was holding them in continuous session until Christmas Eve to pass the foreign aid appropriations bill.

As Christmas approached, the black crepe in which the White House had been draped since the assassination came down, and Yuletide decorations went up in its place. A Christmas tree glittering with crystal snowflakes and myriad lights now graced the oval Blue Room, and one noon President Johnson decided that he wanted to invite every Senator and Representative to the White House that afternoon. With no time for telephoning, the invitation was publicly announced in both houses of Congress, while Lady Bird and her staff frantically set to work directing the setting up of two eggnog bars in the East Room and State Dining Room, complete with fruitcake and coffee. A member of the White House staff called to say that I was also invited, and as dusk fell, we braved a six-inch snowstorm to make our way to the White House during rush hour.

The President and Mrs. Johnson stood in the Blue Room to receive their guests, many of whom were given double-arm grips and back-slaps by the President. Four reporters still remained when the last guests had departed, and LBJ zestfully led them on a tour of the swimming pool and his executive offices. Three years earlier, Lady Bird had sagely observed that "Lyndon's temperament is not exactly suited to being the number two man." Now he was number one and obviously relishing every moment of it.

The old "Lyndon magic" was still at work, and, after his spur-of-the-moment party, the House of Representatives met at the unprecedented hour of 7 A.M. and passed the foreign aid bill. It was Christmas Eve, and after the Johnsons first went to Philadelphia for the funeral of Representative William J. Green, Jr., they flew on to Austin to call on Governor John Connally, who was recuperating from the bullet wound which he had sustained at the time of President Kennedy's assassination. Pushing on to the LBJ ranch, the Johnsons played host to twenty-seven assorted relatives who lounged around the living room, while LBJ insisted on escorting the accompanying press reporters through the ranch house.

Never in my life have I worked as strenuously as during those first few months of the Johnson administration. The day of the tragedy I wrote at my typewriter until long after midnight, completing the first two installments of a six-part series about the new President, which were released for immediate publication. The next day I appeared on an hour-long television panel program about Kennedy and Johnson, went to the White House to pay my respects at JFK's bier, and continued to write day and night until I finished the series on November 26. The next day, I covered the new President's address before a joint session of Congress and began simultaneously to write an article for *Good Housekeeping* magazine and the book, both about

Lady Bird Johnson. On Thanksgiving we went to the Bill Mac-Crackens' only long enough to dine, after which I returned to my desk. As soon as each daily column was completed, I would insert another piece of paper in the typewriter and begin to pour out tens of thousands of words about Lady Bird. During this period, I also interviewed countless friends and relatives of the Johnsons for the book, and Bob and I gave a large party in honor of our good friend Liz Carpenter, who had been named press secretary to Mrs. Johnson.

Thanks to the frenzied typing, one shoulder became locked with bursitis, so that I could scarcely lift my left hand from the typewriter keys; but with their usual thoughtfulness, Liz and the Johnsons arranged for Dr. Travell, who had remained on at the White House, to resume her treatments of me. Miracle woman that she is, my arm was soon restored to complete usefulness.

I had barely completed *Mrs. LBJ* in January when the executive editor of Bantam Books flew to Washington to persuade me to write a book about Jeane Dixon, whose timely forecast of President Kennedy's assassination had won national headlines. Exhausted from the ordeal of the preceding months, I demurred, but neither Jeane nor the editor would take no for an answer. Mrs. Dixon had been insisting that I write a book about her since 1960, when I wrote *Once There Was a Nun,* the story of Mary McCarran, daughter of Senator Pat McCarran, who had been a nun for thirty-two years until after her father's death, when she left the convent to take care of her widowed mother and invalid sister.

Moved by Jeane's insistence, I finally agreed to write a book about her and give her half the money from it, on condition that Bantam would arrange with another publisher to bring it out first in hard cover. The stipulation was accepted, and I resumed my round-the-clock pace with interviews and research on Jeane's predictions. The manuscript for *A Gift of Prophecy* was nearly completed when Bantam changed executive editors, and the new one insisted on deleting most of my references to Jeane Dixon's many wrong predictions, leaving in mainly those on which she had hit correctly. I was too tired to put up a proper argument, but after *A Gift of Prophecy* became one of the most sensational best sellers of the decade, I wished that I had more firmly stood my ground.

President Johnson, on assuming office, had invited all members of the Kennedy Cabinet and White House staff to remain. Most of the Cabinet officers did so, even including Attorney General Robert Kennedy, who bitterly resented LBJ in his brother's vacated seat of power. But the White House staffers began gradually to fade away, and the Texas drawl soon replaced the Boston twang in the executive wing. Walter Jenkins, LBJ's right-hand man since Congressional days, took over as the President's top aide, although the man most often at the Presidential elbow was Jack Valenti, the forty-two-year-old Houston advertising executive who had married the President's favorite secretary. Jack suddenly found himself working day and night for the new prexy even before he went on the payroll. Vice President Johnson, during the ill-fated November trip to Texas, had asked Valenti to ride with him to Dallas, and after the tragedy there he flew back with the Johnsons to Washington, where he remained. For the first several weeks, with no place to hang his hat, he stood on call outside the Presidential office, and he made himself so indispensable that he soon had an office and secretary next door to Jenkins. The Valentis' first child, a daughter, was naturally named Lynda in honor of Lyndon, and Jack now became the first man to see the President in the morning and the last one at night, in his bedroom.

The old political maestro was meanwhile touching all bases, with a something-for-everyone bag of goodies. Texans who had been threatening to walk out on another Kennedy-Johnson ticket were now delighted that LBJ staged his first international huddle in the Lone Star State. Texas liberals were pleased that he took time out to call on Senator Yarborough while in Austin, and Kennedy fans nodded approvingly because he frequently telephoned Jacqueline and put Air Force jets and White House limousines at her disposal. They also took notice when LBJ dispatched a Kennedy brother-in-law, Sargent Shriver, with a personal message to Pope Paul VI while His Holiness was touring the Holy Land. German-Americans were gratified that LBJ gave such a folksy welcome to Chancellor Ludwig

Erhard, and Italian-Americans were happy with his warm reception of President Antonio Segni.

Johnson began consulting former President Eisenhower solicitously, to the delight of Republicans, and economy-minded Americans chuckled with pleasure when he began turning off the lights in the White House to save money. This peculiar economy drive became such a fetish with the new President that whenever he walked into the outer offices, he even switched off the only light in the ladies' restroom, but newswoman May Craig always turned it on again when he disappeared around the corner.

LBJ's "loneliest job in the world" was turning out to be quite a sociable one. The gregarious President surrounded himself with yes-men and even took to dropping in uninvited at feminine cocktail parties and private luncheons when he learned that Lady Bird or some member of his staff was going there. On weekends he took houseguests along to Camp David. He began attending the weddings of the daughters of old friends and even visiting newspaper friends unannounced. If Lady Bird was entertaining women at the White House, it was a sure bet that LBJ would crash the party.

Every time that I wrote a column which pleased President Johnson, he would not only telephone or write a thank-you note to me, but also write to Richard E. Berlin, president of Hearst Publications, to tell him what a "wonderful job Ruth is doing." I feel sure that he must have been flattering and wooing other news writers with equal zest, and no one can deny that it is effective public relations.

Seldom have so many parties been given at the White House, and whereas previous Presidents habitually disappeared into the elevator after the program ended, leaving guests to their own amusement, LBJ would lead the dancing in the East ballroom, often until 2 A.M. Bob and I were formally invited to the Johnsons' first state dinner for royalty, honoring King Hussein of Jordan, and it was a gay, mad night to remember. A jazz buff, the twenty-eight-year-old king sat through a red-hot musical by the Dave Brubeck Quartet, which was so lively that it set the crystal chandeliers tinkling in the East Room. Afterward he glided onto the polished floors of the Blue Room with

Lady Bird Johnson, who is only of medium height but towered above the diminutive monarch.

We female guests were instructed that by protocol a king does not ask a woman to dance. She must invite him, but practically the only one who mustered enough nerve to do so was Trude Feldman, who barely topped five feet and must have made King Hussein feel like a tall Texan by comparison. What His Majesty did not realize was that Trude, who had not been invited to dinner but merely came in afterward as a member of the covering press, is the daughter of Rabbi Moses J. Feldman, ranking member of the Orthodox Jewish community in Los Angeles. Her three brothers and a brother-in-law were also rabbis, and she wrote a column for the weekly Jewish press and the *Jewish World* magazine. The purpose of the king's visit to America was to seek support for blocking neighboring Israel from diverting water from the Jordan River, but he had a daughter of Israel in his arms.

President Johnson had recently received unfavorable publicity for driving eighty miles an hour on the roads near his LBJ ranch while sipping a mug of beer. He asked me to dance, and while we were performing a fox-trot, I pleaded with him to slow down his driving for the sake of the country, if not for himself. Beaming down at me from his great height, he scoffed, "Ruth, I'm a very maligned man. I never drive faster than sixty miles an hour." Both of us knew this to be untrue, but who can argue with the President when she is dancing in his arms at the White House?

One of my two dinner partners that evening was AFL-CIO labor leader George Meany, who was laughing heartily at the predicament of railroad management during the impending strike. When I asked what his own solution would be for the featherbedding problem that was giving management its chief headache, he banged his fist on the table and narrowly missed being speared by a bouncing gold fork, as he bellowed, "If I'd known you were going to use that word 'featherbedding,' I would never have talked to you." Boss Meany continued to talk to me, however, right through the strawberries Romanoff, and two days later he gave me a newsworthy private interview about the strike.

The day after the state dinner I went to a party hosted by King Hussein, and when President Johnson arrived, he clutched His Majesty by the arm and led him through the cocktail-imbibing crowd. He insisted on reintroducing me to the king, saying to him, "Ruth is one of our finest writers in America." To me he said, "Ruth, I want you at my press conference tomorrow. You girls ask the best questions." Another day, striding along the White House corridor with a group of advisers, LBJ saw me emerging from Dr. Travell's office and enveloped me in a bear hug, saying, "Ruth is my favorite newspaperwoman." Dr. Travell, smiling at my embarrassment, replied approvingly, "She's one of my favorites, too."

Mrs. LBJ hit the bookstands in April, setting some kind of speed record in publishing history, and the reviews warmed my heart. Houston *Post* publisher Oveta Culp Hobby, whom I had known when she headed the WAC and later the Department of Health, Education, and Welfare, wrote a two-page review which headed the Chicago *Tribune* book section, and she not only praised the book, but also the author as a newspaperwoman.

Radio commentator Patty Cavin gave a gay party in my honor, with a *This Is Your Life* motif, and in New York I starred on a *To Tell the Truth* television program. Lady Bird Johnson, for the foreword of my book, wrote:

> My admiration for the reporter who goes her daily rounds to cover the news is excelled only by my esteem for one who also has the discipline, energy, and talent to write a book. Such is the gift of Ruth Montgomery whose by-line I have long admired and whose friendship I have long appreciated. It is a new experience to be the subject of a book. The opportunity to write an introduction to one's own biography is an even more novel courtesy. I confess, however, that the experiment has been painless and that these pages have jogged recollections both poignant and pleasant. I hope those who read it will enjoy reading it as much as I enjoyed living it.

On May 2, 1964, I flew to Los Angeles and boarded a Pan American jet for the inauguration of nonstop service to Tahiti, where I spent an idyllic week before stopping for several more days in Hawaii at the new Kahala Hilton, en route back to the mainland. The next day in Chicago I appeared on the Don McNeil *Breakfast Club* radio program and Kup's TV show, before addressing the Book and Authors luncheon of the Chicago *Sun-Times*.

Scores of newspapers were serializing my book, and I also made trips to Cleveland to speak at the Book and Authors luncheon of the Cleveland *Press,* to Philadelphia for the *Inquirer*'s author luncheon, and to Cincinnati for the annual Matrix Table of Theta Sigma Phi. Every day during the next few weeks I was on TV shows and the autograph party circuit, including beautiful Deena Clark's NBC show, while continuing to write my daily columns and work on the book about Jeane Dixon. Patricia and Turner Bailey gave a party in honor of my book about Mrs. Johnson. And Bob and I went to Sargent Shriver's luncheon for the Prime Minister of Denmark and to Irish President Eamon de Valera's party for President Johnson.

Bobby Kennedy's world seemed to collapse for a time after the tragedy which ended his brother's life. He seemed listless and remote. No one could penetrate his aura of gloom until a little boy, with the thoughtlessness of children, said to him, "Hey, mister, your brother got shot."

"It's all right; I have another brother," Bobby responded quietly, and from then on he began to emerge from his cocoon.

On February 4, 1964, I had an exclusive interview with Bobby Kennedy, who was hoping to be selected as President Johnson's running mate despite their mutual animosity. New lines etched his sharply chiseled face, and he seemed deeply sobered by the tragedies which stalked his close-knit family. He was in shirt sleeves in his big Justice Department office, the walls of which were lined with childish pictures painted by his youngsters. A new baby had just been added to Bobby and Ethel's brood.

I reminded the Attorney General that several years previously, when Jack Kennedy was still a Senator, he had said that if anything happened to him Bobby would run for his Senate seat and that if something happened to Bobby, Teddy would take over. Was it logical to assume, I asked, that Bobby would now seek the Vice Presidential nomination as Jack had done in 1956?

Without a moment's hesitation, Bobby replied, "I still would be following in his footsteps if I ran for office in Massachusetts." Inasmuch as Teddy was then occupying Jack's former Senate seat, I asked if he was thinking of the governorship in 1966. "I could run in Massachusetts," he said thoughtfully, "and there's another thing I could do. I'm also thinking of leaving government for a time after the fall campaign, to teach and do some traveling with my children. It would be a different kind of life." His voice trailed off, and a bleak look clouded his eyes. During our conversation, he made it so plain that he would like to be President or Vice President that I asked if he was thinking of running, but he avoided a direct answer by replying, "Lyndon will be elected in '64 and running again in '68." Obviously he had not yet thought of switching states and declaring for Senator from New York.

The Bobby Baker case had been shaping up for some time into a hot political issue. The onetime impoverished page boy had become a millionaire during the years that he served on the Senate payroll as Senate Majority Leader Lyndon B. Johnson's right-hand man. Forced to resign in the face of conflict-of-interest charges, he took the Fifth Amendment rather than answer questioning from a Senate committee, and the Democratic-controlled committee obligingly swept the investigation under the rug. A Justice Department case against Baker could not be so lightly dismissed and was due for trial in the summer of 1964, but was conveniently postponed until after the elections.

Abe Fortas, a close friend of President Johnson's whose nomination as Chief Justice was later to be rejected, served as Baker's defense attorney in a $300,000 vending machine suit against him. Baker had been so intimately associated with LBJ that the latter often said he was "like a son to me," so Republicans were naturally trying to link Baker's nefarious activities with the Democratic President. Then a strange thing happened.

Lyndon Johnson had never been considered a football fan, and on the few occasions when he had gone to any kind of ball game he invariably shared a box with political friends. LBJ was too much of a star performer to like spectator sports. It was intriguing, therefore, when at a Washington Redskins-Baltimore Colts football game the President sat alone in a box, except for the presence of attorney Edward Bennett Williams, president of the Redskins, with whom he engaged in deep conversation throughout the first half of the game.

Bennett was chief defense attorney for Bobby Baker, and a savvy government official said to me, "Where else could the President of the United States talk to the defense counsel for Bobby Baker, without giving away the fact that he was taking an active interest in Baker's defense? If Williams came to the White House or LBJ went to his legal office, the world would immediately know that they were discussing the Baker case. And on the telephone, there's too much chance of eavesdropping. This way, it looks innocent."

On July 10, 1964, I flew to San Francisco to cover the Republican National Convention and while there had several interviews with Peggy and Barry Goldwater in their suite at the Mark Hopkins. The day before his nomination, Barry was sitting in his undershorts having a haircut when he suddenly summoned Mrs. Edna Coerver, his sixty-four-year-old secretary, and asked, "Edna, do I have enough money in my checking account to write a birthday check for Barry, Jr.? He's been so good to help that I want to do something nice for him."

Nelson Rockefeller would not have had to ask such a question, but it was Barry Goldwater, son of a Russian Jewish immigrant and an Episcopalian mother, who captured the Presidential nomination the next day. On his evening of triumph, he ate a rare steak and a salad in his suite, and then sat with his campaign manager to watch the roll call on television. The South Carolina delegation put Barry over the top at 10:43 P.M., at which moment the shirt-sleeved nominee suddenly swung from the TV set to another immediately behind him. Asked why, he grinningly replied, "I want to see if Peggy cries." He was recalling the 1960 convention when, as he withdrew his name from Presidential nomination, TV cameras picked up Mrs. Goldwater sitting in a box, with tears streaming down her cheeks.

But 1964 was a different story, and there was wild jubilation among the conservatives. As soon as Goldwater's nomination was made official, he accepted a few telephone calls; then he took a shower and shaved, in readiness for arriving television crews. Governor William Scranton of Pennsylvania and his family came to the suite, and the two rivals spent fifteen minutes together. Barry, who had repeatedly told me, "I may not be the best-qualified man for the job," was now the GOP standard-bearer, and Governors Romney and Rockefeller went home to sulk. William E. Miller, a lackluster Congressman, was Barry's handpicked running mate.

The two nominating conventions are normally held a week or two apart, but inasmuch as everyone that year knew who the Democratic nominee would be, the Donkey Party conclave was not scheduled for another seven weeks. During the interim, Marjorie Merriweather Post invited Bob and me for a visit to Top Ridge, her fabulous summer home in the Adirondacks, and on August 6 we flew in her private plane, the *Merriweather,* with the Japanese ambassador, Air Force General Godfrey McHugh, the Homer Gruenthers, and several other friends to Saranac Lake, New York. Limousines rushed us from the airport to dockside, where her cabin cruiser awaited to skim us across the sparkling waters of Upper St. Regis Lake, and her private funicular lifted us from her dock to Top Ridge.

At the vast lodge, each couple was assigned a personal footman who escorted us to individual cottages. Ours, perched amid the treetops, contained two spacious bedrooms and baths, plus a telephone with twenty buttons which we could use for summoning cars, boats, golf clubs, breakfast trays, a masseur, or anything that our hearts desired. The personal maid assigned to me unpacked my suitcase, while a valet tended to Bob's. Our clothes were whisked away for pressing, and a reverberating bell summoned us to cocktails in the main lodge whose living room approximated 60 by 100 feet and had a 30-foot ceiling and gigantic fireplaces at each end. Vast picture windows framed a sweeping view of two lakes and a forested mountain range.

After dinner each evening we square danced or watched a movie in the lodge; by day we had a choice of tennis courts, golf, croquet, ping-pong, badminton, shuffleboard, swimming, and fishing, to say nothing of hiking and bridge. Once we went on an all-day picnic, traveling across five lakes, with seven guides rowing and portaging the seven Adirondack canoes to the campsite, where we feasted on charcoal-broiled steaks and Adirondack flapjack pies. Few queens live as luxuriously as Marjorie Post, the Post Toasties heiress, and few are as philanthropic.

The Democratic Convention in Atlantic City, where Bob and I went on August 22, was one of the strangest in living memory. It was also the biggest and most poorly managed. For no reason whatsoever, Atlantic City police would bar credential-laden newsmen from the press entrance to the world's biggest convention hall for periods of up to an hour, and there was little enough news to write about when we did get inside.

For months before the convention, the "Irish Mafia" had been floating trial balloons plugging Bobby Kennedy for the Vice Presidency, although LBJ was not about to have his bitterest foe breathing down his neck during the next four years. But Johnson dared not offend the Kennedyites, whose support he would need during the campaign, so shortly before the convention he told a press conference that he would not tap as his running mate any member of his Cabinet or anyone sitting with the Cabinet. This Machiavellian touch not only eliminated Attorney General Kennedy, but also his handsome brother-in-law, Sargent Shriver, who directed the Peace Corps. A movie depicting the career of John F. Kennedy had been scheduled for opening night at the conclave, but LBJ was taking no chances with an emotional binge that might sweep Bobby into the Vice Presidency by acclamation. He ordered the film delayed until after the nominees were selected, when Bobby would serve as its moderator.

Seventeen-year-old Lucy Baines, who by now had changed the spelling of her name to Luci, was the only member of the First Family to arrive for the opening festivities. The gregarious teen-ager promptly became such a scene-stealer that when her mother and older sister came on August 27 and the crowds cheered Lynda, the latter remarked sarcastically, "I'm Lynda, not Luci." Lady Bird and Lynda made a dramatic entrance by helicopter, landing near the boardwalk in midtown, where a crowd of officials and tourists had gathered an hour earlier. Dozens of Ladies for Lyndon, dressed in matching mulberry-red crepe dresses, tried to pep up the waiting throng while lightning flashed and thunder rolled. Suddenly the heavens opened up, spewing torrents of rain on the fancy hairdos which had painstakingly been acquired for Perle Mesta's big dance that evening. The bouffant coiffures became streaming cowlicks, and as the deluge came down, the hemlines on the mulberry dresses went up, up, up. By the time the sun peeked through for Lady Bird's belated arrival, the red shifts had shrunk so much that only bedraggled petticoats protected the dimpled knees of Ladies for Lyndon.

Perle Mesta was so happy again to have a President who was a personal friend that she rented a large abode and hosted a dinner party every evening during the convention, but her big bash was to be a supper-dance at an oceanfront hotel after LBJ's nomination.

Meanwhile, LBJ was playing his Vice Presidential selection so close to his vest that during that fateful afternoon he summoned both Senators Hubert Humphrey and Thomas Dodd by plane from Atlantic City to the White House. It was a dirty trick. Johnson already knew that Humphrey was to be his man, but he used Dodd as a ploy to confuse newsmen and lend drama to the dull proceedings. It was a humiliating experience for the Connecticut Senator, who later told me that he was as mystified as everyone else about why the President had so abruptly summoned him.

Dodd told me, "The President personally called and ordered me to go to the Atlantic City airport, where a plane would be waiting to fly me to Washington, and that I would recognize somebody there. At the airfield I ran into Hubert, who said the President had told him the same thing. En route to Washington, Humphrey asked me if I had been chosen, and I told him I knew nothing whatsoever."

Arriving together at the White House, Dodd was the first to be summoned into the Johnson presence, while Hubert nervously waited in a parked limousine. Then for forty-five minutes LBJ explained why he had decided on Humphrey instead of Dodd.

"I kept telling him that I never had been a candidate, and please to include me out," Dodd recalled, "but the President kept telling me that I was the last runner-up. I don't know why he did it, unless he wanted Catholics to think he had been giving a member of their faith serious consideration, or that he wanted to appease conservatives by pretending to think he had also considered me."

Lady Bird herself did not know whom her unpredictable husband would select when she left Washington that day for the convention city, but after LBJ landed at the Atlantic City airport that evening, he tipped his hand to reporters en route to Convention Hall. Lady Bird's shining hour began at 11:15 P.M., when, garbed in black silk with ruffled collar, she walked onstage with her husband while Convention Hall went wild with cheering. They were flanked by Lynda and Luci, the latter appearing to copy the Pope by slowly moving her hand horizontally, in a sort of regal benediction, while her parents and Lynda gave the usual arms-up wave of greeting.

The climax had been a long time in coming. For three hours the First Lady presided over the President's flag-draped Presidential box, welcoming the wives of each nominating and seconding speaker in turn and vigorously applauding the endless compliments paid to her husband from the rostrum. One chair remained vacant, but shortly before 11 P.M. Muriel Humphrey slipped into it, and delegates who had not already heard the news of LBJ's Vice Presidential choice quickly figured it out for themselves. Soon thereafter, the deal was signed and sealed by the delegates. The ticket was Johnson and Humphrey.

Perle Mesta's dance that night was an anticlimax. For one thing, it coincided with a reception for Vice Presidential nominee Humphrey, and neither Hubert nor any of the Johnsons came to her ball. Neither did a number of delegates and party bigwigs, who went to the Humphrey party instead. As a result, it was one of the most pleasant parties that Perle ever gave, with plenty of room for dancing and table-hopping under a three-quarter moon on the breeze-swept ocean terrace. As always, there were attempted gate-crashers. One woman, using another's name to gain admission, said, when confronted by the hostess, "You invited me at the April in Paris Ball," to which Mrs. Mesta grimly replied, "I wasn't even there. I've never laid eyes on you before. Now, go!" The young lady scrammed but forgot her gloves and had to return and plead for them.

CHAPTER XXVIII

Barry Bites the Dust

I SPENT a lot of time that fall on the Goldwater campaign trail, which mainly took to the airways, as befits a candidate who can also pilot a jet and who sometimes piloted our campaign plane. The crowds were exuberant and friendly nearly everywhere except in the small towns of New England, where oldsters understandably scowled while the candidate attacked Social Security. At one such hamlet, when our temporary prop plane was delayed in takeoff, I suggested to Barry that he walk back to the door and wave again to the assembled crowd, but his answer was, "To hell with it."

Barry Goldwater was at his oratorical best in the open sky country of the great Southwest, which he loved and where his native wit bubbled up like an oasis in the desert. By late September he seemed to be hitting his campaign stride, as he settled on the issues of peace and freedom, and he constantly taunted President Johnson and "Yo-yo McNamara" for concealing the truth about Vietnam from the people. He also had a neat stack of innuendoes about political scandals in the opposition party, and he said of LBJ's protégé Bobby Baker, "Bobby has a baker's dozen. You get thirteen, but you have to kick back two." Of Johnson's notoriously thin skin, he wisecracked, "I don't know why Johnson can't take criticism. He takes everything else."

Since the Kennedy assassination, Johnson's theme song had been "Let us continue." Goldwater, referring to our recent foreign policy failures in Vietnam, Yemen, Panama, and Cuba, would jibe, "Is this what Johnson means when he says 'Let us continue'? You can't conduct foreign policy while walking the dog on the White House lawn. You can't conduct it while flying around dedicating dams at public expense. And it's kind of hard to conduct it in a swimming pool."

He accused Johnson of sweeping the scandal about his fellow Texan Billie Sol Estes under a red carpet, and with the intensity of an Old Testament prophet he would light into the corruption issue, saying, "Records show that Billie Sol Estes, the Texas wheeler-dealer in illegal cotton acreage allotments, withdrew forty thousand dollars in cash for a trip to Washington in 1962, and records show that he spent six thousand of this for tickets to a hundred-dollar-a-plate Democratic dinner, most of which he turned over to Cliff Carter in the office of the then Vice President Johnson. We never learned whose pocket got the other thirty-four thousand."

The breakdown in law and order was a big issue in Boston, where a masked strangler of women was still at large, and in the vast baseball stadium there one night Barry said, "Nothing is more clear from history than that the moral decay of a people begins at the top. It seeps down from the highest offices to all walks of life. The fast buck and easy morals have become the standards of the day for many." At another huge rally he drew laughs by quipping, "President Johnson has so much power that the Democrats don't know whether to vote for him, or plug him in."

At the end of September Goldwater met with his archrival, Governor Rockefeller, and Rockefeller's second wife, Happy, in Albany, and tensions were high. I was the pool reporter chosen to walk behind Goldwater and Rockefeller through the New York Statehouse, where both stopped frequently to pump the hands of state employees, and it went surprisingly well. The same could not be said for Barry's subsequent meeting with Governor Romney in Michigan. On a sunny fall day we arrived in Midland while Romney was addressing an ox roast, and the Republican governor continued to speak for half an hour without once mentioning the GOP Presidential nominee's name. Finally, on leaving the stands, he merely shook hands and said, "How are you, Barry? Welcome to Michigan." Then, after telling our press entourage that he would not "endorse" Goldwater, he departed before Barry's speech.

A strike had blacked out Detroit's three newspapers for ten weeks during the campaign, but when the Goldwater entourage reached that Democratic stronghold late in the day, tens of thousands of fans who had managed to get the word of his arrival lined the avenues through which his motorcade rolled and, with Fourth of July sparklers, turned the city into a veritable fairyland. Another 13,000 supporters jammed Cobo Hall for the night rally and twice booed Governor Romney, but cheered Goldwater to the rafters.

The ovation that night was so monumental that a newsman later remarked to Barry, "Senator, if you told that audience that you planned to raise taxes, they would still have cheered you." Yet, strangely enough, the Democratic-oriented Washington newsmen who accompanied Goldwater led off their newspaper articles the next day with Romney's snub, rather than with Barry's spectacular reception despite the snub. There is little doubt that the accompanying press shared some of the responsibility for Goldwater's low ratings in the public opinion polls.

After the 1960 campaign, Bobby Kennedy had said, "Lady Bird carried Texas for us." The Johnsons had not forgotten this, and on October 6, 1964, Lady Bird set forth on the unique task of saving the Southland for Lyndon. Never before in our history had a First Lady assigned herself such a difficult political task, nor had any before attracted such enormous press coverage. The Lady Bird Special chugged out of Union Station in Washington, en route to such fascinating sounding Southern hamlets as Wide Water, Drum Hill, Speed, Haw River, Ten Mile, Doctor Town, and Century, and although it was billed as an all-distaff trek, LBJ could not resist getting into the act. As a consequence, our Lady Bird Special pulled out of Washington without the leading lady. The President personally put her aboard a few miles south of Alexandria, where he needed some Virginia supporters, and that evening he caught up with our train again in Raleigh, North Carolina, to make his own speech. President Johnson adored his wife and knew that she was supremely capable, but he simply could not overcome his lifelong habit of trying to run everything himself.

A chill was in the fall air as we boarded the train that early morning in Washington, and LBJ wore an overcoat when he arrived in Alexandria with Lady Bird and Lynda to tell a shivering crowd, "This whistle-stop has been selected as an opener by one of the greatest campaigners in America, and I am very proud to announce I am her husband." Ignoring a few signs about Bobby Baker, the First Lady told the largely friendly crowd, "This is a journey of the heart." That night in Raleigh, when LBJ again took center stage, he said of his wife, "I can catch up with her, but I can never overtake her." Then he returned to Washington.

Our train chugged on through Dixie, and the farther south that we went, the deeper the drawls of the First Lady and Lynda became. At each stop, after Lady Bird spoke, Lynda would take over the microphone to add a folksy touch by saying, "I hope you-all are gonna go out and work for us. Over half the people in this world are under twenty-five, and that means y'all."

Senator Strom Thurmond of South Carolina had recently quit the Democratic Party to become a Goldwater Republican, and at Orangeburg, South Carolina, teen-agers chanted, "We want Barry," while some others waved signs saying: "Blackbird Special." At Charleston a huge sign read, "Fly away, Lady Bird, this is Goldwater country," but the First Lady ignored it. After all, that was why she had come, to change it to Johnson country. By the fourth day of our trek through Dixie, Hubert Humphrey had become the forgotten man of her one-woman campaign. Not once at the dozens of whistle-stops and downtown rallies in five states did Lady Bird mention her husband's running mate—the man who had precipitated the Dixie walkout at the 1948 Democratic Convention.

The First Lady was booed in Savannah, Georgia, and at another nearby stop Lynda angrily shouted into the microphone, "I'm sure those few rude shouts and boos are not from the good people of this state, but from the people from the state of confusion." The boos rose to a crescendo, and Lady Bird winced. But on Friday she finally hit "kissin' kin" territory, and seven of her kinfolks clambered aboard the special train at Pensacola, Florida, for the ride into their home state of Alabama. Throughout the campaign in Alabama, the drawl was thicker than the grits that were suddenly being served in the diner of our train. By this time Luci had replaced Lynda and was doing a better job, although their mother flinched each time that Luci took over the microphone. "She's so unpredictable," she whispered to me, "that I never know what she's going to say."

The Lady Bird Special, whose crowds outdrew LBJ's Dixie Special four years previously, finally pulled into New Orleans, where President Johnson met the train and again cheated his wife out of the spotlight by delivering what would have been her windup address. Then he proceeded to a dinner that night, where he eulogized the late Huey Long to the consternation of practically everyone except his son, Senator Russell Long.

During the height of the campaign, I wrote that only one man could defeat Lyndon Baines Johnson for election to the Presidency in November, and that man was Johnson himself. I said that if the election were held at that moment, even Goldwater's own strategists would concede Johnson's election, yet in his peripatetic efforts to win by the largest landslide since the advent of the two-party system, LBJ was paradoxically risking his own defeat. A wide sampling of opinion in a dozen states prompted me to raise these questions in my column:

Was it helping or hurting the President's image with the electorate when, after a grueling twenty-hour day in New England and a political speech at 1:45 A.M., he flew to Omaha and made two television appearances? What the viewers saw was a haggard-looking President, his voice husky and his manner so weary that he seemed to stagger. Was it helping to read that a President who was leading the polls by an unprecedented margin nevertheless persisted in shaking so many voters' hands that his own were bruised and bleeding? In light of the awesome Warren Committee Report, did it win votes when a President who was without a Vice President plunged into street crowds, carelessly ignoring his own safety while Secret Service agents anguished?

Were voters attracted by press accounts that the President persisted in opening the White House gates and inviting hordes of unknown

President Lyndon B. Johnson and Ruth chat at a party.

Ruth, as Fall Gal of the Circus Saints and Sinners Club, chats with General Lyman L. Lemnitzer, chairman, Joint Chiefs of Staff, and Dr. You Chan Yang *(right),* former Korean ambassador at 1962 dinner in her honor.

More fun at the Saints and Sinners dinner as Ruth meets some of the elaborately costumed participants.

With Clark Clifford, President Johnson's Secretary of Defense.

Interviewing President Johnson in his White House office.

Interviewing Lady Bird Johnson.

With Pat Nixon.

Montgomerys arriving to visit Ruth's family in Indianapolis,
Indiana, for Christmas. Left to right: Ruth's mother, Mrs. I. W.
Shick; Bob Montgomery; Ruth; Paul Shick *(kneeling)* and his
late wife, Mary.

tourists? Was Lee Harvey Oswald the only potential killer in America? Does it win votes to lead a battery of photographers and newsmen into a Boston hospital after midnight, disrupting the sleep of the sick, to pay a political call on convalescing Senator Teddy Kennedy, who had nearly died in a plane crash? Does it help with the voters when the President arbitrarily labels his speechmaking trips nonpolitical so that he can charge the cost to taxpayers instead of the Democratic National Committee?

Are voters reassured when a President who has had a massive heart attack carries on nonstop monologues with the press while walking ten or fifteen laps around the White House lawn, under a broiling sun? Why does he do it? What inner compulsion causes the man who is far ahead in the polls to drive himself so relentlessly? Why is LBJ so irresistibly drawn to the telephone that he calls business executives, legislators, and ambassadors all day long and far into the night? In view of his tremendous popularity and his remarkable record in pushing the unfinished Kennedy program through Congress, was it necessary for the President to barnstorm around the country at the risk of his own health? Could he perhaps win greater support by staying close to the White House during the week, serving as President of all the people, and making admittedly political excursions only on weekends? One third of the Presidents in this century had died in office; another, Woodrow Wilson, so exhausted himself with the rigors of a cross-country report to the people on the League of Nations that he suffered a paralytic stroke and was thereafter incapacitated. President Johnson seemed to be taking needless risks.

I had barely rejoined the Goldwater campaign special, when word reached us of the arrest in a YMCA rest room of LBJ's top assistant, Walter Jenkins, on a charge of homosexuality. All of us who knew and liked Walter were stunned. So was President Johnson, who delayed any public reaction for a day, during which Lady Bird staunchly defended her husband's chief administrative aide. To the credit of Barry Goldwater, he declined to make political hay of the tragic incident. Jenkins resigned, and after LBJ's reelection he helped him secure several lucrative public relations accounts in Texas, including that of the Johnsons' television station in Austin.

The Goldwater plane was meanwhile crisscrossing the country from New York to Los Angeles, from San Diego to Texas to Indiana, touching down in Tennessee, Kentucky, Ohio, Iowa, Pennsylvania, and Illinois. On October 29 we rode a campaign train, for a change, through heavily populated Pennsylvania, and the Goldwaters invited me to lunch with them in their private railroad car. Then we flew on to Cheyenne, Las Vegas, Tucson, Los Angeles, and Phoenix, where we rested a few days in Barry's hometown before pressing on to San Antonio, Columbus, San Francisco, and back to Arizona.

Barry wound up his campaign in Fredonia, Arizona, a small Indian village which he called his "good luck town," and the residents presented him with a handmade kachina doll to add to his substantial collection. Barry graciously gave it to me the next day, and it now dominates my doll collection which I have amassed from countries throughout the world.

We returned to Phoenix the evening before election, where the press corps was luxuriously housed at Camelback Inn to await the returns. The Goldwaters invited me to their beautiful house overlooking the desert and led me to the guest powder room where the walls were papered in snapshots which photographer Barry Goldwater had taken of his friends. Bigger than life-size was an unflattering one of me which Barry had snapped while I was laughing uproariously at one of his pranks during a party in their Washington apartment.

I asked Barry if he thought that he had a chance to win, and he replied, "I believe that I have a chance, but not an overwhelming chance. I'm a fatalist, and I think if I'm meant to win, I will. Otherwise, I won't." Peggy adored her husband but hated the very thought of living in the White House. While Jack Kennedy was still President, I once asked Peggy if she wanted Barry to succeed him, and she laughingly replied, "If you want to know the truth, I told Barry that if he won the nomination and election, I thought he should make a contract with Jackie to stay on at the White House, because she was doing a fine job." Turning serious, she added with a sigh,

"I guess I'd like to live in the White House if Barry were living there."

On election eve the Goldwaters gave a party for the accompanying press at the Camelback, and the next morning we watched them vote. That evening they sent a car for me, and I sat alone with the family in the den to watch the early returns on television. Barry, wearing dirty dungarees and sports shirt, was limping a little from unaccustomed physical exertion. For more than an hour he had been shoveling sand and transplanting sword cactus on his twenty-one acres of land. Earlier, after casting his ballot, he had headed into the desert for a lonely hike toward Squaw Peak Range. Now he was ready to unwind, and when his beautiful daughter Peggy, Jr., asked if she could get him a drink, he blew the perspiration off his forehead as he said, "Just some iced tea."

His wife, Peggy, wearing a flowing muumuu, was busily reading the cards on dozens of boxes of flowers which were being telegraphed from every part of the nation. Barry suggested that she sit down and relax, but she protested, "I'm not tired. Why don't you let me do what I want to?" Laughing softly, Peggy Holt teased, "Who's jumpy now?" The early returns began flashing on the TV screen, and everyone but Barry leaned forward to watch intently. The Arizona Senator picked up a newspaper to read, while the TV commentator reported that on the basis of two percent of the vote, President Johnson had won Kentucky and probably Indiana.

Peggy, Jr., was indignant. Indiana was her mother's home state, and Barry was currently ahead there. "How can they do such a thing!" she exploded. I tried to explain their computerized system of projecting the vote from sample precincts, but Barry said nothing from behind his newspaper. The television voice continued relentlessly, saying that by vote profile analysis Indiana now seemed definitely in the Johnson corner. "Yes, and wouldn't you be happy if it is," Peggy, Jr., snapped at the TV screen.

"Listen to this," Mrs. Goldwater said, as she studied more cards on the flowers. "It says, 'To the loveliest woman in America,' and I don't even know who sent these beautiful roses. They came from

Salt Lake City." She sounded as pleased as a debutante preparing for her first dance, but no one said anything.

Barry reached for an illustrated book on kachina dolls and began explaining to me the significance of the sun-god kachina which had been presented to him at the windup of his 80,000-mile campaign in Fredonia. A telephone mechanic came in to prepare the direct line to press headquarters at Camelback Inn. Barry wondered out loud how he had ever been able to string so many lines across two miles of desert. Twenty-four-year-old Mike Goldwater joined our group as the next batch of bad news flashed on the television screen. A phone rang, and as Peggy Jr.'s husband, Rick Holt, reached for it, Mike said that calls were being answered in the garage.

Peggy, Sr., began checking cigarette lighters in anticipation of the family gathering that evening and noted that one needed a flint. "I'll get one of the boys to work on it," she mused. Barry again suggested that she rest, saying that it was going to be a long evening. She protested again that she was not tired, but ruefully confessed that she had fallen asleep in a deep chair in the den the night before, watching television after the family had gone off to bed. "The next thing I knew it was four-thirty A.M."—she smiled—"but I had a good sleep."

It was time for me to return to press headquarters for my coverage of the returns, and Rick Holt offered to drive me there. Barry got to his feet and said he guessed he'd take a bath. "Why don't you take a steam bath, dear?" his wife asked. "That's what I'm going to do," he replied amiably, as he started down the dramatic glass corridor leading to his well-equipped bathroom. Soon his mother and the rest of his family would be arriving for the family get-together around the four television sets. It could have been just another evening, but it wasn't. Long before the sun would rise in a golden flush across the red-ridged mountains of his native land, Goldwater would know his political fate. The family would close ranks around the man they loved—the man who was looking forward to a long-delayed vacation, somewhere in Mexico, with his Hoosier sweetheart, Peggy Johnson Goldwater.

The next day, twelve hours after he had been expected to do so,

Goldwater strode into the Peace Pipe room of Camelback Inn to concede defeat and read a congratulatory telegram to President Johnson. In that wire he offered to help his victorious rival "in any way that I can towards achieving a growing and better America, and a secure and dignified peace." During the rapid-fire televised press conference he said that he expected liberal Republicans to attempt to wrest party control from him, but he intended to work hand in glove with the GOP Congressional leadership, which has the real power when a party is out of office.

Barry attributed his defeat to three major factors: the refusal of some liberal Republicans to work and vote for the ticket, the vast power base of an incumbent President, and the "vicious" attacks by some columnists and commentators, "who should hang their heads in shame for their misrepresentation of my position."

Goldwater looked fit and full of fight. After the press conference he made a safari into Scotsdale, a plush shopping area near his Paradise Valley home, to buy two paintings by Mark Comer. One painting was of a clown, which he was giving to Peggy and Rick Holt for their new house in Los Angeles. The clown was crying, and in an accompanying note to his youngest daughter, Goldwater wrote, "I voted for Barry." He had not lost his sense of humor in defeat.

Johnson won by the greatest landslide in our history, and one of the most telling counts against Goldwater had been that he sounded "trigger-happy." Barry had suggested defoliation of Vietnam areas used by Communist infiltrators and saboteurs, using strategic atomic weapons if necessary. Johnson, on the other hand, pledged not to enlarge the fighting. History has a way of repeating itself, however, and just as second term candidate Woodrow Wilson had pledged to keep us out of World War I and third term candidate Franklin D. Roosevelt had promised not to send a single American boy to fight on foreign soil in World War II, Johnson soon after the election began escalating our forces in Vietnam from 50,000 to hundreds of thousands. Whether Barry Goldwater would have done the same, we can never know.

CHAPTER XXIX

Tall in the Saddle

How was he gonna keep 'em down on the farm, now that he had invited them all to his inauguration? This was the poser confronting Lyndon Baines Johnson as he prepared to take the Presidential oath for the second time. Throughout the fall of 1964 he had been barnstorming around the country, exhorting the teeming millions, "Y'all come to my inauguration, heah?" What if, like the Pakistani camel driver, they took him up on the invitation?

It was Lady Bird, as usual, who had to deal with the problems created by her exuberant husband. Wading into the dilemma, she tried to devise a way to personalize the television coverage, so that Americans sitting at home in their snug living rooms could feel a "sense of participation," and to this end she held numerous conferences with TV executives.

January 20 dawned bright, clear, and bitingly cold. As I sat in the press section outside the U.S. Capitol to cover the swearing in of President Johnson, I noted that his daughters and his only brother, Sam Houston Johnson, were bundled in army blankets on the steps behind him. William B. Whitley, an official, was scheduled for the honor of holding the Johnson family Bible while LBJ swore the Presidential oath, but Johnson as usual was ready to spring a surprise. Not until Lady Bird stepped to her husband's side and gently took her mother-in-law's Bible from Whitley's hands did the public know what LBJ had arranged. Then, chalking up another "first" for a First Lady, she held the Bible on which her husband's hand rested, and as he concluded with "So help me God," she gazed long and lovingly at him. Dabbing at her misty eyes with a dainty handkerchief, she then resumed her seat, and at the conclusion of Johnson's inaugural address she rushed over to kiss him warmly and murmur that his speech was "wonderful." Perhaps that was the "sense of participation" that she wanted stay-at-home viewers to experience.

Bob and I planned to attend one of the inaugural balls that evening with Hope and Dr. Lee Miller; but since Lee had a bad cold and Bob was understandably bored by inaugural balls after twenty years in Washington, Hope and I went with Dr. Luther Holcomb, deputy director of the Equal Employment Opportunities Commission. The balls, as usual, were a sea of squashed humanity, resembling more nearly ball games than balls. A week later Lee Miller unexpectedly died, and I sadly handled his obituary for local papers and wire services.

Meanwhile, at the Texas-style White House we were being treated to instant diplomacy and instant partying. Former occupants of 1600 Pennsylvania Avenue traditionally announced social functions weeks or months in advance, because a bid to the White House was considered a must, and this permitted ambassadors and local hostesses to avoid a conflict in dates. But President Johnson's penchant for keeping everyone in the dark about his plans until the last moment carried over into the social circuit and was causing havoc.

At the drop of his Stetson hat, the Prexy would decide to spring a party or make a speech. Embassy chatelaines were having their formal dinner-seating charts wrecked at the eleventh hour, because officials who had accepted their invitations weeks before were suddenly drafted for Johnsonian dinners. The White House diplomatic reception the spring of 1965 was a case in point. Social schedules for ambassadors are customarily made out a month in advance, since most of them dine at other embassies or host parties at their own six nights a week.

As a consequence, pandemonium reigned when White House invitations for a 7:30 P.M. reception-buffet went out to all ambassadors and their wives only six days before the event. Hostesses who had carefully built their dinner party lists around one or more ambassadors were stranded without guests of honor. Ambassadors who had already issued invitations to embassy dinners that evening either had to cancel them or daringly say no to the President of the United States. If the diplomatic reception had been a six-to-eight affair, as in the Kennedy administration, or a late-evening white-tie soiree, as was traditional, the dinners could have been held as scheduled. This one, however, came in the middle of the wining-dining hour, with a mere buffet rather than a seated dinner, and the diplomats were furious.

The Johnsons' dinner party for Ambassador to Vietnam Henry Cabot Lodge, Jr., was not only a last-minute affair, but completely off limits to the press. Approximately 175 officials and friends dined at the White House that night, but the guest list was as secret as our Vietnam strategy, and the President was so sensitive to published reports that he had danced until three o'clock in the morning at his previous dinner for the Danish Prime Minister that he barred dancing at the Lodge party. There was something of a national furor at the time over news that the frug, the swim, the watusi, and other far-out dances were now the order of the evening at White House soirees, and LBJ was apparently becoming gun-shy in the face of mounting bad news from Vietnam.

Johnson's penchant for refusing to say whether he would attend a speechmaking affair was simultaneously wrecking the well-laid plans of mice and men. As a result, everyone from Vice President Humphrey to Welfare Secretary John S. Gardner was being sidelined at the last moment, with undelivered speeches in his hot hands. Poor Humphrey was left stranded several times that spring holding a carefully prepared talk that he was not permitted to deliver, because LBJ would suddenly show up with ruffles and flourishes to make a speech instead. One such was the Gridiron Club dinner, where a "funny" but very difficult talk was expected.

On March 11, President Johnson made world headlines with his arrogance-of-power speech at Princeton University, but he did not announce until three hours beforehand that he would attend, and HEW Secretary Gardner, who was the scheduled speaker, hastily had to step aside. To add to the embarrassment, the released text of New

Jersey Governor Richard J. Hughes' speech praised Gardner's address, although the latter had not been allowed to deliver it. What was that again about the "arrogance of power"?

Johnson, a strong individualist who had chafed in the number two position under Kennedy, should have been more sympathetic with Humphrey, another outgoing man, but he seemed never to give it a thought. While Johnson was hospitalized with a virus cold, Humphrey told a Chicago audience of his ordeal after learning of LBJ's middle-of-the-night ambulance ride to a hospital. He said that after being notified of the emergency, he walked the floor in lonely vigil until his wife awakened, after which they sat up talking until dawn.

Johnson was not amused, and a White House assistant confided that Humphrey's "indiscreet" remarks explained why Johnson did not assign HHH to represent him at the funeral of Sir Winston Churchill in London. Whatever the motive, the English were offended by our ailing President's failure to dispatch his Vice President as the logical substitute. Humphrey, a normally loquacious man who had once engaged Soviet Premier Khrushchev in eight hours of conversation, was making a valiant effort to curb his tongue, and like a good soldier in the ranks, he was constantly at the President's beck and call. He was willing to perform every task assigned to him, and more, but that frequently failed to satisfy his Commander in Chief.

Johnson, who liked favorable publicity even more than the next man, had leaned over backward during his own Vice Presidency to avoid capturing headlines that might have detracted from Kennedy's spotlight. One day he told me how he had learned that lesson. As a young Congressman in a hurry, he was overjoyed when a flattering article about him appeared in a syndicated column. Since he had an appointment at the White House that morning, he put the clipping in his pocket so that he could show it to President Roosevelt. On arrival, he noticed that FDR seemed unusually cool toward him, and he soon learned why. The President caustically commented on what he thought of legislators who took too much credit for their own efforts in public print. Grinning ruefully, LBJ recalled, "I got the point in a hurry. It was obvious that he'd seen that write-up, so I stuffed the clipping just as far down in my pocket as it would go."

During his Vice Presidency, Johnson was approached by several newsmen who wanted to write books about him, but remembering FDR's reaction, he turned them down, explaining that the time was not yet ripe. He well knew that Bobby Kennedy and some other members of the "Irish Mafia" hoped to dump him from the ticket in 1964, and he was determined not to give them any excuses to take to President Kennedy.

Humphrey had probably not heard that story. At least, he gave me frequent exclusive interviews in his Vice Presidential office next to the White House, and when I did not call often enough to suit him, he would telephone or write a note to ask when I was coming in to see him. In April, 1966, he told me for quotation, "They say a President and a Vice President get along together for about six months, or a year at most. Well, yet me tell you about this one. Our first year was one of accommodation. The President and I were old friends, but we were getting acquainted at a new level of government. This year we have a much closer relationship than last, and I'm involved even more than before. To me, this is very encouraging and happy."

I asked whether he enjoyed the Vice Presidency as much as the Senate, and he quipped, "That is like asking a movie actor whether he preferred the legitimate stage. Both are enjoyable. There's more freedom of action in the Senate, but here I'm in the center of history. I'm in on important and sensitive discussions at the White House. I'm permitted to make my observations, and I'm called on for suggestions. These are the rich rewards, even though there are some headaches. I'm soft and sentimental about this opportunity. I'm doing something worthwhile. I love this country. I'm almost a roaring patriot about it, even if people do think that sounds soft."

At the beginning of his second term, the problems of the Presidency seemed to be weighing more heavily on Lyndon Johnson; he was holding so many meetings and ceremonies that public tours of the White House were canceled on short order, sometimes five days out of seven. Tour guides were indignant when hundreds of busloads of out-of-town tourists were turned away at the White House gates, and Lady Bird Johnson confided, "Life at the White House is one continuous seminar. I found this out when I began searching for a quiet spot where I could meet with a hundred women from the Job Corps. I looked in the East Room, but Lyndon was holding a ceremony there in honor of outstanding students. Next I spotted the rose garden, but a group of ministers were gathering there to discuss community relations with officials. Then I tried the State Dining Room, but it was being set up for a luncheon and briefing to which the President had invited business leaders. I didn't dare try the second-floor family quarters, because I would have a dramatic plea from Luci to keep everything quiet there while she studied for exams. We finally had our meeting in a far corner of the south lawn."

Not even the Executive Mansion was big enough for Lyndon Johnson, who complained that every time he went to his bedroom to take a midday nap, Lady Bird was holding some kind of beautification meeting in the oval room next door. Visiting schoolchildren wept because they could not tour the White House, and Liz Carpenter commented, "When you get a hyperthyroid administration like this one, you have got to expect a lot of pulsating all over the place."

Luci Johnson meanwhile was planning to beat her older sister to the altar. Lynda had been engaged to be married when her father became President, but shortly after moving to the White House she broke her engagement. Now Lynda was having dates with Hollywood actor George Hamilton, but Luci, who relished center-stage spotlight, was floating on her own private cloud with a former Senate page boy, Patrick John Nugent of Waukegan, Illinois, and friends and hangers-on immediately began scheduling parties in her honor.

Then, abruptly, the White House issued a statement asking Luci's friends to cancel their parties for her. Some felt that owing to the seriousness of the Vietnam War, it was unwise for Luci to be so lavishly wined and dined; but immediately after the press announcement Luci flew to Wisconsin as guest of honor at a swinging, frugging ball, and she continued to maintain a hectic social schedule. Those of us in the know realized what actually lay behind the White House action. Barbara Howar, a swinging Washington matron, had already issued invitations for a big party honoring Luci and was re-

ceiving reams of national publicity as "a close friend of the family,"
until she went a step too far and began telling interviewers how
useful she was being to Lady Bird as well as Luci in selecting their
wardrobes. Barbara, a generation older than Luci, had to cancel her
party, but the others proceeded as scheduled.

At age eighteen, Luci was the liveliest Presidential daughter since
the Teddy Roosevelt era when "Princess" Alice kicked up her heels,
smoked cigarettes, jumped into a swimming pool fully clothed, and
so stirred up turn-of-the-century society that her President-father
once remarked, "I can do one of two things. I can be President of
the United States, or I can control Alice. I cannot possibly do both."

Luci, who had adopted the Roman Catholic faith to marry, became
a bride at an enormous cathedral wedding on August 6, 1966, one of
the most scorching days that Washington has ever known. Lynda,
who had gradually emerged from her Plain Jane wrappings under
the appraising eye of George Hamilton, thereafter found her heart's
desire in Marine Captain Charles S. Robb, one of the White House
military-social aides, and was married at the White House in December, 1967.

A commission appointed by President Johnson and headed by
Chief Justice Earl Warren had meanwhile declared that Lee Harvey
Oswald was the sole murderer of President Kennedy, and several
authors were planning to write books about the tragic event in Dallas.
One of them was Jim Bishop, author of the best-selling *The Day
Lincoln Was Shot,* but Jacqueline Kennedy decreed that there should
be only one book and that she would select the author. The first two
authors who were approached turned down her terms, but William
Manchester grabbed at the chance, and the subsequent controversy
which raged about his book was due to three errors of judgment.
The first occurred when Jacqueline Kennedy granted Manchester the
exclusive right to interview friends and relatives of the late President
and instructed them not to discuss the subject with anyone except
Manchester. Perhaps the most pertinent comment on that error of
judgment came from Jim Bishop, who remarked, "The Kennedys
are trying to copyright the assassination."

The second error was committed by Manchester, who should have realized the impossibility of meeting Jackie's terms. And the third error occurred when Jackie and Bobby Kennedy, despite their stipulation that they must approve the manuscript, declined to read it. Instead, they had a few friends comb the work for passages which might be offensive, and these were read to them out of context. Quixotically, Jackie had granted Manchester a ten-hour tape-recorded interview describing her personal thoughts and feelings about the tragedy but then became irate because he used the material in his book. The tone of the book was violently anti-Johnson, yet even a Kennedy partisan who actively disliked LBJ and flew back on the plane from Dallas to Washington told me that he found nothing to criticize in the behavior of President or Mrs. Johnson.

Having by now completed my book about Jeane Dixon, *A Gift of Prophecy,* I began work on an illustrated one about White House flower arrangements for state occasions, to be called *Flowers at the White House.* Homer Gruenther, a Presidential assistant during the Eisenhower, Kennedy, and Johnson administrations, had urged me to write the book, and Mrs. Johnson and Liz Carpenter made available the exquisite color photographs which eventually graced it.

Always cooperative, Lady Bird enthusiastically wrote out for me her views on floral arrangements and the use of flowers in the Executive Mansion. I wrote to Jacqueline Kennedy in New York, also requesting her views to include in the book, but my letter was answered by her secretary, Pamela Turnure, who merely enclosed a mimeographed release bearing on the subject which had been issued during the Kennedy administration. This seemed typical of Jackie's haughtiness, which had earned for her the caustic title "The queen in exile on Park Avenue, awaiting restoration of the crown."

How different her reaction when the book was published early in 1967! My publisher had mailed Mrs. Kennedy a complimentary copy, as was done for all those mentioned in the book, and I had just autographed another copy for Jackie, when I received a letter from Pamela saying, "Dear Ruth, Mrs. Kennedy was simply enchanted with the copy of your book about flowers at the White House—so much so, that she wonders if she could possibly get three more copies. She would like to have one for the Kennedy Library and one to save for each of the children when they are older. I am sorry to trouble you with this, but I thought you would like to know of her enthusiastic response to your fine book."

Smiling to myself as I recalled her lack of cooperation in preparing the book, I telephoned Pamela and said, "I have autographed a copy for Jackie that I am mailing today. She can give the book which the publisher sent to the Kennedy Library, and I'll ask that two more copies be sent for Caroline and John, Jr. Incidentally, the books are for sale in all bookstores."

Jackie's reluctance to spend her own money was by now becoming general public knowledge. A rather recent innovation was a $10,000-a-year widow's pension, which had been designed to prevent the widow of a President from suffering economic hardship. The pension was not automatically paid but had to be requested by a former First Lady, and Jacqueline surprised many by immediately filing a petition for it, although she was the principal beneficiary of her husband's $10,000,000 estate. Besides this, Congress voted Mrs. Kennedy a one-year $75,000 office allowance so that she could answer the avalanche of sympathy mail which flooded in after her husband's death, plus Secret Service protection for herself and her children and free postal privileges.

No one at first questioned the correctness of this Congressional action, but after Jackie moved to New York, the Secret Service protection became a sizable budgetary item. She began traveling widely to skiing resorts here and abroad, spent a vacation in Argentina and another in Spain, where she was the guest of the Duchess of Alba at Seville's gala spring fair, and visited Aristotle Onassis on his yacht in Greek waters.

Year after year Congress kept renewing its unprecedented generosity, and a swelling volume of mail to legislators began to ask why. Jackie's secretary revealed that by then her public mail consisted largely of requests for her appearance at some charitable event, and since she declined them all and did no official entertaining, many taxpayers could not understand why the U.S. government should finance two secretaries and a Park Avenue office for Jackie, particularly in view of the government's economy drive which even called for elimination of the school lunch program for poor children. Jackie's office allowance was eventually reduced to $50,000 a year and finally discontinued, but all other emoluments including Secret Service protection remained until her remarriage.

In February, 1967, Jackie's so-called friend Robin Douglas-Home wrote an article about her for *Queen* magazine in London, which was widely reprinted in America. It was not a pretty story. The Englishman-turned-tattler, who had spent innumerable hours with Jackie in Italy and Washington, wrote that even at the moment of JFK's murder she had noted his bravery, saying, "Governor Connally was squealing like a stuck pig. Jack never made a sound." Recalling a period in 1962 when he and Jackie were guests of Lee Radziwill in Ravello, Italy, the author described "the complete transformation that came over her when one was alone with her. Flesh and blood instead of a symbol, she no longer tried to disguise the protean quality of her character, the paradoxes, the irreconcilable desires, the incompatibilities, the illogicalities, the frustrations, the damned outlets, and the impossible idealism. The next moment, without any warning, she was the royal, royal First Lady to whom it was almost a duty to bow to pay obeisance. Then again without warning, she was deflating someone with devastating barb, and deriding the pomp of politics, the snobbery of a social climber. It was Pavlovian treatment."

Douglas-Home also dredged up what he called the "trouble and gossip" about her supposed love affairs while First Lady and the nearly forgotten gossip that Jackie's father-in-law had offered her a million dollars not to divorce Jack, by saying that she "scoffed" at the reports. Picturing her as the imperious queen awaiting restoration of the Kennedy dynasty, he slyly added that she seemed not to realize that if Bobby Kennedy became President, it would be Ethel and not Jackie who would share the throne.

CHAPTER XXX

The End of the Beginning

RETURNING from a lecture tour connected with my latest book in December, 1965, I was distressed to learn that our close friend columnist George Dixon was in the hospital with what was described as a mild heart attack. Bob and I immediately sent flowers and telephoned his wife, Ymelda, since he could not receive visitors. They were the last flowers that he personally received, although the mortuary overflowed with wreaths a few days later, at his funeral.

It was almost too much! We had lost three intimate friends, including Hap Seitz and Lee Miller, within eleven months. Before the twelfth month elapsed, there would be four. Newspaper columnist Marguerite Higgins had been seriously ailing since midyear, after picking up a little-known tropical disease while on a trip to Vietnam, and by year's end she was desperately ill. A week before Christmas I took her a rosy-red bed jacket and a gaily bedecked Yule tree for her room at Walter Reed General Hospital, and we had a wonderful visit together. Christmas Day, after Bob and I dropped off presents for Bill and their two children, we went to the hospital to see Marguerite again. It was the last time.

Bill Hall, Marguerite's husband, insisted that we proceed with our long-arranged plans for a trip to Egypt, and since Hope and Lee Miller and Bob and I had always spent New Year's Eve together, Hope was going with us. We saw the old year out and the new year in at a supper club beside the emblazoned Sphinx, with the pyramids silhouetted against the dark sky beyond, and then flew to Abu Simbel,

Aswan, and Luxor. On our return to Cairo a cable awaited us telling
of Marguerite's death. The message from Bill Hall urged us not to
return for the funeral, and we received it too late to go anyway; but
it was a sad homecoming.

I was now writing another book, *A Search for the Truth,* and on
February 25, 1966, I went to Indianapolis to receive the Woman of
the Year award of Theta Sigma Phi. The following month I flew
to Waco, Texas, where I was honored as Woman of the Year by the
Laurel honor society of Baylor University and made a speech. In
April I flew to Dallas, addressed a thousand women members and
guests of the Foreign Affairs Council, then on to Indiana University
to receive its best nonfiction award for *A Gift of Prophecy.*

That summer Bob and I bought a lovely house surrounded by
water at Virginia Beach, Virginia, and I also enjoyed seminars there
at the Edgar Cayce Foundation, about which I had written several
series for Hearst Headline Service. It was a busy summer and fall.
We went to parties hosted by the Sargent Shrivers in Maryland, to
an after-the-theater supper dance given by Perle Mesta at Voisin's
in New York, and to another of Marjorie Post's square dances at
the Army-Navy Club. Later that fall I flew to Los Angeles, where I
was named California Woman of the Year by Theta Sigma Phi. We
went home to Indianapolis for Christmas, and Hope Miller came
down from Washington to spend New Year's Eve with us at Virginia Beach.

Early in the new year *A Search for the Truth* appeared on bookstands and best-seller lists. Besides writing my columns, I was flying
around the country to make speeches and appear on television pro-
grams. The Indiana Society in Washington awarded me its outstanding Hoosier award at a gala luncheon party, and television cameras
moved into our Georgetown house to make movies for the *Here's
Barbara* TV show.

Boston, Philadelphia, New York, Baltimore, Columbus, Cleveland,
Chicago, and the West Coast. I began to feel like a railway conductor,
except that I was flying to make a series of personal appearances,
autograph parties, lectures and television. My family had not wanted
me to write *A Search for the Truth,* fearful that those who disbe-

lieved in psychic phenomena might consider me a crackpot, but the public response to it was more gratifying than anything I had ever before written. Now I was even being invited to speak from the pulpits of Protestant churches throughout the country and on innumerable college campuses, including Notre Dame. Letters poured in from every section of the country, saying such heartwarming things as, "This is the most important book that I have ever read, except the Bible," "This book has changed my entire life for the better," and "Your book, which came into my hands by chance, has saved me from suicide."

The subject matter of the book dealt primarily with life after death and the strong possibility of communication between the two phases of eternal life. Marguerite Higgins died before its publication, but during our last talk at Walter Reed she had questioned me closely on the subject and expressed the wish that she had taken time to learn more about my interest in the psychic field. I had become fascinated with the subject and especially enjoyed the sessions with college students, because of their enthusiastic response. These young men and women would be the leaders of tomorrow, and their bright, inquiring minds seemed hungry for more knowledge on a subject which they did not find in college textbooks.

The Laurel honor society voted me the Most Valuable Alumna of Baylor University, and Professor Guy B. Harrison, director of Baylor's Texas History Collection, established a special Ruth Shick Montgomery collection at my Alma Mater to house my papers and manuscripts. This, too, seemed to demonstrate man's new enlightenment in this dawning Aquarian Age, for during my campus years at Baylor University such a divergence of thought from orthodox views would have been looked upon askance by the Baptist trustees and professors.

My newest book, *Here and Hereafter,* came out in August, 1968, and it, too, appeared on best-seller lists. On publication day I was interviewed on the *Today* television show and afterward on Johnny Carson's *Tonight* show. The subject was reincarnation, and after a wide swing through the East and Midwest, I flew to California for other television appearances.

In late October, I began a speaking tour, lecturing in Kansas City and Houston and Austin, Texas. Arriving at Love Field in Dallas at noon, I was met by Rudolph Johnson, who was taking me directly to a press conference and television show before my evening's address. Starting into a restroom to tidy my appearance for television, I slipped on a gooey concoction of hand lotion which someone had spilled just inside the entrance door. My right shoulder and arm were broken into the socket, and I spent five days in a Dallas hospital before I could be moved home to another hospital bed.

Fortunately for deadlines, I had given up my syndicated column at the beginning of 1968, and in the farewell column had written:

New Year's is a time for reverie as well as revelry, and because this is to be our final column, we are indulging in a nostalgic backward glance at the nearly quarter-century during which we have covered the Nation's capital. The Second World War was raging on both fronts when we picked up our press credentials for the White House, Capitol and Embassy Row. Our mortal enemies then were Germany, Japan and Italy, but the hour-glass has been upturned. Today they are our valued friends, whereas France has repaid our heroic rescue with crass ingratitude [de Gaulle was still President then], and our wartime Soviet ally is now the deadly foe.

Ten months after D-Day, Franklin D. Roosevelt died, and we attended his funeral in the White House East Room. A generation later we sadly stood in the same room, at the bier of another fallen chief.

V-E Day came three weeks after FDR's passing, and V-J Day followed in three months. Since America alone possessed the devastating atom bomb, the world was once again made safe for democracy. Or was it?

We covered the trial of Axis Sally, who was convicted of treason for broadcasting Nazi propaganda from Germany during the War; but nowadays Stokely Carmichael goes unprosecuted for spouting equally virulent anti-American propaganda from enemy territory in Cuba and North Vietnam, while our men die in battle.

There was never a dull moment in those early post-war years. We flew to Argentina and obtained the first exclusive interview with President Juan Peron, but he subsequently wrecked his country's economy and now lives in ignominious exile.

On the first of many European assignments we flew in a coal plane in the Berlin Airlift, which provided that embattled city's only supply line. Russia eventually lifted its blockade, but the even more shameful Berlin Wall now mocks the cause of peaceful coexistence.

America went to war in Korea to make Asia safe for democracy, but after three bloody years of fighting we settled for a divided country, whose artificial boundary is still being infiltrated by Communists. Now we are engaged in an even bloodier conflict in Vietnam to make Asia safe for democracy, and no end is in sight.

While covering one of President Truman's work-and-play vacations at Key West in early 1952, we hopped over to Cuba to report the Batista revolution. Cuba was strongly pro-American then, but seven years later came another revolution, and now it is a Communist bastion at our doorstep.

We covered the anti-British riots in Egypt which preceded the ouster of King Farouk, and a year later traveled beside President Naguib on his trip down the Nile to launch Egypt's land-distribution program. In those days Egypt hailed America as friend, but President Nasser has since broken off diplomatic relations with us.

The McCarthy era came and went, while we wrote tens of thousands of words about scores of spotlighted Congressional hearings. Today it is another McCarthy, of opposite political bent, who is giving a Democratic administration political indigestion.

We accompanied Vice President Nixon on his celebrated tour of Russia, and although he looked like a winner in his kitchen debate with Nikita Khrushchev, the next year he lost a more crucial debate to John F. Kennedy, and with it the White House.

Political conventions and Presidential campaigns have occupied us quadrennially during the passing years; but although windswept airports replaced the cozier whistle-stops, the banners, bands and impassioned oratory remain virtually untouched by time. Even the cast of characters seems hauntingly familiar.

Nixon is running again. Harold Stassen has declared his availability as he's been doing since 1952, and Nelson Rockefeller is looking as hopeful today as in '60 and '64. Lyndon B. Johnson will be a candidate as in '60 and '64, and a future Humphrey-Kennedy battle is shaping up, to suggest the '60 headlines.

A Democratic President with a low rating in public opinion polls is flaying Republicans in the 90th Congress, much as Democratic President Truman fought his underdog election status a generation ago by lambasting the Republican 80th Congress.

Yes, the more things change, the more they remain the same.

But life was not the same in the capital city of the free world. Law and order seemed to have broken down there, as elsewhere in our troubled land. Some of my friends were being slugged and mugged as they walked their dogs. Women were being raped in bright daylight as they strolled in a Georgetown park, prayed in a church, or tried to hail a taxi. No longer was it safe to saunter alone along the historic path beside the Georgetown canal which George Washington had surveyed or to venture out after dark. The once-beautiful capital of our nation was becoming infamous for its crime, rapacity, dirty streets, and befouled air. Washington wasn't much fun anymore.

Even for Lyndon Baines Johnson, some of the zest had gone out of living. Three years after capturing the Presidency by the greatest majority of votes in our history, he had reached his nadir in public opinion polls. If anyone had a kind word for him, it was scarcely spoken above a whisper. The Vietnam War which he had drastically escalated had become the most unpopular confrontation in our history, and victory remained elusive. Young men of fighting age were burning their draft cards. Both blacks and whites were rioting in the streets, looting, and setting fire to the big city ghettos. The cost of living was mounting steadily, and inflation was stealing the pensions and savings of our senior citizens. Unrest was everywhere. The President and members of his Cabinet were booed on college campuses. The once-docile Congress was beginning to turn a deaf ear to the exhortations of our Chief Executive and to dodge the reach of his long arm.

LBJ had every reason to doubt that he could be reelected, and his was a proud nature that could not easily withstand voter rejection.

He also yearned to win the Vietnam War. Early in 1968 he surprised the nation by withdrawing from the Presidential race. Senator Eugene McCarthy became a full-fledged candidate, and shortly afterward so did Bobby Kennedy. Johnson, who wanted to be succeeded by neither of the two, gave his blessing to Hubert Humphrey's candidacy. The race was on, but America was not done with violence, and on a dreadful evening in Los Angeles after Bobby Kennedy had won the California primary, a disgruntled Jordanian named Sirhan Sirhan shot him dead.

The nation was once again plunged into mourning, and television, which had recorded the fatal shot, gave full coverage to Bobby's funeral in St. Patrick's Cathedral and the sorrowful train ride back to the capital, where his body was buried near that of his President-brother in Arlington.

Humphrey won the Democratic nomination in Chicago, while the host city reverberated with riotous violence. A birthday party had been planned for President Johnson to climax the convention, but feelings ran so high and blood so hot that it was unsafe for him to attend. Was this America the Beautiful?

Richard M. Nixon captured the Republican nomination and went on to victory in the fall election. On January 20, 1970, Lyndon Baines Johnson returned to the LBJ ranch to begin rewriting history. Now it was a Republican President who must sink or swim with the problems of war, crime, pollution, rioting, and inflation.

These are sorely troublesome times, yes; but therein lies the challenge. How can we grow unless there are obstacles to overcome, problems to surmount, hate to conquer, and love of brotherhood to awaken? Dick Nixon has been called a man of destiny, but that could be said of almost any man who has led our country since the days of the Founding Fathers. Perhaps it can be said of any of us, each of whom has a role to play in trying to leave this embattled world a better place than he found it.

During our formative childhood years, we had little opportunity for free choice. We were at the mercy of parents, teachers, and adult society. But unless we are willing to remain eternally in that embryonic stage, we must begin to free ourselves of outworn shackles and try to exert our inborn power for good.

Freed from the inexorable tyranny of daily deadlines, I am living now in Cuernavaca, Mexico, where Bob and I have acquired a Spanish-Colonial casa atop a flowering barranca. The distant peak of snowcapped Popocatepetl is eternally framed in the archway of our veranda, and our mountain air is sweet and clean. A large portion of my heart remains in my native land, but perhaps it is good now and then to remove oneself from the eye of the hurricane, in order better to understand the problems within the whirling vortex.

The first cycle of my life has ended. Perhaps wistfully, I hope that the new phase now beginning will achieve more purpose, more depth, more *raison d'être*. Time, for all of us, is running out.

Index